THE QUARTERBACKS

Other Books by Mickey Herskowitz

The Camera Never Blinks, with Dan Rather
This 'n That, with Bette Davis
Cosell, with Howard Cosell
Self-Portrait, with Gene Tierney
Behind the Scenes, with Michael Deaver
Catcher in the Wry, with Bob Uecker
Back in the Saddle Again, with Gene Autry
Confession and Avoidance, with Leon Jaworski
All You Ever Wanted to Know About Sports
One with the Flame
The Golden Age of Pro Football
The Legend of Bear Bryant

T·H·E Q·U

THE UNCENSORED

ARTERBACKS
TRUTH ABOUT THE MEN IN
THE POCKET

MICKEY HERSKOWITZ

WILLIAM MORROW AND COMPANY, INC.
New York

Recognizing the importance of preserving what has been written, it is the policy of William Morrow and Company, Inc., and its imprints and affiliates to have the books it
publishes printed on acid-free paper, and we exert our best efforts to that end.

Library of Congress Cataloging-in-Publication Data

Herskowitz, Mickey.
    The quarterbacks : The uncensored truth about the men in the
  pocket / Mickey Herskowitz.
      p.   cm.
    ISBN 0-688-07387-5
    1. Quarterback (Football)   I. Title.
  GV951.3.H47   1990
  796.332'25—dc20   90-36053
                                                                  CIP

Printed in the United States of America

First Edition

1 2 3 4 5 6 7 8 9 10

BOOK DESIGN BY GLEN M. EDELSTEIN

To Sid Gillman, who saw the beauty in the passing game and enhanced it; to Don Klosterman, whose own promising career ended on a ski slope, but who understood as well as anyone the mentality of those who played the position; to Joe Namath, who made us look beyond the numbers; and to Bart Starr, who exemplified the best of the breed, this book is dedicated

ACKNOWLEDGMENTS

To approach the men in the pocket from an angle slightly off-center required the support of literally several teams of people. Ben Arthur, who can track a trail with the best of them, was extremely helpful with the early research and interviews. Jim Carley, a former pro football beat writer, came through at the wire to plug some missing holes.

Rick Mauck and Vincent Marino of the National Football League office in New York, Tim Williams of the NFL Alumni staff, and Susan Kuthe of NFL Properties Creative Services in Los Angeles, all provided valuable services, from locating long-retired players to digging out timeless photographs.

Additional thanks are due Jim Walden for raiding old files, and Michelle Lichlyter for baby-sitting the computer that turned out the pages.

There are no thanks large enough to cover the contributions of Bill Adler, the most prolific literary agent in the business, who shaped the idea and pushed it along; and Adrian Zackheim, an editor whose patience and insight kept us going on third and long; and Pamela Altschul, who was there for us down the stretch.

CONTENTS

★ 11

PROLOGUE

From the glory that was (Bob) Griese to the grandeur that was Roman (Gabriel), the quarterback has been at the center of pro football's universe. More is expected, or demanded, of him than of any other athlete in the vast canopy of sport. He is the object of our admiration and scorn, the bearer of our hopes and fears.

It is a fiction to pretend that football is a game that depends on eleven players working in harmony. Simply check out the reaction of a team whose starting quarterback has been shelved. They treat it as lightly as one would a plane crash.

In short, quarterbacks are a source of endless fascination and debate. The fashion in recent years has been to compare high-priced athletes—which certainly includes your typical pro quarterback—to our show business stars. In terms of potential fortune and fame, the comparison is valid. But an actor or a singer performs in a controlled situation. A star quarterback performs in a totally uncontrolled environment. Bodies are hurtling and thudding all around him.

The tension mounts before the game begins, continues as the game progresses, and, depending on the outcome, may linger for an indefinite and distressing period of time.

What sort of men choose this life? It is a career short lived at best, promising pain, real pain, and even the prospect of permanent injury. A Joe Theismann suffers a compound fracture of the leg. A Joe Montana undergoes major back surgery. A Neil Lomax goes out with a hip whose socket will need replacing. A concerned and anxious public asks gravely, "Will he be back in time for the playoffs?"

In the end each has to ask himself, Was it worth the grief? Was the roar of the crowd and the color of the money worth the years of discomfort and misery after the last clock has run out?

On this particular day, Terry Bradshaw, who led the Steelers to four Super Bowls in the 1970s, is taking inventory of his body. "I just had an MRI," he reports, referring to an instrument that electrically stimulates aching muscles, "on my lower back. Bothers me all the time. My wrist gives me constant trouble where I broke it. I also broke my neck once and that always hurts. I crawl out of bed every morning and have to roll around on the floor and twist and turn and pop my body to get myself going. But that's just part of it."

Any regrets? you ask, expecting he would have a few.

"Oh no," he says. "Football was the greatest thing that ever happened to me. It is the most intense emotional relationship I've had other than with my kids and my wife. It was the greatest passion I ever had. It was great. That's how crazy we are."

They are relentlessly interesting people, quarterbacks, even the dull ones, because they perform their art amid fierce collisions, always where we can observe their worst moments. We empathize with them. We see, if we do not quite feel, what it is like to stand in the pocket when the pocket is collapsing all around you.

Since Slinging Sammy Baugh threw his last pass in 1952, roughly two thousand quarterbacks have passed through the National Football League. The numbers alone restrict us to a list of players whose stories are either so different, or so representative, they begged to be told. I have chosen to cover the period from Baugh's time forward, making the turn, the transition, to the modern passing game. I have tried to be attentive to the incident here, the anecdote there, the encounter that defined a career.

Bill Walsh, now retired to the television booth but until recently the man who coached three fourths of the San Francisco 49ers' dynasty in the 1980s, credits Sid Gillman with the innovations that changed the passing game. "A lot of the things we did," he says, "went back to Sid Gillman football. Sid developed a system using all receivers that are eligible on most plays. We used our backs and tight ends as our main receivers so much of the time. We looked for those kinds of matchups more than some other teams. The routes we run, that most teams run, grew out of Gillman's ideas."

Sid Gillman coached off and on, mostly on, for forty-five years, including stints as head man of the Los Angeles Rams, when Norm Van Brocklin was his quarterback, and at San Diego, where he employed, among others, Jack Kemp and John Hadl.

It is Sid's proud boast that he is the only man to play in the first College All-Star game and to coach in the last one. On his honeymoon in 1935 Gillman took his bride, Esther, to Chicago for the game and played in a downpour, during which he impressed upon her the terrific location of their seats. The next day, with his bankroll down to twenty-five dollars, Sid blew fifteen of it on a movie projector he saw in a pawnshop window.

That was fifty-five years ago. Sid still has both the wife and the projector. He inherited his interest in film from his father who owned movie theaters in Minnesota. In the late 1950s, when he was head coach of the Rams, Sid started the first film exchange in the NFL.

His colleagues long regarded him as the premier student of technical football. It was his creative use of film footage that opened new horizons for the passing game. Gillman was in awe of the particular talents of the players he had, especially his throwers and receivers. The air game reigned supreme. "It wasn't a question of innovations," he insists. "We had Dutch Van

Brocklin, gawdamighty, what a passer he was. We had Tom Fears and Bob Boyd, the sprinter, and Elroy Hirsch back out of retirement, and a great back, Ron Waller.

"The main thing was Fears. We were just beginning to understand how 'moves' are made by a receiver. Fears was one of the greatest 'move' men in the history of the game. He didn't have much speed, but he could turn 'em on their heads. We studied Fears and we began to coach what he was doing."

Later in San Diego, Sid discovered another pair of splendid receivers, the graceful Lance Alworth, known as Bambi, and big, tough Dave Kocurek. "If Lance had played the piano," Gillman once mused, "he would have probably sounded like Arthur Rubenstein." One can only speculate how nice it must have been to play for a coach who knew who Arthur Rubenstein was.

Said Kocurek: "He was the best passing coach ever. He had films of all the great receivers, and he'd devote a reel to each particular pattern. He'd say, 'O.K., here's the post pattern,' and you'd see Tom Fears, Dante Lavelli, Billy Wilson, all of them running it."

Difficult as it may be to imagine today, professional football was not even exposed to two thirds of the country, not even on television, until the 1960s. In those days the new American Football League played a bombs-away brand of ball, with coaches such as Gillman, Al Davis, Hank Stram, and Weeb Ewbank leading the way.

It may take no more dedication to play quarterback, or to coach it, than any other position, but certain images are hard to shake. The quarterback is by necessity a leader of the team, whatever his nature, and some coaches lament the passing of a more combative type: Bobby Layne, Van Brocklin, George Blanda, Billy Kilmer. "Heck," says John Madden, the former Raiders coach turned TV analyst, "those guys were the field generals. They had control of what was going on out there. They would even spit at guys."

And yet, for once, a Hollywood stereotype isn't far off: The quarterback is often among the best-looking fellows on the team, starting in high school. He dates the best-looking girl, usually a cheerleader or baton twirler, and marries her, or someone like her. Check it out.

There was a renewed surge of interest in the passing game in the 1980s, and in the men at the controls. The likes of Dan Fouts, Tommy Kramer, Dan Marino, and Joe Montana took turns at leading the league. Changes in the rules made it more favorable to put up the ball, and the coaches schemed to outwit one another.

The results were often wild and spectacular. In the 1980 season Minnesota introduced a play called Squadron Right to beat Cleveland as time ran out, sending every available receiver downfield and then letting Tommy Kramer hang the ball like a weather balloon. It was deflected near the goal line and caught by Ahmad Rashad for forty-six yards and the winning touchdown. The Vikings had moved eighty-six yards in fourteen seconds with no time-outs. Snap City.

More and more teams turned to the use of gang or group reaction. There was the Maniac Blitz, when the defensive unit sent *everybody* in an effort to sack the quarterback, leaving no one back to keep an eye on the end zone except the photographers. The tactic led to a few sacks, several touchdowns, and some terrific pictures before it was abandoned.

And, of course, inflation struck the NFL in the 1980s. Nothing dramatic, understand, but the nickel defense went up to a dime, in a manner of speaking. Where once a nickel purchased a large amount of pass defense, some teams discovered they now needed more, as long as such aerial gunners as Kramer, Fouts, and Jim Zorn insisted on throwing forty or fifty passes a game.

So we began to see teams inserting as many as seven backs in obvious situations, while rushing four, or fewer. Most of this resulted from the rule change that limited defensive backs to one bump, or chuck, on a receiver and within five yards of the line of scrimmage. At some point the league also banned the use of stickum, a substance as sticky as axle grease used by receivers to help them hang on to the ball. Asked what effect the ban might have, Raiders safety Lester Hayes replied, "You'll see fewer guys catching passes with their elbows."

But the chaps who take the snaps are and always will be the object of our attention. "There's a lot of temperament in football," Tommy Prothro, then coaching the Chargers, once noted. "I would guess the most sensitive of all are quarterbacks. There's a reason for this. They are the most credited, discredited, booed, cheered, revered, hated people in the game. Far too much of what happens in football is linked to them. So when something happens, they would tend to take things more personally than the rest."

Everyone has an opinion on quarterbacks, of course, including other quarterbacks. To begin with, we wonder if we will see the quality in the 1990s that was evident in those of a generation or two ago.

"Oh yeah," says Bradshaw, who had to rebuild his career twice on his way to the Hall of Fame, "they don't change much. From one era to another, the Sammy Baughs, the Otto Grahams, the Joe Namaths, they could play for any team. Roman Gabriel. John Brodie. A Ken Stabler or a Dan Fouts. They could do it all in any era. Time diminishes their importance because people don't remember them. You ask someone who Sammy Baugh was, and he can't tell you. But if Baugh were in his prime today, he'd still be able to throw it eighty yards. He'd still be just as great."

Joe Theismann, the former Redskin, doesn't think the product coming off the assembly line today is equal to past standards.

"You used to have half a dozen or so exceptional quarterbacks," he says. "Unitas, Bradshaw, Starr, Hadl, Jurgensen, Namath. If they played well, the team won. Today the primary job of a quarterback is not to win games, it's to make the right decisions and not lose them."

Marv Levy, the Buffalo coach, believes that the defenses are so sophisticated that you simply can't compare the current crop with the passers of another day. "Sonny Jurgensen was a great quarterback, a great passer," says Levy. "He looked at a strong zone, weak zone, and man-to-man free safety. There isn't enough

time for me to explain all the coverages there are now. If anything, there are more good arms. But they are going against more
good defenders."

For this and other reasons we have seen the rise of the quarterback coach in the last decade. One of the better known of the
breed is June Jones, in Detroit, where he helped install an off-
fense known as the Run-and-Shoot, a formation that sends four
receivers scattering all over the field. The Lions called their version the Silver Stretch. It may be one of the trends worth watching in the 1990s.

You may also want to keep an eye on June Jones, who played
in a brief NFL career in Atlanta as a backup to Steve Bartkowski.
He was the kind of marginal talent but free spirit who gives the
game a certain texture, and who frequently makes the best kind
of coach.

He vividly remembers the first game he ever started for the
Falcons in the late 1970s, against the Houston Oilers. "I was an
emotional guy," he says, "and I'd get fired up for the games.
Well, Gregg Bingham was a linebacker with Houston at that
time, at the top of his career. I gave the ball to Bubba Bean over
the right side, and the whistle blew and everybody stopped, except Bingham. He took a cheap shot at Bubba while he sort of
stood up.

"So I ran into the pile and pushed him out of the way, and
we got into a verbal deal. We came to the line on the next play,
and I got up under the center. Then I stopped and I walked over
to the right guard, over to where Bingham was, and I looked
across the line at him and I said, 'We're running right over your
ass on this play. Right now! We're going to bury your ass right
here.'

"He just looks at me and beckons with his hands and he yells,
'Come on, come on. Bring it on. Bring it on.' So sure enough,
we ran the play right at him, and my whole team is looking at
me like, 'What the hell is going on?' I pivot and hand the ball
off to Haskel Stanback, and Bingham comes up and stuffs the
right guard, stuffs Haskel, and we get thrown for a loss on the

play. Haskel just got up and looked at me and said, 'June, please don't do that anymore.' "

No one ever said that playing quarterback was all ninety-yard drives and long touchdown passes and trips to Disney World. Of course, some of it is.

☆1☆ THE PATRIARCH

Fifteen years after football made its organized debut as a commercial venture, Sammy Baugh arrived in Washington and showed the game its future. It was Baugh who made the forward pass a routine play from scrimmage.

When coaches close their eyes and imagine the classic quarterback, they still see Sammy Baugh: tall and lean, with the hardness of a Texas ranch hand, which he was, and is. In Baugh's life, football was a transient thing—one might almost say a passing thing.

Baugh still owns over seven thousand acres of ranchland at Rotan, on the vast west Texas plains an hour north of Sweetwater. He has lived there since 1941, on the land that he bought with the money he made playing pro football.

He played sixteen seasons when the sport was at its crudest and roughest and meanest, without breaking a bone. Three years ago, he suffered a fractured left arm when he was blindsided by a bull. "It was kind of stupid," he confided. "Most times you get hurt it's something you did that's a little stupid. A cow got out the gate on us and I was gonna head the dang thing off, and a bull followed her and run over me from the back and I didn't even see it. I'm always cautious around bulls, but I wasn't too cautious that time and I broke my arm. That was my fault, not the bull's.

"I'd rather be hit by a football player, anytime. But that's the same way you get hurt in football. When you get hit from the blind side."

When you study the casualty reports among quarterbacks today, it isn't easy to imagine how conditions could ever have been any worse. But then you examine the rules under which Sammy Baugh played, and you are reminded of a scene from an adventure-comedy movie. With bullets slamming through the walls, one character says to another:

"I've got good news and bad news."

"Give me the bad news first."

"There is no way we can get out of here alive."

"What the hell is the good news?"

"We're not going to be here long."

This is the way Slingin' Sam remembers it: "The thing that hurt when I came into pro football in 1937, and it hurt all the boys that threw the ball, was that the rules didn't give any protection to the passers. Those linemen could hit the passer until the whistle blew. If you completed a pass out there and somebody's running fifty yards with the ball, well, that damned bunch could still hit you. In other words, a passer had to learn to throw and move. You would never see him just throw and stand there, looking. You had to throw and start protecting yourself because those sons of bitches were going to lay you right flatter than that ground every time.

"If you were a good ballplayer—a passer or whatever—they tried to hurt you and get you out of there. I believe they did that more so than today. See, we had only twenty-two or twenty-three men on a squad and they were playing both ways, offense and defense. So if you lost two good ones, you were dead."

Maiming an opposing team's star player was simply a basic part of the game plan. The tactic they often used was called the bootsie play, a cute name for such a mean deed. "Everybody would hit one man and just try to tear him to pieces," said Baugh. "I don't mean they ran this kind of play very often, but if they came up against a guy that was giving them a lot of trouble, they'd run the bootsie play every now and then and just stay after him.

"Like I said, the passers never could relax after they threw the damn ball. Nowadays, if a guy is not already in the act of hitting you when that ball goes in the air, he's not allowed to hit you. But back when I started it was just like a boxing match—you were just dodging and ducking and hitting. It looked awful at times. The coaches—and our coach [Ray Flaherty] said the same thing—told the team, 'Put that son of a bitch on the ground every time he throws the ball.' That was just a cardinal rule all through the league."

To the owners of that era, struggling as they were to survive, the safety of their players was not exactly uppermost in their minds. An early exception was George Preston Marshall, who owned the Redskins and appreciated what a unique property he had in Sammy Baugh. "If we don't put in some kind of a rule," he told his associates, "all the passers are going to get killed."

In the first game of his second season Baugh went down with a separated shoulder. The next year, 1939, a rule was adopted assessing a fifteen-yard penalty for roughing the passer.

Although Baugh has been acclaimed as the greatest thrower of footballs the sport has seen, that description may not do him justice. He may have been the most extraordinary talent ever to play the game. He was a great defensive back and punter, who in 1943 led the league in passing, punting, and interceptions.

"We kicked different than they do now," he said. "We were taught to kick the ball out of bounds all the time. If you didn't, that safety man would run the ball back down your throat because your offensive line couldn't cover a punt like they do today. We had that short punt formation where you kicked from only nine yards back, so your boys didn't release till they heard the thud of that ball. Today, on that deep punt formation, the center throws the ball back and everybody hits and goes."

Baugh had few if any equals at putting the ball out of bounds inside the 5 or 10 yard lines, the so-called coffin corner. Even before he turned pro, he had mastered the art at TCU. In the first Cotton Bowl ever played, won by TCU over Marquette, 16–6, on New Year's Day in 1937, he did it all day—with one exception.

The TCU coach, Dutch Meyer, instructed Baugh to kick away from the Marquette safety, Art Guepe, a cocky little scatback who later coached at Vanderbilt. "So I was kicking the ball out of bounds," recalled Sam, "and every time Guepe would pass our bench he'd say, 'Dutch, tell Sam to kick that ball to me.' And all during the game, Dutch kept telling me, 'Don't kick it to him.' But somewhere along the line I didn't get the ball out of bounds, and that son of a bitch ran it back. I remember him going over the goal line with that punt and throwing that ball as high as he could and jumping up and down, and I don't know if we ever laid a hand on the little pisser."

What is fascinating about Baugh's historic career is that it happened at all. He had no interest in pro football; in truth, he didn't really know what it was.

Twice an all-American, Baugh was Washington's first pick in 1937, in the first player draft the National Football League ever held. Baugh remembers being flown to Washington by George Preston Marshall and turning down an offer of four thousand dollars. "Down in Texas," he said, "no one knew anything about pro football. I didn't know if I could make it. Dutch Meyer had offered me a job coaching the freshman team at TCU, and I told Mr. Marshall I was going to stay in Texas and coach."

Actually, what Sam really wanted was to play major-league baseball. He had been a terrific prospect as an infielder and lost a baseball scholarship to Washington State when he blew out a knee sliding into second. Knee surgery was almost unheard of at the time, and his doctor told him to keep a mudpack on the knee. He did, mixing the mud with vinegar, and by the end of the summer the knee wouldn't bend. The scholarship fell through.

The summer after his senior year Baugh played third base in a semipro tournament in Denver and attracted the interest of Rogers Hornsby, the Hall of Fame second baseman who was then scouting for the Cardinals. Hornsby signed him to a contract for the next season, and a contented Sam Baugh moved on a week later to play football in Chicago, leading the college all-stars against the Green Bay Packers.

Given the chance to mix with other players from around the country, Baugh was surprised by the number who were committed to play in the NFL. "Most of them were like me," he said. "They hadn't been away from home—not even out of the county they were born in—too often. And I realized I could play better than ninety-nine percent of them. I became a little more confident about whether or not I could play pro football. As it turned out, we beat Green Bay and then Mr. Marshall got after me pretty hot.

"I didn't know how much pro players were making, but I thought they were making pretty good money. So I asked for eight thousand dollars and finally got it. Later, I felt like a robber when I found out what Cliff Battles and some of those other good football players were making."

Cliff Battles, Turk Edwards, and Wayne Millner, all future Hall of Famers, were making around three thousand dollars. "If I had known what they were getting," said Baugh, "I'd have never asked for eight thousand. But Mr. Marshall never did tell me, 'Well, So-and-so is only making so much.' He never did say that, and I thought more of him because he hadn't."

Battles quit the game when Marshall refused to give him a small raise, after he had led the league in rushing for the second time, in Baugh's rookie year.

Baugh didn't approve of the flamboyant Marshall's business methods, but he was a realist. "Of course, nobody was making a lot of money out of football in the thirties," he said. "The owners weren't making money. That's why I'll always think a lot of Marshall and George Halas and Art Rooney and those kinds of people—they stayed in there when it was rough. They stayed with it and made a great game out of it."

The arrival of Slingin' Sammy Baugh in Washington was an event. The thin-as-a-whip Texan stepped off the plane decked out in high-heeled cowboy boots and a ten-gallon hat. Only Baugh and Marshall knew that he had never worn this costume before; he was doing so now at the insistence of the owner, whose Redskins needed all the publicity they could get. The team was preparing for its first season in the nation's capital after moving from Boston. Sam was an immediate hit with photographers and newsreel cameramen. Before he ever threw a pass, he was the NFL's most photographed player.

A few observers wondered about his sturdiness, his ability to survive the punishment that was then the most consistent feature of the pro game. At six feet two and 180 pounds, he looked frail, but Baugh lacked neither confidence nor toughness.

His coaches became sold the day Ray Flaherty diagramed a play on the blackboard, concluding with, "And when the end gets right here, Sam, I want you to hit him in the eye with the ball."

"Which eye?" asked Baugh in his Texas drawl.

When push came to shove, as it often did in that era, he stood his ground. He didn't object when an opposing player knocked him down after he had delivered a pass; he expected it. But when a Green Bay tackle drove his fist into Baugh's face, he warned him not to do it again.

On the next play, the lineman ignored the warning and added a knee to the groin. Baugh's teammates were enraged, and Turk Edwards, their tackle and captain, offered to retaliate. "I'll take care of him myself," Baugh assured him. "Don't try to block him on the next play. Let him come through."

The tackle blasted through for the kill, and Baugh stood there, his arm cocked, until his tormentor was only a few feet away. Then he threw, a bullet pass that struck the tackle right between the eyes and knocked him cold. "He stood there for a split second," says Sam, "and then he just keeled over straight as a board. I thought I had killed him. Scared the daylights out of me. Of course, he recovered and when he came back he kept doing the same thing, so it didn't help a bit."

Those years were the prime of Sammy Baugh. The Redskins played for the championship five seasons out of his first nine. But mixed in with that success was an embarrassment that would linger forever: a 73–0 plastering by the Chicago Bears in the 1940 title game.

And when the carnage had ended, Baugh would put it in ripe perspective with a comment in the losing locker room. One of his receivers had dropped a touchdown pass that would have tied the score in the first quarter, and reporters crowded around to ask Sam if the outcome would have been different if the pass had been caught."

"Yeah," he replied, "it would have been at least seventy-three to six."

Decades later Baugh would say, "I have my own ideas about what happened in that game. I think it starts with the fact that we had played the Bears three weeks earlier and had beat them seven–three. Boy, it hurt 'em. Leaving the field, both teams had to go down the same steps, and I remember some of those Bears were crying. Their pride was hurt bad. I remember Bulldog Turner coming down those steps and saying, 'You just remember one thing—we'll be back in three weeks.'

"The week of the championship game, the weather was so bad in Chicago that I believe the Bears had to work inside. They couldn't work as hard as they wanted. In the meantime, we had beautiful, sunshiny weather in Washington and we worked like we were in training camp. We worked like dogs. I think we left a lot of our football on the practice field."

Nor could their cause have been helped when Marshall, after the Redskins edged the Bears in the regular season, gloated that the Bears were "crybabies and quitters." Halas pinned the newspaper clippings to the bulletin board before the teams met again for the title.

That game would go into the books—and stay there—for the most points and worst defeat in the history of the sport. After the Bears scored their tenth touchdown, the officials had to ask Halas not to kick for any more extra points. They were running out of footballs.

The Redskins had to wait two years for payback time. With Dick Todd and Wilbur Moore at halfback, and with virtually the same cast that had been beaten in the 73–0 game, they met the Bears again in the 1942 championship game. It was Ray Flaherty's last game as coach before entering the navy, and he decided against making any pep talk. He simply wrote in chalk on the blackboard, the numbers as large as he could write them, "73–0." That was the only message the players saw as they dressed in grim silence.

The Redskins won, 14–6, handing the heavily favored Bears their only loss of the season. Baugh passed to Wilbur Moore for thirty-five yards and one touchdown, and got off a quick kick that measured eighty-five yards from scrimmage.

During the war years, the Redskins remained contenders only because Baugh was deferred from service under the "essential occupation" rule. He worked his Texas ranch during the week. Then he would fly east on Friday, practice on Saturday, play on Sunday, and fly home after the game, in the days long before jet aircraft, on planes that made five or six stops. Farmers and ranchers were exempt from the draft.

Meanwhile, the teams were switching one by one to the T, spurred on by the impression of one game, the Bears' humiliation of the Redskins in 1940. Most football historians believe the modern era began that season, when the Bears established their streamlined version of the standard T, with the quarterback under the center and a man in motion.

Clark Shaughnessy, a true offensive genius, was between college jobs when Halas enlisted his help with the Bears. The first time he diagramed a play, with a halfback hitting the line without a blocker in front of him, the players laughed out loud. They thought he was crazy.

Baugh had come into the league as a single-wing tailback. Up to that time, the quarterback position did not exist as we know it today. The quarterback might call the signals, but he lined up as a blocking back.

Baugh took a direct snap from center, and when he wasn't passing, running, or quick-kicking, he did a little blocking himself. "It about killed me," he says, of the single-wing sweeps that required him to take out an end.

This was the game Baugh knew for seven seasons, yet he was a reluctant convert when the club decided to install the T formation in 1944. Marshall brought in Shaughnessy to teach his players the finer points, as he had done for the Bears earlier in the decade.

The Redskins struggled that year as they tried to master the T and finished in third place. At first Baugh hated the formation and doubted he would ever feel comfortable snuggling up to his center. Shaughnessy assured him that he would learn to love it, that when they introduced it to the Bears, after a few weeks Sid Luckman cried out of frustration—the same Sid Luckman who would later set the standard for that position.

Soon the ball handling and play fakes came more easily, and in time Baugh would feel that the T had extended his career by years. "For a while I could have played in top hat and tails," he said. "The wear and tear on a T quarterback was about half what it was on a tailback."

During most of the early years of pro football the teams used the short punt or the Notre Dame box before shifting to the single wing. All of these were primarily running formations.

The rules of the game were gradually changed to favor the forward pass. The ball grew slimmer and easier to throw. In 1943 the adoption of the free substitution rule meant that pass-catching specialists could be used without regard to their ability to play defense.

Each new wrinkle in the offense, of course, was intended to put pressure on the defense, to expose a weakness, to force an adjustment. It was an endless game of chess. First, the offensive teams began splitting an end to one side, getting him away from the traffic in the middle. The running game grew less dominant, and eventually one of the two halfback positions was recycled. They moved this position outside the end and called it the flanker.

The defense was constantly struggling to adjust. The outside linebackers had to react to the threat of the wide receivers. With most teams using the so-called Eagle defense, with a five-man line, the responsibility for stopping the run over the center fell to the middle guard (now known as the nose tackle).

The middle guards were, accordingly, roughly the size of New Hampshire. Ed Neal of the Green Bay Packers weighed 324 pounds and broke empty beer bottles over his forearm to more easily dispose of them, making him an early volunteer in the antilitter, environmental campaign. Les Bingaman, of the Detroit Lions, was about the same size and could flip the top off beer bottles with his thumbnail. But the era of power football was ending, and a new style evolving, quicker, wide open, built around the men with the golden arms.

Baugh had such confidence in the passing game that he didn't hesitate to throw from his own end zone, as he did in the 1945 championship game. Two fluke plays won it for the Rams, 15–14, in their last game in Cleveland, in six-degree weather.

A pass by Baugh hit the back of the goalposts for what was then an automatic safety, and a placekick by Bob Waterfield, the Rams' quarterback, hit the crossbar and bounced through. Before the next season, the Rams would move to Los Angeles, and the rule would be changed to make such a pass an incompletion.

In the postwar years great quarterbacks seemed to roll off the assembly line. Waterfield in 1945 enjoyed the finest rookie season any quarterback ever had. A year later, Otto Graham began his career in the All-America Conference.

Paul Christman, from Missouri, reported to the Chicago Cardinals in 1945 and led them to a championship in 1947. Around that time, a weathered-looking graduate of Ole Miss named Charlie Conerly was breaking in with the New York Giants. Angelo Bertelli and Glenn Dobbs started their careers with the Los Angeles Dons, and George Ratterman began his in Buffalo.

Frankie Albert, the first of the college T quarterbacks under Shaughnessy, at Stanford, had taken his left-handed artistry to the San Francisco 49ers. By 1948 two more superb prospects had signed with the Bears, Johnny Lujack of Notre Dame and Bobby Layne of Texas. On New Year's Day in 1949 Norm Van Brocklin led Oregon into the Cotton Bowl, and a few months later he joined Waterfield on the Rams.

This wave of talent turned the game more and more toward the pass. And each in his time would be measured against Sam (not Samuel) Adrian Baugh.

They were emerging too as people, as personalities. In 1939

Hollywood plucked Baugh, who had a distinct Gary Cooper-ish look, to star in a western serial called *King of the Texas Rangers*.

"Tom King, that was supposed to be my name," said Baugh. "Actually, the picture was one of those serials that they used to show in weekly episodes, and I never knew what the damn thing was about. We'd have to be at the studio about six o'clock and get made up. You had a script, but I can't remember very few days they ever stuck to it. They'd tell you what to study for the next day, but then you'd get there and maybe the weather wouldn't be just right so they'd go to something else in the script. I got where I never would even look at the thing.

"I think I was there about six weeks. I rented me a little apartment over there near the studio. Everyone out there was real nice, but there wasn't a thing in Hollywood I was interested in. I didn't care about nightclubs. I did go to a few saddle shops and places like that, but I was just glad when the goddamn thing was over.

"I saw some of them episodes, but never did see 'em all together. I still to this day don't know what I was supposed to be doing in that picture."

As long as the Redskins had Baugh—and they had him until 1952—they were a team to be feared. But they suffered from uninspired coaching, and from being the last NFL team to integrate its roster. Marshall was no racist, but the Redskins had a radio network that reached through the Deep South and he believed he would alienate his listeners by playing blacks. (Running back Bobby Mitchell integrated the team in 1960, after pressure was put on Marshall by the Kennedy administration.)

The glory years were behind him when the club decided to honor Baugh with a special day in 1947. He was given a new station wagon and other gifts before the game, then he put on one of his finest performances. He hit eleven of his first thirteen passes, threw for six touchdowns and 355 yards in a romp over the Cardinals, who would win the Western Conference.

One of the charms of the pro game in that era was the sometimes whimsical way in which coaches were hired. By 1949

Baugh had played under five coaches, including a former career naval officer, a retired admiral named John Whelchel, who lasted seven games. "Turned out to be a real nice fellow," said Baugh. "All the players liked him, although he wasn't up on his football as he should have been."

That year the Redskins were breaking in a rookie quarterback as Baugh's understudy, Harry Gilmer, out of Alabama. In the league opener, Baugh had been shaken up and was on the bench in a game they were losing badly to the Chicago Cardinals. When the Cardinals stretched their lead to 30–0 in the fourth quarter, Baugh began to relax, grateful that his day was over. Just then the admiral walked over and nudged him. "Sam," he said, "you better get back in there a'fore this thing gets out of hand."

The NFL had adopted the two-platoon rule, and later in the season George Preston Marshall concluded that the admiral had his athletes playing out of position. In short, he felt Washington's best offensive linemen were on defense, and its best defenders were on offense. He told his coach to straighten out his personnel.

"Well, the admiral didn't pay any attention to him at all," said Baugh, "and we were out there working one day when here comes Marshall in that big black car of his. He looks at us for a while, then he comes out and stops practice. He said to the admiral, 'I thought I told you what I wanted done.'

"The admiral didn't say a word. He just turned around and walked off the field and got in his car and left. Well, that kind of threw Mr. Marshall. Meantime, we just stood around. Finally Mr. Marshall told me and a couple of others to get in his car. We were going back to the hotel, and he was madder than hell. 'How could you let this happen?' he yelled at us. 'How could you let this man ruin the ball club?'

"We said, 'Hell, Mr. Marshall, he's the coach. We're just the players.'

"But George said, 'Hell, I hired him to be a *disciplinarian*. I didn't hire him for a goddamn coach.' "

The Redskins would go twenty-five years without returning

to the playoffs, from 1946 until George Allen's Over-the-Hill Gang broke through in 1971. But Baugh's records would outlast the memory of even the poorest of Washington's teams. Fifty years after his arrival, he would still hold or share a total of eleven.

In 1939 he completed 70.3 percent of his passes, and that record lasted until Brian Sipe broke it in 1972. Three of his punting records are still in the books, including his single-season average of 51.4 yards per punt in 1940. And he shares the record for intercepting passes in one game, with four. Keep in mind that he didn't throw them, he *caught* them. We can just about guarantee you that this is a record no quarterback will ever threaten.

There was an entertaining, although not exactly happy, sequel to the career of Sammy Baugh. When he retired to his ranch, his contact with football was to be low-keyed and at his convenience. A coaching tour at Hardin Simmons, near his home, filled that description.

Baugh's name was not one that would have popped into mind as a prospect for a head coaching job in pro ball. But when you get down to it, the only qualification a fellow needs is an owner who will give him the job. And along came Harry Wismer, the colorful former sportscaster who in 1960 had the rights to the New York franchise in the freshly minted American Football League.

The team, called the Titans, existed mostly in Wismer's apartment, if not his imagination. Operating on the thinnest bankroll in the league, Wismer in the early months made his living quarters the team offices. The ticket staff was in a hallway. The coaches had the dining room, and the publicity director, Ted Emery, occupied a butler's pantry between the kitchen and the one bathroom available to the staff. If anyone wanted to use the bathroom, Emery had to get up, squeeze past the cook, the mimeograph, and wire-service machines, and leave the area.

All of which may seem to have little to do with Sammy Baugh's coaching status, but to the contrary, it did. Baugh operated under the same severe limits, and many felt he did an outstanding job to lead a miscellaneous New York team to two consecutive 7–7 seasons.

The Titans had a handful of legitimate pros: Don Maynard, a Giants castoff who would make it into the Hall of Fame as a wide receiver; Bill Mathis, a rookie running back from Clemson; Al Dorow, an NFL retread at quarterback; and Art Powell, a veteran end who had played well in Canada.

Those were sometimes comical and always unpredictable times. The crowds at the old Polo Grounds were so small, and the attendance figures so clearly padded by Wismer, that writers noted that thousands had shown up disguised as empty seats.

Wismer had hired Baugh because he thought the great quarterback's name and reputation would sell tickets. When Wismer launched a subway advertising campaign, the pictures on the posters were Harry's own. He figured he was better known than any of the players.

In that environment no coach could have survived. But before Baugh disappeared into the sunset, he became embroiled in, of all things, a quarterback controversy. He had established a decent passing attack, with Al Dorow putting the ball up an average of thirty-one times a game. After a game with Buffalo, Baugh tongue-lashed his quarterback for starting a fight in front of the other team's bench. Wismer was upset, feeling that a fight had public relations value, and he sided with the player.

Harry was an agitator and a lover of intrigue; he could tell you the serial number of the Unknown Soldier. He cooked up a press conference for Dorow and two lesser players, and they blasted Baugh for his coaching failures. Among their complaints was that they had no playbook.

Baugh admitted it. "Before you can have a playbook," said Sam, "you first have to have paper."

But Baugh was liked and admired by most of the players, and a meeting was quietly held and a plan adopted. In the next game, the players decided to "open the gates" on Al Dorow. When a team opens the gates on a quarterback, the blockers take turns letting the opposing rushers get through, making sure that at least two reach the passer every time he drops back. It doesn't take much of this form of punishment before a quarterback figures out what is going on—if he is conscious.

Sammy Baugh learned of the plot and put a stop to it. At the end of the 1961 season, Wismer hired Bulldog Turner and Baugh again went home to the range.

Except for a brief excursion as coach of the Houston Oilers, and a part-time college job or two, he has stayed there ever since.

☆2☆ LEADERS OF
THE BAND

There was Waterfield. And Graham. And Van
Brocklin. And Unitas. Now some say Bart Starr.
Others say Tittle, but he never won the big one.
But for those of us who know the game, there
was only one quarterback . . . Bobby Layne.

Howard Cosell.

Bobby never lost a game in his life. Time just
ran out on him.

Doak Walker.

Time may be the only thing that ever dared to run out on Robert Lawrence Layne, pro football's original Macho Man, the last
quarterback to play without a face mask or protective pads. "I
like freedom," he said, meaning in movement as well as thought.

And Cosell's fine sentiments were probably no less sincere for
having been said not in public, but to Bobby himself. He would
have wanted it that way, frankly. Layne hated crowds. It was
an interesting conflict in the nature of a man who spent the

better part of his life in front of crowds, adored by most, booed by some, but always sensitive to their alternating currents.

Layne helped usher in the golden age of professional football when he led the Detroit Lions to a championship season in 1954. Layne and his teammates and a moody genius of a coach named Buddy Parker shared something remarkable that year. They built a team, and with it an idea that took root and grew and became bigger than their own time and place. For it was one thing for a metropolis such as New York to accept pro football. But when you captured Detroit the rest of America would not be far behind. This was a workingman's game in a workingman's town. And there was never a bigger blue-collar hero in the whole blessed firmament of sports than Bobby Layne.

Texans practically invented the word "heroic," and Layne, a Texan, had been a hero since high school, if not before. In Dallas, he played in the same Highland Park backfield with Doak Walker, later his Detroit teammate. They were a wondrous pair. Layne ran and passed. Walker ran and caught. Both of them kicked, blocked, and played defense.

Bobby was a blue-eyed, tousled blond whose talents divided the University of Texas campus fans nearly in half. They just could not decide if he was greater as a football or baseball player— as a pitcher, he was unbeaten in four seasons.

But his future was in football. Even in his relatively innocent amateur days, he could give a bungling teammate a look that would stop Big Ben. Nobody used the word "charisma" back then. But anyone could see that Bobby had presence; he had an aura, which consisted of equal parts sulfur, gunsmoke, Texas natural gas, and bourbon.

In Texas he courted and married a lovely coed named Carol Krueger. Many years later, Carol would say, "If I am ever reincarnated, I'd like to come back as Bobby's chauffeur. That way I'd get to see all the places he saw."

At least she was there at the start, for every blessed mile. Bobby Layne came to the National Football League by car, sharing the driving with his wife and his college coach, Blair Cherry. En route to the camp of the Chicago Bears, Layne would hop out

of the car at every gas stop to work on his techniques. His wife
would snap the ball and Bobby would pivot and go through his
fakes while Coach Cherry observed and offered criticisms. All
through the Midwest, they left behind a trail of service station
attendants who concluded they had then seen everything.

There was always a separate category for Bobby Layne. Other
quarterbacks had a more graceful form, threw longer or prettier
passes, were faster or stronger. But none pushed, drove, threatened, scolded, or inspired like Layne. He led, as few have
ever led.

"Now Layne," said Red Hickey, the former 49ers coach, "as
bad as he looked throwing the ball, was a winner. You'd work
him out and you wouldn't want him. But you'd want him in
your huddle. Players feel that way about a quarterback. When a
leader is in there, they'll perform, they'll go."

Bobby agreed: "There's something about being a winner. You
can spot a winner by the way he walks down the street. When
you're a winner you don't have to park your car yourself, somebody parks it for you. When you're not a winner you have to
stand in line for picture shows, but when you're a winner you
go in the back door with the manager."

Some might find the idea quaint, this reverence for winning.
But Bobby was part of pro football's last picture show, the era
before the small screen took over and the stadiums overflowed
and the money cascaded through the roof.

What Layne did best was win, pure and simple. Well, maybe
not always pure and certainly not always simple. He had a par-
ent-child relationship with his offensive line. Lou Creekmur, who
was an all-pro tackle for the Lions in the 1950s, remembers how
it was: "If you ever missed a block, Layne made sure everybody
knew about it, guys on the field, guys on the bench, everybody
in the stadium knew it. He would get the number of the guy
who creamed him, figure out who was at fault, and call you
right out of the huddle. He'd stand there, raving at you and
shaking a finger in your face, and you wanted to punch him. A
couple of times we had to grab people to keep 'em from hitting
Bobby. But off the field there was nothing he wouldn't do for

us. He bought us steaks. He showed us respect, that was the main thing."

No one ever accused Layne of being a diplomat in the huddle. Once, during his term with the Steelers, he exploded at Ed Beatty, his center. "Beatty," he roared, "once, just once, take out your man and we'll declare a damned holiday."

Years later Layne would wince when such stories were repeated to him. "I never got on anybody for dropping a pass or getting beat by his man," he said. "Those things happen. What drove me nuts was somebody missing a block or an assignment."

In short, he felt his research in the field of human relations spoke for itself. "One year at Detroit," he said, "I quit getting on the guys and they went to Parker and asked him to make me get on them again. Said it made them play better. I was trying to be a good guy that year—the guy with the white horse and the white hat. But it's more fun the other way."

It was Yale Lary, the fine Detroit safety, who explained how the Layne brand of leadership worked: "When Bobby said block, you blocked. When Bobby said drink, you drank."

That, too, was part of the legend. Layne once beat a drunk-driving charge when his attorney persuaded the judge that the arresting officer had mistaken Bobby's Texas drawl for drunken slurring. The incident, which involved an early-morning collision with a parked car, led to some not so gentle needling. When Layne walked into the Lions' locker room a day or so later, he was greeted by a sign erected by the equipment manager, Friday Macklem: AH ALL AIN'T DRUNK, AH'M FROM TEXAS.

Layne was not insensitive to his reputation and defended his late habits on the grounds of an inner time clock that had to be served. "I'm the kind of guy," he once said, "who can't go to bed early. I don't need more than five hours sleep. If I go to bed early, I wake up early, maybe five o'clock, and if there's a game to play that day I play it over in my mind maybe a dozen times."

In truth, he was unselfish, unsparing of himself, and almost schoolboyish in his devotion to his teammates. "We had a team of leaders," he said. "The fellowship between our players was practically legendary. We all thought the same way. You could have all the fun you wanted to, but when you went out to play, you had to win. We looked forward to practice, we looked forward to games. We even looked forward to training camp. Damn, it was like going on a vacation when we went to training camp. Guys got there *early* just to get up there and get their hands on the football. Today that spirit is gone. I think the reason is money."

Certainly, the game Bobby Layne knew and revered is gone. So are the Bobby Laynes who played it. Once after a disappointing season, Layne offered to take a $2,500 cut in his next year's contract. The Lions knew it was no stunt, no grandstand play. Nor did it embarrass the management to accommodate him. It was, of course, a different life-style that the players pursued, and a different code by which they existed.

This was an era when the size of a team's monthly phone bill might determine whether or not it broke even. As one of the league's highest-salaried stars (twenty-five thousand dollars), Layne attracted a reputation for free spending. Yet it upset him if anyone misjudged his motives. "I never tried to be a big shot," he said. "But I had enough sense to realize I made more money than anybody else on the club. So I always allocated a certain part of my salary to spend on the team. I mean, I didn't try to pick up every tab, but I tried to pick up more than my share.

"I tipped good, but I got good service. I never owned a Cadillac. I never owned a boat. Never had a diamond ring in my life and never wore any rings or stickpins or crap like that. I don't think I dressed fancy. But I did carry around a little spending money.

"I tried to encourage togetherness, and I think we had it. As soon as one game was over, it was a past thing. Yesterday's newspaper. Forgotten, win or lose. We went on to the next."

Before there was a players association, the Lions took their labor issues directly to the ownership. "They met with us," Layne recalled, "and I believe the topics were who had to buy the shoes, the players or the owners, and how much laundry money we should get. They had agreed to twenty-five dollars a week, and we were going for more.

"Finally, Night Train Lane stood up in the back of the room and said, 'Am I under the consumption that this is all we're gonna get?' Everybody cracked up and that was that."

An era was ending when Layne began his pro career in 1948. Jet travel, national television, and respectability would come to the game in the next decade. By the time he retired in 1963, the boom was just around the corner. He had played fifteen seasons; a year each with the Chicago Bears and the woeful New York Bulldogs, then on to eight more in Detroit and winding up with five years in Pittsburgh.

In 1950 Detroit purchased Layne for fifty thousand dollars (plus another player) from the New York Bulldogs, a struggling franchise owned by Ted Collins, the manager of singer Kate Smith. Layne said he learned in New York that he could take a hard blow, that he could get hit and not get gun-shy. Bobby did not enjoy this part of his education, but felt he had earned it fairly.

The Detroit coach, Bo McMillin, had been the storied quarterback of the Praying Colonels of little Centre College, who upset Harvard in 1919, when Harvard and Yale dominated the sport. By 1945 Bo had coached Indiana to the Big Ten title, and three years later, his recruitment into the pro ranks had been regarded—by the Lions' ownership, at least—as a coup. He was signed to a five-year contract and fired after three. He believed in long practices, three or four hours, and he did not believe in such things as field goals, feeling that to kick for points was somehow unmanly.

Layne begged McMillin to use Doak Walker, a reliable kicker, inside the 20 or 30 yard lines when a field goal might have won the game. McMillin never budged. Nor did he accept the advice of his assistant coaches, who wanted to modify the Lions' system. "He had numbers no one could get straight except him," said Layne. "Hell, the coaches couldn't remember what the plays were, much less the quarterback. He had a 'ninety-eight' where the left halfback ran over right guard, and a 'ninety-seven' where the quarterback threw a pass. Nothing had anything to do with anything."

Most of all, the Lions resented the dreary practices on a public playground in a tough part of town, with no shelter from the freezing winds of a Detroit winter. McMillin bundled up in an aviator suit, complete with flight boots, cap, and gloves, while the players shivered and cursed.

The Lions were a mediocre team in 1950, and one of the owners invited several of the players to explain what had gone wrong in a 6–6 season. Three of the players, Layne, Doak Walker, and Cloyce Box, said pointedly, "We can win with Buddy Parker." Parker had joined the coaching staff that season after having been fired by the Chicago Cardinals. The owners paid off McMillin, who moved to the Philadelphia Eagles. No one knew then that he was a dying man, with fewer than fifteen months to live.

The promotion of Parker slammed the door on one era and opened up a new one. He and Layne had a rare chemistry, and common insights. They were both hard-nosed Texans who saw the game as a contest of wits as well as brawn. "Buddy was the smartest coach I was ever around," said Layne. "He was able to do things with a pencil and paper that people did later with computers. No one was ever better at grading a film."

Layne did not work at being colorful or difficult or special, which may explain how he could manage to be all three. In whatever he did, on or off the field, a sense of mischief was evident. He delighted in making up little trick plays, and he saved a beauty for the New York Giants, one he was confident would work against the defense they liked to use. He called it the Wait a Minute play.

As Layne bent over the center, halfback Tom Tracy suddenly shouted, "Wait a minute!" Then without moving from his crouch, Bobby looked around.

"What's the matter?" he called out.

On the word "matter," the center snapped the ball directly to John Henry Johnson, who ran for a touchdown. Unfortunately, an official was faked out by the play and called the Lions offside.

It is fair to conclude that Layne was not the sort who responded well to regimentation. When his sons, Rob and Alan, were old enough, he brought them to training camp on the theory that the trip would give their mother a rest and teach the boys self-reliance. This was probably true on both accounts.

Rob was eight the first time he joined his father at the Lions camp at Ypsilanti, Michigan. He palled around with head coach Buddy Parker's son, Bobby, who was a year or so older. Although most of the team helped out with baby-sitting, the boys were free to roam much of the time.

For years to come Layne would connect what he called the hardest workout of his life with "the night the boys missed curfew. We were getting ready to play the college all-stars," he remembered, "and Buddy was worried about it. He told us the only way those college kids could beat us was if we weren't in shape. So he said, 'I'm going to work you.'

"We had a scrimmage on the Saturday before the game, and that night we were supposed to be in at eleven o'clock. We never had a curfew during training camp, but that night we did, on account of the college all-stars. And Buddy decided to make a bed check.

"The veterans were all on one floor. The rookies were above us on the third floor, and they were all scared to death and in their rooms. Well, Buddy started to walk down the veterans' hall and the first five or six rooms he checked were empty. His son and mine shared a room, and when he got to it the door was open. He looked inside and the kids were gone. Someone heard Parker cry out, 'My God, even the kids aren't in yet!'

"What had happened was this. Sonny Gandee [an end] had taken them to a drive-in movie, and he was so tired he fell asleep. The boys didn't have the heart to wake him, so they spent most of the night there.

"After breakfast the next morning, I thought I'd get cute, so I lined the guys up and marched 'em out to practice, everybody who had been out the night before, including the kids. Buddy wasn't amused. We had a lot of coaches there taking notes."

Addressing the truants, Parker told them they had a choice of paying a fine of a hundred dollars or going through a special workout. A special workout was one designed to leave every player on his hands and knees. Layne could better afford to pay the fine than the others, but he said he would take the workout. The others went along.

"Well," Bobby went on, "we knew it was going to be rough. There wasn't a football on the field. We ran hundred-yard dashes and played leapfrog where you jumped over each other's butts, and we pushed the blocking sled the length of the field five times, and rolled ourselves down to the goalpost and back, two hundred yards. Talk about getting sick. Guys were throwing up and getting dizzy and running into fences.

"We'd throw up, turn green, and roll a little farther. But we all made it. All finished the workout. I said, 'Fall in,' and started forming a line. Guys were throwing up and falling in. But Buddy came over to me and said, 'If you're feeling so good maybe we ought to start over. I said, '*Fall out.*'

"One of the things I remember is that Harley Sewell wasn't one of the guys who missed curfew. But he didn't say anything. Later Buddy asked him why he went through the workout, and Harley said he didn't want to miss anything."

Layne was the first pro football player to have a social identity, an image, a personality known and understood by the public. His name and picture appeared in places other than the sports pages. Now and then he made the gossip columns, and the pages where items from traffic court were carried. The stories were not always fair to Layne and he resented them. It was a hard way to make pro football better known, but in the 1950s all ways helped.

Layne liked good music, good food, and good company, and he saw his after-dark activities as an extension of his football routine. He led his teammates in both pursuits.

Harley Sewell, an all-American guard from Texas, joined the Lions in 1953 and became a favorite of Layne's. One night in training camp, Bobby barged into Sewell's room just as he was getting undressed for the night.

"Rookie, put on your clothes," said Bobby, "we're going to town. I need some toothpaste." Sewell pleaded that he was ready for bed, but to no avail.

"I went out with Bobby to get some toothpaste," he recalled, "and got to bed three days later."

But Sewell, who became Layne's roommate, also offered a disclaimer. "We had our fun on Monday at the Stadium Bar. But when we were on the road Bobby was always in by bed check on Saturday night. We got up at six in the morning and Bobby would order lots of coffee up to the room. Then he had me go over the ready list [of plays]. We already knew it, but that was his way of working off energy."

With Buddy Parker's blessing, Layne molded the Lions and gave them a character that transcended yards gained and won-lost records, a flair of his that endures in memory. It was a grand partnership. "Buddy used to warn us," said Layne, "about drinking, carousing, and playing cards for money. He said, 'I know very few guys who can do two of them well, and not many who can do one of them well. But if you ever try to do all three around here, you're gone.' "

Parker had a deviously calculating mind. Once, when a railroad switch engine idled back and forth on a track that passed the Lions' practice field, Parker looked up to see the engineer and the fireman watching the workout. He promptly stopped the practice until the train pulled out. "For all I know," he said, "George Halas could be sitting in the cab of that old locomotive."

It was Parker who introduced the two-minute offense to the NFL. That is, he was the first coach to design an offense for crunch time and to work on it daily. He had noticed that many teams let down in the last two minutes before the half and the last two minutes of a game. He thought a team could organize itself to take advantage of that tendency. But Buddy conceded that no theory was worth much without execution. "What made it work," he said, "was the fact that I had the Big Guy." The Big Guy, of course, was Layne.

The Lions made their move in 1951, finishing second and stirring the city. "Detroit was a baseball town and a hockey town then," said Layne. "They hadn't had a winner for so long— what I call a winner is a championship team, and they hadn't had one since 1935. Gordie Howe was coming into his great years with the Red Wings. George Kell and Fred Hutchinson were the stars for the Tigers. We got them excited that year and won it the next."

The 1952 title game against the Browns turned on one play. From the Lions 33 yard line, Cloyce Box lined up wide to his left and ran a deep pattern down the middle. Layne faked a handoff to Pat Harder over left guard and slipped the ball to Doak Walker, heading between the tackle and end on the right side. Walker then cut back to the middle, and the slender Box took out both the cornerback and safety.

Walker's sixty-seven-yard run was his first touchdown of the year, but it gave Detroit a 14–0 lead and set up a 17–7 victory at Cleveland. Suddenly the Lions were the NFL champions, the hottest thing to hit town since the V-8 engine.

After the game, Layne was so keyed up that he and Carol piled their belongings into the car and headed south, driving straight through to their house in Lubbock, Texas, without stopping to sleep. Pro football players couldn't afford two houses in the 1950s, or first-class air fare, and they did not hang around after a season ended. These were the simple truths.

If you asked Layne to select a favorite play, he would offer you a dozen. (When Norm Van Brocklin was asked this question in a magazine interview, he replied that his favorite play was *Our Town* by Thornton Wilder.)

Layne's historic play occurred in the 1953 NFL title game. The Browns led, 16–10, on a pair of field goals by Lou Groza. With barely four minutes remaining, Layne did what all great quarterbacks must do: He raced the clock. On fourth down he passed to Jim Doran for eighteen yards to the Cleveland 33. Then he called a time-out and huddled with Parker.

Doran, who played mostly defense, was in the lineup at tight end for the injured Leon Hart. The Lions had been waiting for this moment all day. Layne trotted back onto the field, looked around at the tense faces waiting for his next words, and said with a grin, "Gimme a little time, boys, and we'll party tonight."

Doran lined up wide, with Box taking the tight end's spot. Box ran an out-pattern toward the right sideline, and Layne gave him a look to fake the cornerback. Then he lofted the ball to Doran, streaking downfield for the winning touchdown. It was the kind of dramatic, perfect, inside-reasoned play that typified the Lions of that period.

Even the wives got into the spirit of that victory. Recalled Layne: "Chlorophyll was real big that year. You had it in toothpaste, chewing gum, everything. So we had a slogan: 'Chlorophyll will put more sock in your jock.' The day we beat Cleveland in the championship game, all our wives sat up there in the stands, wearing hats that they'd made from jockstraps dyed green. Some tied a bow in 'em, some of them wore them as a band . . . and it was pretty cute."

The Lions missed a third consecutive NFL crown in 1954. In a rematch with Cleveland, the Browns raced in front, 21–3, after fifteen minutes and never looked back. The final score was 56–10. Explained Bobby: "We were pressing for three in a row, and everybody went to bed at ten o'clock. I woke up at four like an owl." (Ravaged by clean living, Layne did not often repeat the mistake of going to bed too early.)

That night after the game, Parker went home with a few drinks in him and headed downstairs to the game room in his basement, where a portrait of Buddy hung on the wall. He took out a pocketknife and quietly slashed a cut all the way through the painting.

The next year was a wasted one for Layne, who tore up a knee and was in and out of the lineup. The Lions finished in last place. They rebuilt the defense around linebacker Joe Schmidt and carried the 1956 race down to the twelfth and final game. The season ended in Chicago, in rhubarb and violence, a source of dark suspicions to this day.

The intrigue began at the Edgewater Beach Hotel, home of Guy Lombardo, Coleman Hawkins, and the Mickey Finn, if the Lions are to be believed. "We all ate together and stayed together the night before the game," said Parker, "and Layne was the only guy who got sick. He vomited all night. What are you going to think? Somebody at the hotel must have slipped something to him. Layne had never been sick in his life."

With a title on the line, Layne started the game. In the second quarter, he made a handoff and watched the runner hit the hole. At the same time he was blindsided by Chicago end Ed Meadows and taken out of the game with a concussion. Various Lions spent the rest of the day taking shots at Meadows, and Lou Creekmur was to remember later that he smashed Meadows's jaw. But what shows in the record book is that the Lions lost the conference title by a half game, 38–21.

Years later Layne said of the hit by Meadows: "The lights just went out. I'd be the last guy to say he meant to do it. But I'll put it this way: He could have avoided it.

"A lot of the guys went out of their way to avoid hurting a guy. Hardy Brown of the Forty-niners collapsed a lot of people with the shoulder shot he gave, but he was kind to me. I'll say that. Ol' Hardy would say, 'Gotcha, don't move.' And I'd say, 'Don't worry, buddy, don't worry.' "

Layne could appreciate a good blow fairly struck, the aesthetics of it. He especially admired Larry Wilson, a Hall of Famer at safety for the St. Louis Cardinals. "Larry was the guy who perfected the safety blitz," he said. "You had to have some kind of death wish to invent the safety blitz. But Larry Wilson may have been the toughest guy pound for pound who ever played this game. He'd stand there across the line and his mouth would be open. He didn't have any teeth, which made him look like Popeye.

"He worried the hell out of coaches with the safety blitz, and quarterbacks weren't exactly immune either. We were playing the Cardinals and Buddy says he's got the solution. Parker was always maneuvering. You had to set your alarm at midnight to get up before Parker.

" 'What we gonna do,' Buddy told us before the game, 'is take care of Larry Wilson real early with that safety blitz. He turned to John Henry Johnson and said, 'John Henry, we want you to uncoil on him. We're gonna hide you someplace in the backfield and when he comes, pop him.'

"Sure enough, Larry Wilson comes with the safety blitz, like, on the third play of the game. We got John Henry hunkered down low in the backfield and all I can say is, 'Here he comes!'

"Larry Wilson busts through and John Henry unloads. Legal, but brutal. Wilson went down like he was hit by a train. He's just laying there stiff. I actually thought he was dead. They finally brought him back to consciousness and hauled him off the field. I sort of regretted it, and I told one of the guys, 'You got to admire Larry Wilson for what he tried to do. I hope he's not gonna miss too many weeks.'

"Well, he didn't. As a matter of fact, what he missed was one play. He was back in for the one after that. And two plays later, you know what they came with? That's right. Larry Wilson and the safety blitz.

"I just told John Henry, I said, 'I'll be damned.' And John Henry said I took the words right out of his mouth."

They are joined together, all pro football players are, in a fellowship of pain. That subject always led Layne to Dick Stanfel, Detroit's peerless offensive tackle of that era. "Once we were playing the Forty-niners," said Bobby, "trying to get in for a score just before the half. We ran a sweep to the sideline and Stanfel comes back to the huddle, wheezing and hacking and out of breath. He's real hoarse and he mumbles to me, 'Bobby, gimme a time-out.'

"I was a real hardass about those things, you know, so I just said flat out, 'The hell with your time-out.' I called another play. Stanfel made his block and then he had to go off the field. The doctor looked at him and later diagnosed it. A broken back. Dick Stanfel made this block with a broken vertebra, and you know what I felt like, don't you, because the next day Dick was wearing a cast up to his neck."

Along with the blood and guts, Layne remembered the good and funny times: Jim Hardy, the backup quarterback, renting a plane in 1953 to buzz the practice field, and dropping 144 jockstraps on his teammates; and the coaches getting into an argument over how much Les Bingaman weighed and taking him to the freight depot to find a scale that went over three hundred pounds. "He weighed in at around three-forty-nine," recalled Layne. "Buddy had guessed he was close to four hundred, and that hurt Bingo's feelings."

In a curious turn of events, Parker and Layne were soon to part company in Detroit, only to team up again in Pittsburgh. At a preseason banquet in 1957, Parker shocked everyone by abruptly announcing his resignation. He felt he had been caught in a cold war between two (or more) groups of Detroit owners. He sensed that he was losing control of the players, and the season was doomed.

His bitterness had been building for a long time. "Lyle Fife had been president of the club," he said. "There were twelve owners, and they partied together, socialized together, wives and all. So when Fife got divorced, the rest of the wives didn't want to have anything to do with the new girl he married. That's the way things were in those days. Edwin Anderson became president. And Fife had his own faction."

One group kept an apartment near the team offices, and a few favored players had keys to it. Layne was not among them.

So an electric field surrounded Parker when he went to the annual boosters' banquet that summer of 1957. He received a message asking him to stop by the hotel suite of Lyle Fife before the dinner. When he walked into the room, the first thing he saw was Tobin Rote, a quarterback he had just traded three players to acquire, drinking with the owners.

For Parker that was the last straw. It developed that he had left another championship team behind, the last title the Lions would win to this day. They won it with Parker gone, replaced by George Wilson, and with Layne injured part of the season. The new quarterback was Tobin Rote.

Parker landed in Pittsburgh, and in 1958 Layne rejoined him. They had a few more laughs and a few more tears, but no more titles.

The move required at least a mild adjustment. "At Detroit," said Bobby, "everything was first wagon. In Pittsburgh, hell, they couldn't even boo like big leaguers. The fans got on me one game and Ernie Stautner really let them have it in the newspapers. So now the whole town is on Ernie. Next week we're playing at home and Ernie is the captain. We line up to run out from the ramp at crappy old Forbes Field. Ernie goes first. You know, shoulders back, knees up, the works. The fans booed. Ernie figured he could cope with that because the rest of the team was coming out behind him. He kept running and finally he looked back to see how far behind the rest of us were.

"There wasn't another player out of the ramp. We just decided we were gonna have a little fun with Ernie and let him go out there solo. The fans were just blasting the hell out of him, and we're standing there in the shade, laughing and giggling. Now I call that some kind of ingratitude on our part, but that dumpy old stadium did that to you."

Bobby fought to instill in the Steelers his own pride and passion for winning. He was incapable of sanctioning defeat, even in preseason. After one such loss, Parker and Layne stoked the fire for several hours over drinks. Then, arms around each other's shoulders, they rode like vigilantes through the halls of the men's dormitory, Buddy pounding on doors and shouting at whomever was inside, "You yellow son of a bitch, come out here and tell me why you can't play football."

Behind one of the doors was Charlie Bradshaw, a huge offensive tackle with hands like catchers' mitts. Rising out of a sound sleep, Charlie sat up in bed and slowly, coldly, said across the room, "If I have to get up, I'm going to open the door and *kill whoever is out there.*" Parker and Layne, weaving slightly, continued down the hall.

They were a pair, Parker with his rages and Layne with his raspy threats. In Pittsburgh, Bobby roomed with another ex-Lion, Tom Tracy. They stayed out late one night before a game against Philadelphia, hitting it up at the soda fountain, and the next day Layne handed off to Tracy eighteen times. When Tom the Bomb scored his second touchdown of the day he was hurt diving into the end zone. He limped off the field and, sucking air, slumped heavily on the bench.

Layne kicked the extra point and came walking by Tracy on the sideline. He glared and said, "Dammit, Bomber, why don't you stay in shape?" And he kept right on walking.

There always seemed to be an extra dimension to Bobby Layne, his moods, his actions, his words. He was the quarterback people hated to bet against. Handsome in a rugged, Western way, this muffin-faced blond was one of a kind.

The one vexation of Layne's career seems to have been the sportswriters. Like Ted Williams, baseball's stormy petrel, he regarded them as a menace to freedom, meaning his freedom. They were always hovering, like fruit flies. Myron Cope, a writer and radio talk-show host who lives in Pittsburgh, won Layne's confidence. But Myron knew that such friendships were fragile.

"Layne saw the press as one great mass of gossipmongers," he wrote, "waiting to feed on his traffic tickets and nightclub celebrations. His argument was that the press had no consideration for the feelings of his wife and two sons. On one occasion, while the two of us sat in a parked car outside his apartment at three A.M., he stated his argument plaintively, keeping a grip on his temper. But at a table in Dante's (a team hangout in Pittsburgh) he sometimes would turn on me, remembering that I was a member of the press, and denounce me in the strongest possible terms. I would leave the table, and when I refused an invitation to return, he would insist. Finally, I would approach the table. He would utter the beginnings of an apology, but then his pride would stop him and again he would explode with a denunciation of me. I would return to the bar. Even at those times, I always liked him. One does not expect even temperament from genius."

At the end of the 1962 season, Parker told Bobby it was time to retire, saying, "I wanted everyone to remember Layne as a great player. It was time to quit, to go out on top."

Said Layne: "I didn't realize it, but I had lost a step. You can throw and you can think and you feel the same, but you can't move. Buddy was afraid I'd get hurt."

When he quit, Layne held the NFL records for passes attempted, completions, yards gained, touchdowns, and interceptions.

Age allowed him to show his sentimental side. He could not conceal his delight when he was invited back to Detroit, in January 1982, as the official coin flipper for Super Bowl XVI, the first Super Bowl to be played in the north. The old stadium was gone, of course, replaced by a modern domed one in Pontiac. No matter. He was pleased to be returning to the past, to the team nearest his heart, the 1952 Lions. The honoring of Layne coincided with the thirtieth anniversary of their breakthrough season.

He was still a free spirit, but time had tempered the fires, exposing a sentimental streak as wide as a football field. His closest friends also knew that Bobby was battling cancer.

"I looked around," he said, "and Bob Smith had come up from Tulsa and Cloyce Box from Dallas and Harley Sewell from Arlington, Texas, and Dorne Dibble from Detroit and Doak Walker had flown in from Denver . . . I mean just a whole bunch of guys I had played with. Guys I didn't expect to see. They'd gone there to be with me." He paused to let that thought sink in. All these great guys, great football players, taking time out from their busy lives, maybe leaving their wives at home alone with the kids, or breaking a business date, or putting a cork back in a bottle, to share a memory and a toast with Bobby Layne. Touchdowns in the sky, old-timer.

All Layne ever wanted, he once joked, was to live "a fast forty." He managed that and a few years more. He was fifty-nine when time ran out on him in December 1986 in a west Texas hospital. He left behind, among many other things, the best explanation any athlete ever gave of how a game can grab you by the throat and heart. You could print the quote on cards and make a bundle selling them to ex-jocks to hand out, whenever they are asked if they miss the cheering and the shouting.

"I'll tell you what I really miss," said Layne. "What I miss is the guys. That's what I miss more than anything. I miss going to training camp. I miss the road trips and the card games. I miss the fellowship. The locker room, the places where it was a pleasure to be. The practice sessions. I miss the bar where we'd go for a beer after practice. I miss having that beer with the guys. I miss the ball games. I mean, when you've got a whole team looking forward to everything, when you've got guys showing up for practice early and staying late—well, you've got something there. We had that perfect thing for a while. What I miss now is my teammates."

WHO'S THE BOSS

The quarterbacks closest to Layne, in on-the-field temperament, were Norm Van Brocklin and Johnny Unitas. They were salty and sometimes profane and in questions of leadership they did not take in partners. Sonny Jurgensen and George Blanda fit part of the mold. Of the new generation, Jim Kelly and Bubby Brister have shown promise; they lead with emotion. Kelly's Buffalo teammates accept his blistering criticism, then hover around him after a game or a practice at a favorite pub.

In the heat of a game, Van Brocklin was another whose acid tongue led to confrontations. After an opposing lineman had roughed him, the Dutchman often invited the villain to meet him outside after the game, dates that were never kept. He would cool off in the locker room. No one accused him of being stupid.

Yet he could not resist baiting them. Once against Cleveland, a tackle named Chubby Grigg nailed him for a loss on a pass play. When Dutch ordered him to "get off me, you fat slob," Grigg reacted by silently smashing his fist, like a club, against the hollow of Van Brocklin's back. Grimacing with pain, Norm demanded, "Now why the hell did you hit me in the back?"

Said Grigg: "If you don't like getting hit on the back, then take off your nose guard."

Nor did his teammates escape the lash of Van Brocklin. When

Tom Dahms, a Rams tackle, missed a block that caused Dutch to be buried for a loss, he carried his anger with him to the sideline. There he picked up a Dixie cup filled with water and flung it in Dahms's face. Players on the bench covered their ears, waiting for the explosion. But Dahms, fifty pounds heavier, shrugged it off. The Rams understood. They knew that Van Brocklin's temper, and his urge to win, demanded expression.

Dutch never lost either instinct, not through the rest of his playing days which ended with the Eagles, or in his later, turbulent times as a head coach of Minnesota and Atlanta. Among those quarterbacks who were regarded as special, as winners, Baugh, Van Brocklin, Otto Graham, and Bart Starr would go on to coach in the NFL. None would approach the glory of their playing days; perhaps that was too much to expect.

John Unitas had his own idea of leadership. "A quarterback doesn't come into his own," he once said, "until he can tell the coach to go to hell."

Any leader of men needs a quality called mental toughness, without which he is doomed to fail. Jim Parker, the Baltimore tackle, recalled a game against the Bears, when "my man, Doug Atkins, got through and smashed Unitas across the nose. Blood squirted all over the place and Alex Sandusky scooped up some mud and stuffed it up John's nose to stop the bleeding. When I came into the huddle I almost got sick at how he looked."

The referee stuck his head in the Colts huddle and said sympathetically, "Take all the time you need, Unitas."

John looked up and said, "Get the hell out of here so I can call the play."

☆3☆ THE PARTY IS NEVER OVER

After Bobby Layne, but before Jim McMahon, there was Joe Willie Namath, known throughout the five boroughs as Broadway Joe. His style and skill made him a star. But eight words made Namath a legend: "We're going to win Sunday. I guarantee you."

That promise was spoken on the eve of Super Bowl III at some kind of mom-and-pop banquet in a suburb of Miami, Florida. There was no murmur of shock that night, no feverish reaction in the audience to Namath's prediction. He had been saying it all week, that the New York Jets, a 17- to 19-point underdog, would unfrock the almighty Baltimore Colts. People had been falling down in helpless fits of laughter, reviving only long enough to press their bets on Baltimore.

In fact, that boast was probably not Namath's best line of the evening. During the after-dinner speeches, Larry Grantham, the solid and serious Jets linebacker, had asked for a round of applause for the players' wives, "who have sacrificed so much during the season." Then Namath went to the mike and asked for a hand for the single girls of New York, "who sacrificed just as much as the wives and complained a helluva lot less."

Of course, as football historians have so well documented, Joe

Namath delivered on his guarantee. He did not have a big day passing, but he ran the attack with nerve and precision and the Jets plundered the Colts, 16–7, in what may have been the most important pro game ever played. It showed that the upstart American Football League had caught up with the snobby old NFL and ushered in the new golden age of national exposure and television riches.

If a single athlete can be said to have established an entire league, it was Namath that shimmering sunny day in Miami's Orange Bowl. In the steaming, delirious New York locker room, Weeb Ewbank was asked if he had really believed his Jets could bring it off.

A portly, grandfatherly type, the old coach said, yes, he had made up his mind that very morning after leaving church services. He had paused on his way out and, after complimenting the minister on his sermon, decided on an impulse to ask the question that was on the minds of millions of fans across the country. "Reverend," he asked, "who do you think will win the Super Bowl this afternoon?"

According to Weeb, the preacher lifted his eyes, raised his arms, palms up, and said soberly, "Whomsoever the Lord nameth."

Indeed, Joe Namath was the chosen one in those years, a drawing card when the AFL needed one to survive. Of course, the foundation built by the Jets is not recommended to most athletic teams. Having created a superstar out of his talent and their ballyhoo, the Jets experienced one championship season. And the publicity flowed like nothing anyone had ever before seen. The words about Broadway Joe and his New York Jets rolled off the presses like peanuts tumbling through a vending machine.

His personality, his independent ways, and one football game all came together to stamp Namath as the most distinctive quarterback the sport has known. He might have been the best if his knees had not failed him. He is one of those cases in which people can only guess at what he might have done if his legs had remained sound. (One tends to feel the same way about Mickey Mantle. On ailing legs, Mantle made it into the Hall of

Fame; with healthy wheels he might have joined Ruth and Cobb as three of a kind.)

The Jets did not win consistently behind Joe, and the figures tell us little. He completed 50 percent of his passes and threw more interceptions than touchdowns in his career. If you measure a quarterback by how much his team wins, then you can't mention Namath in the same breath with Otto Graham or Unitas or Starr, or with Montana and Elway in the 1980s. After the winning Super Bowl, Joe and the Jets finished above .500 only once. They were constructed less as a team than as a jewelry box for Joe Willie.

But you cannot judge Namath only by the record. You had to see him, his style, the dart gun release, the way he could bring a crowd to its feet. His talent was chewed up by time and injuries, and by the social distractions and the deals that grew so big the game itself seemed incidental.

It was fun to be young when Joe Namath was young and the Jets were winning the Super Bowl, so long ago that they had just gotten around to using Roman numerals.

Namath played his last college game for Alabama, against Texas, on New Year's Night in 1965. The knee problems that would haunt the rest of his career threatened to keep him out of action. Twenty-odd years later, witnesses can recall few moments more electric than watching Joe come off the bench in the second quarter and trot onto the field. A national championship was on the line and Alabama trailed by two touchdowns. You didn't need to know Joe's number, his solid white shoes gave him away. The crowd went nuts. So did Alabama. But Texas held on, stopping Namath twice at the goal line in the final minute to win, 21–17.

Leaving the field, jostled by the fans who swarmed around them, Namath tried to tell his coach, Bear Bryant, that he *knew* he had scored on his second dive. Bryant shook his head and Joe moved on. The next day, the Bear repeated what he told his young quarterback: "I told him to get in the locker room. If you can't jam it in from there without leaving any doubt, you don't deserve to win."

It was a hard code, but Namath learned from it.

The next day Namath was on his way to New York, and soon he would have the image the public thought it knew best: the fast-living, fast-talking Broadway Joe. On the flight from Miami, bound for his first press conference as a pro, he was needled by a New York writer who asked, "What was your major at Alabama, Joe, basket weaving?" Namath shook his head. "No, basket weaving was too tough," he said, "so they put me in journalism instead."

From the beginning, Namath had his knockers, his doubters. All the hype turned off some of the other quarterbacks, including John Brodie, then in his prime with the 49ers. By 1971 Joe had made a movie and missed most of two seasons with injuries. Brodie said to a friend, Don Klosterman, who had been the general manager in Houston and was then with the Colts, "What is this stuff about Namath being a great quarterback? I can't see it."

At the time, nobody had seen Namath lately except possibly Ann-Margret from the back of an easy-rider hog—she was his costar in a low-budget motorcycle flick. Detroit's Mike Lucci had crumpled one of Namath's famous bum knees and knocked him out of action until week number eleven. His return coincided with a visit to New York by Brodie and his San Francisco mates. Namath played barely two quarters, whistled three touchdowns through a good 49er defense, and almost pulled a victory out of a 24–21 defeat. The favored 49ers were shell-shocked at the end.

Klosterman sent Brodie a short telegram the next day: "NOW YOU HAVE SEEN JOE WILLIE."

That was vintage Namath: playing hurt, lots of heroics, but not quite enough to save a flawed team.

In his later seasons, as observers tried to square the record with the reputation, it was tempting to say that Joe Willie was not very well understood. I never quite saw it that way. I thought he was remarkably easy to understand. There was little mystery to him at all.

He was partial to blondes, Johnny Walker Red, soft llama rugs, restaurants where the waiters spoke with an accent, and friends who did not try to analyze him. He set a new standard for candor when he was asked how he spent the night before Super Bowl III, and he said he spent it in his room—with a blonde and a fifth of scotch.

His prowess with the ladies was no myth. One day as an Alabama senior, bored with whatever class he was in, he decided to kill the time by compiling a list of the girls he had slept with. The roll had reached three hundred by the time the bell rang.

An airline hostess once wrote a story about spending the night with Joe. She described the experience as unsettling. Joe was like a nervous passenger, she said, who continually monitored the engines. In bed, he kept hearing noises, jumping up, checking the door. This was in the early 1970s, when not many fellows had bedroom reputations worth writing about.

No football player in history, including Red Grange and O. J. Simpson, was marketed more effectively than Namath. Deep in his gypsy soul, Joe wanted to think that material things didn't matter. But he made a lot of money, enjoyed it, and—for what he gave to the sport—earned every dime.

His friends were fond of claiming that Joe "never changed." That's baloney—all of us change. Joe did, in many ways for the better. He went through his wild period of Fu Manchu mustaches and big business deals and tacky movies. He went through a period of not talking to the press. He retired three or four times and once, for revenge, he called a news conference at 9:30 in the morning.

As an athlete who aroused wild reactions in people, he was in his time in a class with Muhammed Ali. For years his elders, and a few writers, wanted Joe to cut his hair, correct his posture, and drink milk shakes. Joe's response was to stop reading the papers. In a revealing moment, he said: "I haven't enjoyed being interviewed in years. If I read something bad about myself I don't like it. And if I read something good I feel like I don't deserve it."

Interviews bored him anyway. He reached a point where he thought there was nothing left to say. But if you approached him from the side, if you did not leap instantly to areas he regarded as sensitive, if you began, say, by asking him about basketball, or growing up in Beaver Falls, he would talk all day.

You gained an insight into Namath, incidentally, when you learned that he was the captain of his high school basketball team, a six-foot-two guard who could dunk the ball, and the only white guy in the starting lineup. When he quit the team in his senior year in a dispute with the coach, the four other starters quit too.

In one respect Namath didn't change. He made the Beaver Falls all-star team in basketball, and the day came to pose for the team picture. The squad was positioned in several elevated rows, and the photographer peered into his camera. Suddenly the man jerked his head up and said, pointing to the top row, "You up there. Please remove those dark glasses while I shoot the picture."

There was no response. "You," repeated the photographer, "the one with the goatee. Take off the glasses."

Joe Namath removed the glasses, slowly and casually, and held them alongside his head. "Look, mister," he said with Jimmy Cagney cool, "if you want my picture, you take it with these glasses on."

For his time, for a decade that urged young rebels "to do your own thing," Broadway Joe was perfectly aimed. He was one of the symbols of the Woodstock generation, and within days of his arrival in New York he had a four-hundred-thousand-dollar contract, a new Lincoln Continental, and a knee operation. According to Dan Jenkins, who later wrote a novel called *Semi-Tough*, the hip line in New York that summer was: "Sorry, Sybil, I can't make your party. I'm going to the taping of Joe Namath's knee."

Namath was not quite like any of the super sports celebrities the Big Apple had embraced before him—not Jack Dempsey, Babe Ruth, Joe DiMaggio, or Sugar Ray Robinson, to name the most obvious. They were grown men, wearing hats, when they achieved the status that Joe had handed to him. They were less hip to their times and more or less aloof from the crowd. Joe thrust himself into the middle of it. Their fame came more slowly, with the years of earning it. Joe Namath just happened.

Sonny Werblin gave him the contract and the car and paid for the knee operation, and helped the happening along. Werblin, who salvaged the franchise after Harry Wismer had gone broke with it, created Namath the way Louis B. Mayer created Jean Harlow. Werblin had made his fortune in show biz and he believed in the star system. He gave Namath the richest contract ever paid to a rookie up to that time, and instead of concealing it or underplaying the money involved, Sonny waved it like a flag.

Contrary to popular belief, Joe gave serious thought to signing with the St. Louis Cardinals. He suspected that the Cardinals, who had an established passer in Charley Johnson, were fronting a deal for the Giants, who had nothing. "They weren't that far off in money," he said, "but they had it laid out wrong. Like, I had to do a radio show for part of my salary. I couldn't believe that. I said, man, I'm just a football player and what I make will be for football, only."

Meanwhile, Bear Bryant tried to keep his mind on the big picture. Bryant reminded him that Weeb Ewbank had won a couple of championships in Baltimore, and if Joe still had any interest in winning, he might give that some consideration.

Werblin knew instantly that he had something special in Namath, not only for the talent in his arm, but for his integrity. "In all my career," he said, "I never met a man whose word meant more than Joe's. I can remember when we were trying to sign him. I called Bear Bryant about it. He asked me if I had Joe's word. I said yes, but that I'd like to have something on paper. Bear said, 'You don't need it. If he gave you his word you don't need the paper.' "

Werblin applied a pet phrase to Namath. "Bigger than life," he said. "Some people are bigger than life. Babe Ruth. Clark Gable. Frank Sinatra. So is Joe Namath. They are people who can do the darndest things and it turns out right for them." There was a wistful edge to those words. Werblin rescued the Jets from bankruptcy, rebuilt them, and sold out one year before their trip to the top.

Namath wasted no time proving himself to his teammates. "When Joe got here," said Winston Hill, the mountainous offensive tackle, "he told us that he got all the money he could and he assumed we all did as well as we could too. He said he didn't want to hear about the money. If anyone wanted to fight him, he'd go outside with them, but inside or on the field he just wanted to win."

This was before the win that came with a guarantee, before Bachelor I invested in a bar called Bachelor's III, before he endorsed popcorn machines and after-shave lotion, and modeled panty hose and a full-length mink coat. It was before the surgeon's scalpel gave his knees the look of an aerial view of the Burma Road.

On September 18, 1965, the Jets came home to Shea Stadium for their second game of the season. Namath had not played in the opener. Nor did he start that night against the tough Kansas City Chiefs. New York trailed, 7–3, when the call went out to Joe Willie.

His first pass as a professional was thrown right down the middle to Don Maynard for a touchdown. Namath passed well enough to win, but the Jets didn't beat the Chiefs that night. The fans didn't seem to care. From the moment he entered the game they screamed and roared. All they were doing was saying, "Welcome, Joe Willie, we've waited for you all our lives."

And so the era of Bachelor I had begun. And as Sonny Werblin alluded, there would be rebellion along the way. He would clash with Pete Rozelle after it was discovered that Bachelors III had become a hangout for gamblers, and Joe was ordered to sell his interest (which he eventually did). There was a scuffle with a sportswriter, and a bust for driving while intoxicated in Miami.

By then Joe was partly a victim of his own image. Namath insisted he was sober, and a Breathalyzer test seemed to support him. It showed that his alcohol content was one fifth of the level required to produce intoxication. Joe was not the kind of drinker who could get cross-eyed from smelling the bar rag. Nothing might have come of the incident, except that when the officer asked to see his license, Joe said, "Aw, come off it . . . you know who I am."

Now policemen can be very sticky about such things even if they know who you are. It's as though they don't believe you have a license and sure enough, Joe didn't. He said he left it back at his hotel and he offered to go and get it. But the officer said, "Sorry, Joe, how can you drive back to your hotel when you don't have a license to drive?"

(Namath later explained that this exchange was what made him lose his temper, because back in Beaver Falls when a cop stopped you and you didn't have a license he gave you forty-eight hours to go look for one. They had some interesting laws in Beaver Falls.)

It was at this point that Joe used language generally reserved for a late hit by a defensive tackle. And that's when the officer booked him.

But this much could be said for Broadway Joe: When he said, "You know who I am," he wasn't being arrogant. He simply was attesting to the fact that he was not Willie Sutton speeding away from the Florida National Bank. Joe Namath never popped off, in public or in private, about being Joe Namath. He took very few bows for a guy entitled to take a lot of them.

Although Namath did not seem to have a political bone in his body, he was viewed as an antiestablishment figure, and some-how his name popped up on the notorious Nixon "enemies list." Chuck Bednarik, the grizzled old Philadelphia linebacker, attacked him as "a long-haired creep." His locks were thick and shaggy and curled over his ears and down the back of his collar. But it wasn't unsightly. Said Joe: "I've always believed in honesty—I got that from Bear Bryant—and there was a lot of bullshit going on in pro football at the time. People were being judged because they had long hair . . . silly little things."

He was far from a square when he landed in New York, but he admits readily that the nickname Broadway Joe was too big for him and he had to grow into it. "One day we came into the locker room, and there was a copy of *Sports Illustrated* on everyone's stool. The cover had a shot of me standing in front of Times Square, with the bright lights, and me in my football uniform. Sherman Plunkett (who weighted 340 pounds) picked it up and said, 'Broadway Joe.' It sounded so nice coming from Sherman."

Few players ever generated more excitement, some of it by deeds and some by words. Writers who felt that the Namath image leaned too heavily on booze and broads flocked to him nonetheless and competed to record his every move. (Joe refused to come out of the shower to talk with reporters after the Jets defeated the Giants in the first meeting of the teams. In a burst of creative journalism, Sid Hartman of *The Minneapolis Tribune* got into the shower with Joe and interviewed him.)

The son of a Pennsylvania coal miner discovered that what some people saw as eccentric behavior could be turned into a profit. When an electric razor company offered him ten thousand dollars to shave off his Fu Manchu mustache, which made him look like a Chinese warlord, he quickly agreed, explaining that "I had to shave it off eventually, anyway."

When thieves broke into his East Side apartment and made off with fifteen thousand dollars worth of clothes and jewelry, he shrugged it off and the story never even made the newspapers. Included in the haul was the mink coat he had received as a gift after modeling it for a publicity photo. "That was the only time he wore it," reported a friend. "Never had it on again. I think he would have worn it if the cut had been a little more mod. But the thing looked like those raccoon coats they used to wear to football games."

For all the commotion he caused, his football gifts did not go unappreciated. "Joe Namath," said Vince Lombardi, "is the greatest pure thrower of footballs I have ever seen."

Norm Van Brocklin was the last quarterback who meant as much to his team as Namath did to his—and who won a championship. "Namath is the best, quickest, sharpest passer in football," said Dutch during the week of the third Super Bowl. "It takes a passer like him to beat a team like the Colts."

An anonymous NFL scout may have offered the final word on Namath: "He has the quickest arm in the league, probably the quickest ever. And he's got quick feet. Nobody sets up faster than Namath. He's in charge of the game. He's the complete quarterback and nobody can touch him—but what good is he if he can only play four or five games a year?"

There it was. The injuries kept coming: two operations in his first two years on the right knee, a fractured wrist, surgery on the left knee, a separated shoulder . . .

Bury him not with wounded knees.

Four years after they had astounded the oddsmakers and won the world championship, the Jets would finish four and ten. It was Weeb Ewbank's final season. The players knew the omens were poor from the start.

The women, mostly young girls looking for Joe, were all over the training camp. After a rough workout, a wide receiver was relieving himself when he heard a high voice say, "That's really a big snake." Two pretty girls were hiding in the toilet. Pandemonium broke out. With childish screams, the Jets players rushed for their towels and scattered in embarrassment. Two of the trainers escorted the girls out of the locker room.

In September in the second game, Namath separated his shoulder against the Colts. His season—and the team's—was wrecked. That was a depressing year, 1973. Ewbank cried when he cut Don Maynard, the team's all-time leading receiver. Maynard cried too. The Jets lost their last game under Weeb, in the snow at Buffalo, as O. J. Simpson broke Jim Brown's rushing record. A sobbing Ewbank told the team that football was a wonderful game and he was sorry he failed them. The players gave him a gold watch and a lawn mower as retirement gifts.

The line had grown old in New York and they could no longer protect the quarterback. Namath took a pounding, but the closest he came to criticizing his teammates was an occasional sharp remark. After he had been flattened on one play, he walked slowly back to the huddle and addressed his offensive line, "I picked up the linebacker that time, how about you guys getting the next one?"

His pain was constant. Before every game both knees had to be drained of fluid—the sight of the large hollow needle alone made some of his teammates turn their heads. After every work-out he iced them down.

In the endless attempts to define the source of his celebrity— was he a rebel, a hippie, a Beatle?—his best quality may have been slighted: his pure courage. George Young, the Giants general manager, was working for the Colts when they lost the third Super Bowl to the Jets. He remembers the exact day that Namath converted him, November 10, 1974.

"The Jets were playing the Giants," said Young, "and I remember this one play. I never really cared for Namath, but he called a naked bootleg around left end. Well, everybody went right and he sort of limped into the end zone for the points that tied the score [the Jets went on to win in overtime, 26–20, at the Yale Bowl]. He looked like a guy with two wooden legs. I had never realized how bad his knees were, but you could really see it from the press box. It was like slow motion. It took a lot of courage to play with that."

The Jets picked up halfback Abner Haynes, near the end of what had been a colorful and, at times, a notable career. Haynes took a pitchout from Namath against the Raiders, just as the Jets' blocking broke down. Abner looked up and saw four or five Raiders bearing down on him like a pack of wild Australian dogs. And to the horror of the Jets quarterback, Abner tossed the ball right back to him. Namath disappeared under the Raider charge.

Later, in the locker room, he was asked if the move surprised him. He nodded what was left of his head and responded, "Have you ever had a fried egg jump out of the pan at you?"

There were other surprises in the dozen seasons of Joe Willie, not all of them on the field. But he grew in patience and class. When new coach Lou Holtz announced he was benching Namath in favor of Richard Todd, in November 1976, Joe was surely expecting it. We all were. Even so, another egg jumped out of the pan at him. Holtz said he was turning to Todd in the interest of the team's "peace and tranquillity."

And on that note, Joe gave his regards to Broadway. Signed as a free agent by the Rams, excited about getting a fresh start in the shadow of Hollywood, he didn't play a down the last two months of what would be his last season. But he never complained, never stirred the kind of trouble that one in his position could easily have done.

So the Namath career ended in irony. In Los Angeles he wound up on the bench with a team more talented than the one he had left. In training camp Joe had roomed with Pat Haden, the young Rhodes scholar who would soon take his job. Haden was asked what their social life was like.

"On a typical night," he said, "we made a bowl of popcorn and watched the eleven o'clock news. Then we watched Johnny Carson and went to sleep after the monologue."

Joe may or may not have slowed down off the field. But as a quarterback he was nearly immobile. No one ever threw a straighter pass, tried harder, or made fewer excuses. Many athletes have a fear of getting out too late, exceeded only by their fear of getting out too soon. Namath didn't overstay his time. He was entitled to one more shot with a winning team. Too bad the script didn't accommodate him.

From time to time over the next few years, we encountered Joe in his public appearances, and in his role as a television analyst. The crowds still flocked to him. The affection that passed between Joe and the people who had come to see him was genuine. The loyalty he inspired among his fans is apparently a lasting one.

Once a writer staying in the same hotel observed in the lobby an attractive blonde he had noticed earlier in the airport. Later she approached him near the house phones and said almost tearfully, "They won't give out Joe's number. Do you know what room he's in?"

"Eight-two-four," he said.

She threw her arms around him and cried, "How can I ever thank you?"

The writer thought and thought, but nothing came to mind.

Namath waited until he was nearly forty to marry. His bride, a beauty named Deborah, was seven years old when the Jets upset the Colts. Their first child, a daughter, was born a year and two months after Broadway Joe was inducted into the Pro Football Hall of Fame in 1985, in a class that included Roger Staubach and O. J. Simpson.

Today Off-Broadway Joe is a contented Connecticut squire, living on a farm ten minutes from the Long Island Sound. Joe Namath, whose eye rarely missed an open receiver or a nice pair of legs, now can't see beyond a four-year-old blonde named Jessica. Horses, cats, and dogs run free on five acres of land, a world removed from the heyday of his East Side bachelor pad.

His contract with NBC ran into the 1990s; he owns an interest in a cellular phone franchise and a shopping center in Tuscaloosa. He is secure financially and secure in his life-style. One by one he outgrew his youthful stages: the night life, the acting bug, the idea of having it all. "You've seen a four-month-old puppy running around," he said, "looking to get into everything? Then he gets older and he doesn't look so hard. That's the way I am."

Please, Joe, leave us with a few illusions.

DANTE'S
INFERNO

Dan Pastorini could throw a football farther than Namath and may have enjoyed as much luck in the romance league. If his career was less celebrated—either career—it must be noted that he suffered two disadvantages. He worked in lesser markets and never led a team to the Super Bowl.

At least, Pastorini had a sense of proportion. What he remembers are the zingy things that never show in the highlight films. Such as the time he threw four interceptions, *three* of them to defensive linemen, an NFL record. And the fact that in his first five years as a Houston Oiler he played under four head coaches.

One of them, Bill Peterson, was famous for his halftime pep talks. Before one game Peterson announced he would lead the team in the Lord's Prayer, whereupon he knelt on the floor, bowed his head, and began, "Now I lay me down to . . ." The coach paused. He looked around the room with a pained expression. He shook his head. "Naw," he said at last, "that's not it."

It might belabor the obvious to point out that there were many other occasions when the Houston team did not have a prayer. Pastorini recalled the weekly bruises of the 1972 season, when his fiancée, the buxom actress June Wilkinson, later his wife, was appearing on the stage in Dallas and flying to Houston on her days off, which were Mondays. Routinely Dan would leave his car for her at the airport, knowing he would be too beat up after Sunday's encounter to drive down and meet her. He was even too battered to make love. "She had to do it for me, if you know what I mean," he said.

Of course, one may argue that losing can't be all that unbearable when one can go home to June Wilkinson for consolation. But Pastorini spoke for his teammates when he said, "Someday I'll be in the position other quarterbacks have been in, playing in the Super Bowl, and this will make great stuff for the interviews. I'll look back and say, 'Gosh, remember when we were one-and-thirteen and people laughed at us?' "

It didn't happen for Dante Anthony Pastorini, super young prospect and heir to the family restaurant's secret recipe for Chicken Pastorini. When he broke into the NFL there were those who thought he had a chance to rank with the best of his generation. Few quarterbacks had his cannon of an arm, his artistic potential, or his generous heart.

The week the Oilers reached the playoffs for the first time in ten years, in 1978, Pastorini treated his entire offensive unit, starters and reserves, twenty players, to dinner. After three hundred dollars' worth of prime rib had been consumed, Dan raised his wine glass and toasted his guests. He thanked them for the protection they had given him that season. It was a short speech but a touching one, when you consider that he was leaving the party early to check into a hospital, where a team of doctors would decide if he needed an operation.

If the occasion offered a trace of irony, Dan and his friends didn't notice. In a sense it typified his career, his days of wine and Novocain. He postponed the surgery. He played against Miami wearing the now-famous flak jacket to protect three cracked ribs, and with a brace on his knee. He also had a tender elbow, wrist, and ankle.

The flak jacket, made of the same material as a bulletproof vest, is now almost standard equipment for quarterbacks and receivers with upper body pain. Its inventor, Byron Donzies, walked into Pastorini's hospital room wearing one, accompanied by a friend holding a baseball bat. He had read of Dan's injuries and thought his product, not yet on the market, could help. He demonstrated it right there.

Usually, a fan walks into your room in such a getup and you call for the nearest SWAT team. But Pastorini was intrigued. From his bed, he watched Donzies take a shot from the bat without flinching. "Get me one of those!" Dan yelped.

Football coaches do not as a rule like to talk about luck. It is rather like talking about the occult, and psychic experiences, things you can't diagram on a blackboard. "To get through a season unhurt," said Bum Phillips, "a quarterback has to be lucky. Dan never was. He might get hit just once in a game and that one time would get him hurt. But if it was just a question of pain, he'd play. Dan has a high threshold."

Added Carl Mauck, the veteran center: "What he went through that week was the gutsiest thing I ever saw. He was hurt in five places. They had to put him under anesthesia at the hospital to check out his knee. He was feeling a lot of anxiety, not knowing if he would be able to play. He had come so far, gone through so much bull, the one-and-thirteen seasons. We knew what it meant to him. You see a guy on the field with as much wrong with him as Dan had that day, he didn't have to say anything. That was his finest hour."

Indeed it was. Pastorini threw for 261 yards in the first half, a club record, and completed twenty of twenty-nine passes. The underdog Oilers knocked off the Dolphins at Miami, 17–9, and around the NFL the flak jacket was the hottest fashion news since polyester. Of course, the jacket alone didn't do the trick. Years later he admitted to taking twenty-four shots of Novocain, twelve before each half.

Like Namath, no one ever accused Dan Pastorini of lacking courage. What they questioned was his judgment, his timing, his nightclubbing, his maturity.

"Sometimes he would let his emotions get the best of him," said Mauck, his closest friend, "and he would say or do things he'd regret later. Part of it was just the fact that he has a big heart. He helped a lot of guys when they were down that nobody knew about. Once he helped a sportscaster who was broke, going through a divorce, and needed to get to the West Coast. Dan loaned him the money."

Lending money to a sportscaster may not strike you as a sign of maturity. But along the way, Dan figured out the American way of fame. "People would say to me, 'When you came to Houston who did you replace?' Well, the quarterback before me didn't just have a good career, he had a great career. Charley Johnson. But people forget. And when I'm gone they'll ask the same question of the quarterback who comes after me. And that's why I try not to take it all too seriously."

The fans did not always understand his commitment, a fact that troubled him from the day the Oilers drafted him out of Santa Clara in 1971, hailed as the deliverer of a franchise that had become a chronic loser. The Oilers played to a lot of empty seats. Coaches came and went. One coach learned he had been fired when he walked into the office and his secretary handed him the middle drawer of his desk.

When the Oilers came within a game of the Super Bowl in 1978, Pastorini had arrived. He was brilliant as the leader of a team that won twelve games with a lineup that was constantly changing. They lost their first three wide receivers to injury, including the game-breaking Billy "White Shoes" Johnson.

At midseason, Bum Phillips signed two receivers, one off a cement truck and another out of a rec center in Atlanta. A starting defensive end, James Young, was on leave from his job as a Houston fireman. The Oilers were in great shape if a fire broke out.

There was nothing predictable about them, except that Earl Campbell would get the ball on the goal line, Phillips would never lose his temper, and Pastorini would play hurt.

In 1979 the Oilers again went to the American Conference finals, and again they lost to the Steelers. The fans forgave Dan his youth and good looks and cheered his courage. Alas, that would turn out to be Dan's last game for Houston. As someone once noted of a temperamental actor, he learned to say hello when it was time to say good-bye.

"He was no prima donna," said Phillips. "He was always his own worst critic. No matter what anyone wrote or said, he was twice as hard on himself. He worked hard. He didn't just loosen up his arm, he worked out with the linemen. What he had a hard time handling was praise. You start to bragging on him and right away he'd want to talk about someone else."

In his travels through the league, Carl Mauck had snapped the ball to Johnny Unitas and Bob Griese. "Dan had a superior arm," says Carl. "At reading a defense and using the people around him, he was their equal."

"I never denied that I liked to have a good time," says Pastorini. "But I wasn't trying to be a Broadway Joe, or even a Westheimer Dan." Westheimer is a winding, bustling Houston street on the arty side of town, heavy with restaurants, bars, and clubs. But Houston isn't New York and the town pretty much shuts down at midnight. The mere fact that Dan found so many ways to stay up late impressed people.

"Some of that image," he says candidly, "I think had to do with my marriage to June." The statuesque, British-born actress was ten years older than Dan. The marriage was in trouble the first year. If women found him irresistible, Pastorini returned the favor. He dated Vegas show girls, Hollywood starlets, had a fling with Farrah Fawcett. He appeared in two movies, one with Margaux Hemingway and Lee Majors, and in one unforgettable scene was eaten by tiny fish.

But it wasn't the night life or the high life that shortened his career, or brought him down a few yards short of his own goals. There was the strange quality of his luck, and a streak of the daredevil in him that he could not control, and did not want to control.

He may have established a new category for the *Guinness Book of World Records* by injuring himself in three different modes of transportation: cars, boats, and bicycles. Even his best intentions had a way of backfiring. No one ever had a more colorful season than Pastorini did with the Raiders in 1980. He separated a shoulder when his bicycle jumped a curb during a charity race, had his head stitched after his car collided with a careless tree, posed less than fully clad for *Playgirl* magazine, and fractured his leg in a game that he somehow managed to fit into his crowded schedule.

He suited up with the Rams and the Eagles and retired after twelve seasons. No one was really surprised when Dan announced that he would try his hand as a professional drag racer, or that he would be good at it. He was rated among the top ten drivers by the National Hot Rod Association, hurtling himself down drag strips at speeds in excess of 250 miles an hour.

In his first month on the circuit, Pastorini nosed out Don "Big Daddy" Garlits in a national qualifying heat. His car was named Quarterback Sneak.

SNAKE BIT

Over the years, many a quarterback hoped to be the inheritor of the Namath mystique. Some would tell you that Kenny Stabler succeeded, if not in the quality of his arm then in the thickness of his address book.

Stabler was a confessed party animal whose approach was refreshing: He never tried to conceal his night life, never apologized for it. Anyone who lived as fully and openly as Stabler needed a philosophy, and the Snake—his nickname since high school—had one that was nearly poetic:

"People always thought my life-style would ruin me," he said. "Yeah, I liked to get out and get after it. So what if I'd go out and drink, shoot pool, chase women, stay out late, not come home. All the time I'm doin' that I'm bein' nice to people. I go into bars and sign autographs and shake hands and shoot the bull. What's wrong with that?"

It was his proud boast that he liked to study his playbook by the light of a jukebox, and no coach—no wife, either—ever really reformed him, although some managed to hold down the score.

His trade to the Oilers seemed like a match made in honkytonk heaven. They were training in San Angelo in the summer of 1981, and Stabler rode into town sitting tall in the saddle of a young bronco, his blue eyes squinting against the late-afternoon glare of a west Texas sun. The imagery worked fine, except that this Bronco was built by Ford. Still, the outdoorsman could run that baby over washboard roads, through shallow streams, and up into the high country, and never spill a drop from a can of Coors.

The truck had a customized black paint job, with a tiny coiled reptile decorating each door. Underneath the symbol appeared two words, "The Snake," in print no larger than a newspaper photo caption. A modest touch. Still, you knew: Don't tread on him.

Stabler had come to the Oilers in exchange for Pastorini, one of pro football's most stunning trades, the first time that starting quarterbacks in the NFL had been swapped man for man. Like pegged trousers, wide neckties, the Watergate plumbers, stereos you can wear on your head, sugarcoated cereal, Sonny and Cher, and supply-side economics, it seemed like a good idea at the time. Regrettably, it turned out to be a trade that helped neither team.

What Pastorini had to show for his two years in Oakland were mainly a broken leg and a shoulder operation. Then there was the question of style.

Stabler was a little bit country, Pastorini a little bit rock 'n' roll. Stabler rolled in from the playing fields of the Gulf shores in Alabama, what is known as the Redneck Riviera. He was, as nearly as anyone could tell, delighted by the change of scenery. The Snake was never given to wild mood swings. Casual observers were seldom aware when he was feeling low, or even when he was wildly happy, partly because it was hard to read the mood of a fellow who, for weeks at a time, could only be reached by telephone, except on those days when he wasn't answering the phone.

For Stabler, the thrill was gone in Oakland, where he had exchanged insults with his boss, Al Davis, over contract matters. And Davis, who always favored the vertical passing game, believed Stabler's arm had lost a few yards. There was no question that he looked forward to playing for a coach—Bum Phillips— who seemed to be a cross between Uncle Remus and Hoss Cartwright. He described his first private audience with his new coach:

"Right after the trade I came back from a press conference and walked into his office. He had his cowboy boots propped up on the desk. He had on a pair of ragged old Levi's and a cowboy shirt and his hat was cocked back on his head. He was spittin' tobacco juice into a Coca-Cola cup. I said right there, that's my kind of guy. He's just an unpretentious cowboy who happens to coach football."

The Oilers wanted Stabler because Phillips felt they were a move away from overtaking Pittsburgh, the team that had kept them from the Super Bowl in 1978 and 1979. With Oakland, Stabler had beaten the Steelers.

Another factor was the restlessness of Pastorini, who had been through troubled years in Houston and had been looking to escape. Finally, he demanded a trade, and when Bum accommodated him he had second thoughts. Phillips reassured him, "I think this will be the best thing for you, Dan." The trade was on again. Then Dan thought some more and tried to call back; Bum's phone was off the hook.

"It's funny," says Stabler today, speaking for the two of them. "But sometimes a player will practically dare a team to trade him, and when it does he feels betrayed."

No matter how many such stories one's brain can stand, we are still surprised by how complicated these relationships between a coach and his quarterback can become. Bum Phillips had taken a lot of heat for Pastorini. Phillips thought much of the criticism was unfair. He defended Dan's escapades. He covered up his injuries. And at least once he took Dan's side against a member of his own coaching staff. When he fired Ken Shipp, his offensive coordinator, Bum made no attempt to finesse the decision. "Anytime it comes down to a choice between an assistant coach and my quarterback," he said, "I'm going with my quarterback. I know where I can find lots of assistant coaches."

In Bum's view Pastorini was never quite the maverick or hellraiser so many imagined him to be. But Pastorini moved in an electric field in Houston. There was the matter of a simmering feud with tight end Mike Barber, a sort of underground drama that kept the town gossips occupied for two seasons. When Barber complained in public that he was not being used enough as a receiver, Phillips blamed it on the game plan.

A French inspector might have suggested, "Cherchez la femme." The root of the problem, the rumors went, was that Barber had dated an ex-girlfriend of Dan's (in fact, to make the story more interesting, she was the ex-wife of Atlanta's quarterback, Steve Bartkowski).

So here came Stabler, into a town whose taste for barbecue and cold beer and country music suited him fine. In fact, writing country-and-western songs was one of Stabler's own amusements. In a period of twelve years he had composed a total of three. You get the idea that he either didn't have much spare time, or he didn't rush himself when the creative juices were flowing.

Stabler was too shy to expose his work to what he calls "a real singer," although several counted him as a friend. After all, Willie Nelson never jogged up to Stabler and tried to show him how far he could heave a football.

Most country music is based on universal themes: pain, weakness, love, whiskey, pickup trucks, good or bad-hearted women, and moving on down the line. Stabler's compositions were no exception. His favorite was a song he wrote "about hangin' out in honky-tonk bars and meetin' some lady, gettin' to know her, and sayin' good-bye the next morning. Pretty soon it gets old. Everybody gets tired of that life-style sooner or later."

The song may or may not have been autobiographical. Let the record show that you didn't have to be a bartender to enjoy Stabler's trust. He seemed to offer it automatically to anyone who hadn't crossed him.

Once in an interview, he was asked what kind of dreams he had. (Now, you can sometimes tell if an athlete has any imagination by how he responds to an unexpected, whimsical question. Of course, you ask some athletes what kind of dreams they have and they will pitch you out the nearest window.) Stabler's eyes lit up. "I had one the other night," he said. "I dreamed that I was on this river with my friend Randall Watson. He and I are pretty close. And we're up there in this place where we can get away from people. And we're sittin' and fishin' and all of a sudden Dan Rather comes out of the woods. Honest to God! And he's wearin' a coat and tie and tennis shoes. He came up there and shot the bull with us. And I kept waitin' for a camera crew to pop out of the woods and ask about my tax returns."

After he finished describing his dream, Stabler leaned back

and smiled and said, "Boy, I really like these questions. Got any more?"

Of course, there were other questions he found far less entertaining. An expensive divorce had left him strapped for cash, and he resented the refusal of Davis to renegotiate his contract. "We have no problem with Stabler," Al announced grandly, "as long as he plays like the great quarterback his agent says he is."

In fact, the trade was perfectly timed to allow both teams to unload discontented players.

Stabler's personal life was, to put it mildly, disorganized. He couldn't set foot in California until his lawyers had, in effect, cleared out the zone. His ex-wife had sworn out a warrant against him for unpaid child support. In New York, headlines in the *Times* announced that the NFL was investigating his friendship with a "known gambler" said to have connections to the wrong kind of Italians.

The story went nowhere. Stabler never denied having encountered the fellow two or three times in hotel lobbies, but that was as juicy as the disclosures got. The readers felt cheated. Any story that included a Snake and an apple, especially a Big Apple, ought to have a moral to it.

But for all his reputation as a hell-raiser, Stabler was a gentleman, soft-spoken, respectful. He would hang back in a crowd. In 1970, his rookie year, he kept calling George Blanda "sir."

Of course, Ken didn't have the flowing gray hair and beard then, the look of a Confederate cavalry officer. He and Blanda had played under Bear Bryant nineteen years apart, George at Kentucky and the Snake at Alabama. More than teammates, they were benchmates and soulmates. They played golf together and shared space on the sideline while Daryle Lamonica started at quarterback.

Stabler became the league's most successful left-handed passer since Frankie Albert. He was deadly at the 15- to 18-yarder, a whiz at seeing the whole field, at "looking off" a defensive back and finding a secondary receiver. At bringing his team from behind in the final minutes, coaches and scouts rated him with Staubach and Unitas and Layne, a list now joined by Montana and Elway.

John Madden believed in him, marveled at the way he could trot over to the sideline with seconds left and the game tight and Madden himself going crazy, take a swig of Gatorade, and say, "Boy, John, the fans are getting their money's worth today."

There was always an immense calmness about Stabler, even as his first season in Houston ended miserably. They were blown out in the playoffs in the wild card game by his old Oakland teammates. Phillips was fired and Stabler, sensing he would not be wanted by the new regime, announced his retirement.

Then one of the game's little embarrassments struck the Oilers. The projected starter, Gifford Nielsen, was injured. The accident that removed Nielsen caused some observers to sit down and reflect on the Meaning of Life. Here was a young trouper who had waited without a whimper for three years to show he could do the job. A product of Brigham Young, a Mormon, his habits were impeccable. He did not smoke, drink, swear, or run out of the pocket. Finally, he gets his chance and in the first five minutes of a practice game he bangs up his shoulder and is lost for a month or more.

The injustice of it all strikes you as profound. If a straight arrow like Nielsen can't catch a break, what hope do the rest of us have? If one is going to wind up in a sling anyway, one might as well live like Dan Pastorini or Ken Stabler.

Stabler gave up his promising career as a professional tannist and left the sun-kissed shores of lower Alabama to answer his team's distress signal. Without training camp, Stabler passed for three touchdowns to upset the Rams on the road in the season opener. It was to be the high point of his Houston service. The Oilers finished 7–9 and gave the Snake his release.

He found his way to New Orleans and reunited with Bum Phillips, who was operating a kind of Seaman's Mission. There he threw his last pass, at thirty-eight, and this time he retired for keeps.

In mid-1987, he made a sentimental trip to Lake Tahoe to

attend the tenth reunion of the Raiders' Super Bowl champions. He was reliving old times the first night with some of his former comrades, when he felt an arm slide around his shoulder and hug him. He turned to find Al Davis grinning at him.

"How you doing, Lefty?" he asked.

"I'm doing great," Stabler said, "but I've been wanting to tell you, I have just one regret about my football career. I wished I had kept my mouth shut and finished my career with the Raiders."

He had one other regret. "I wish I had been in my prime when I came to Bum. We'd have won a lot of games. No one was more loyal to his players.

"At Oakland, we never had a losing season under Madden. He was just like you see him now on television. When we'd watch the game films, he'd give us sound effects while he commented on the action.

"Madden was a great coach because he won with guys who were mentally incompetent. You know what they said about the Raiders. We were the only team in pro football whose team picture showed both a front and side view."

THE MAC ATTACK

By 1989 the predictable doubts had hardened: Was Jim McMahon overrated? Had injuries ruined his career, robbed him of his cheekiness, made him a one-year flash? Was this the replay of a familiar show biz scenario: a star whose act the public stopped buying, once he stopped delivering?

He was Mad Mac, football's first punk rock quarterback. He was outrageous, but funny and appealing, when the Chicago Bears won the Super Bowl in 1986. When they fell short, he was merely outrageous. Off the field, his market value dropped sharply.

This, of course, is part of the phenomenon of the quarterback in the age of high-stakes advertising: as an instrument of delivering a message, merchandise, or groceries. Whatever else his future may hold, they can't take this away from Jim McMahon: He has been the most commercial quarterback in the history of the sport.

It's true. You can look it up. McMahon's income outside of football in 1987, the year after his Super year, was estimated at three million dollars. "If he was really the money-grubbing type," claimed his lawyer, Steve Zucker, "he could have easily doubled that."

As it was, McMoney settled for the class stuff, hair mousse, Hondas, Miracle Whip, a Grid Warrior poster, sunglasses, foot powder, Coca-Cola, a low-cost wristwatch, and personal appearances that were billed at a thousand dollars an hour. Madison Avenue observers noted that Zucker had not adjusted his client's prices from the glory days. "He was charging two hundred thousand dollars for one commercial," said one source, "and half a million for an ongoing deal. The average for a big sports name is fifty to a hundred thousand. Who needs him?"

Our first reflex is to say, we do. The Bears do. Mike Ditka does. Or did. But that was a continuing and riveting story—always another dawn. When Ditka opened camp in 1989 by announcing that the Bears had *three* number one quarterbacks, the other two being Mike Tomczak and Jim Harbaugh, McMahon retorted, "I don't pay any attention to that bullshit. If I'm given the chance, I'll be the starter."

The marketing wizards predicted that his value, in 1989 and beyond, depended on whether he started for the Bears—or anywhere else. As the world soon learned, anywhere else turned out to be San Diego, and in a curiously symmetrical way everything went to hell for everybody.

The Bears traded McMahon to the Chargers on the eve of the 1989 season, letting him go for a third-round draft pick, with conditions. If the Chargers won ten games the pick would have been a number one. Not to worry. For a time, it appeared the two teams might have to scramble to win ten between them.

For the first time in the Ditka era, Chicago did not win its division, lost four games in a row, and was eliminated from the playoffs with three weeks to go. San Diego, which hasn't won a title since Sid Gillman was the coach and Lyndon Johnson was president, never got around to grooming a successor to Dan Fouts.

McMahon was not the problem, nor sadly was he the solution. He jumped into the starting lineup on less than a week's preparation, shrugged off an injury or two, and in December yielded the starting job to rookie Billy Joe Tolliver.

Summing up, the Bears crashed, the Chargers ranged from mediocre to inept, and McMahon misspent a season in the tropics. Even after San Diego cut him, Jim had his backers.

"When he's healthy," said Bart Starr, "I don't know of anyone who has been a better leader than McMahon. My gosh, look at the record. The Bears almost never lost when he was healthy."

In games that McMahon started, the Bears won forty-six and lost fifteen. Those were wipeout numbers, but the flip side was that he had become a question mark at thirty. He was in the final year of his contract. He had started only twenty-one games the past three seasons.

Yet there was nothing fragile about him. He got his injuries the old-fashioned way, playing hard and taking chances. Not everyone bled for him, of course. He had always been the kind of unrepentant loudmouth people love to see humbled.

Of course, he had replicated Joe Namath. He engineered a dream season, won the Super Bowl, and turned the establishment on its ear. No one since Namath had taken over a game, a town, a week, the way McMahon held New Orleans, the New England Patriots, and the news media hostage in Super Bowl XX.

Not necessarily in order of importance, there was the running battle with Commissioner Pete Rozelle, who fined him five thousand dollars for wearing an Adidas headband in a playoff game on national television. The next week McMahon wore one that bore one hand-lettered word, "Rozelle." He had the public dangling from the chandelier, wondering what he would do in the Super Bowl. What he did was model a series of the terry cloth sweat bands, none of which offended public taste or violated one of the league's sacred rules: no free advertising.

One could hardly protest a white headband that read "POW-MIA." Some were vague but meaningful, such as the one that said "Pluto," the nickname of former teammate Dan Plater, who was battling a brain tumor. At least one was decorative, with little Christmas lights that blinked on and off. By the end of the week Rozelle had called him a folk hero.

All harmless fun. The moment McMahon hit town you knew he was going to hit them with his R-rated material, somehow related to his unusual injury. He was suffering from a bruised buttock—sometimes referred to as a pain in the ass. He demanded that the Bears fly in his personal acupuncturist, Hiroshi Shiriashi, to give him treatments. And one historic afternoon when a helicopter hovered over the Bears' practice field, Mac dropped his pants. "I was just trying to show him where it hurt," he explained. League records go back only to 1920, but McMahon is believed to be the first pro football player ever to moon a helicopter.

Finally, there was the press conference his lawyer called so that Jim could deny he called the women of New Orleans "sluts," as a local TV sportscaster had quoted him. True or not, pickets showed up in front of the Bears' hotel the next morning with signs that said "HEY! MCMAHON! PUT YOUR HEADBAND OVER YOUR MOUTH." And "MCMAHON HAS NO CLASS. HE ONLY SHOWS HIS ——." Even the hookers in the French Quarter were furious with him.

Suddenly, fans were copying his butch haircut and his black-mirrored glasses with the wraparound straps. The glasses, it should be noted, were not a prop. McMahon has been sensitive to light since he was six years old, when he accidentally stuck a fork in his right eye.

There were some who thought McMahon, like Namath, had deliberately stolen the spotlight to take the pressure off his team. Others believed he was simply being himself, pointing out that the Bears figured to be at least three touchdowns better than the Patriots. What pressure? The poor Patriots. They couldn't get a word in. They stood around like Vanna White, waiting for someone to ask if they wanted to buy a vowel.

Everyone else jumped into the spirit of the moment. A Patriots fan wandered through the stands at the Superdome, wearing a headband with "McFaggot" scribbled on it.

The game was a blowout, Bears by 46–10, with McMahon scoring two touchdowns, and Refrigerator Perry getting the last one at the goal line. Walter Payton, the NFL's all-time leading rusher, appearing in his final game, didn't score. The press struggled heroically to keep its composure and failed. A Chicago writer mused: "What was it Hunter Thompson wrote about a national political convention—'it's still not weird enough for me?' Well, *this* is."

No one quite knew what to make of Jim McMahon. He had led the Bears to an 18–1 season, and if he didn't keep denying it you would think he was making a statement, striking a blow against the overblown and the pompous, all things artificial and phony.

"He likes to be disgusting on purpose," said Ken Margerum, the wide receiver. "It gives him a kind of mystique. I think that's healthy."

"Football is such a mind game," added center Jay Hilgenberg, "and Jim plays it to the hilt. Nobody knows what he's thinking, where he's coming from, or what he's going to do next. When he's in there, that gives us a big edge."

This is at bottom a Catholic kid from a poor neighborhood in San Jose, who wanted to play for Notre Dame. When the Irish didn't recruit him, he signed with Brigham Young, where he never quite managed to blend in. He broke seventy-one NCAA passing records, but he chewed tobacco, drank beer, and wasn't discreet about it. He also scandalized the authorities with his language. When a Utah writer asked him for his fondest memory at Brigham Young, he said, "Leaving."

He married a Mormon girl, a stunning blonde named Nancy, and has been from all accounts a model husband and father. Nancy tries to reel him in now and then, but mostly she adjusts. He vowed to quit chewing tobacco, and she believes he will. In the meantime, she kept paper cups located strategically around the house.

He was Chicago's fifth pick in the first round in 1982, the first quarterback the club had taken in the first round since Bob Williams of Notre Dame in 1951. "Our first *real* quarterback," said Jerry Vainisi, then the general manager, "since Sid Luckman."

Mike Ditka remembers his first impression of McMahon. He pulled up to the team's training complex, Halas Hall, in a limousine and walked into the coaches' office with a can of Budweiser in his hand. What did Ditka think? "I thought he was thirsty. What are you gonna think? I knew right then he wasn't out to impress anybody with his good manners and good behavior."

McMahon knew what Ditka wanted. He also was shrewd enough to know he couldn't give it to him. "Ditka was at Dallas a long time," says Jim, "and he wanted someone like Roger Staubach. Stable. Works within the system. I like Mike as a person. I would have loved playing on the same team with him. But he had his reasons for the way things should be done and I have some of my own. Sometimes they didn't mix. I think he finally knew that I wasn't just trying to do things that would upset him."

Of course, there were times when they did seem to be competing in a game of one-upmanship. One year Ditka put in a dress code for road trips, shirts with collars. McMahon showed up in a backless T-shirt with a priest's collar tied around his neck. Then Ditka *gave* everybody on the team a golf shirt with an inscription of the front: "Are You Satisfied?" McMahon cut off the collar and the sleeves and wrote across the back of his: "Yeah, I'm Satisfied."

In many ways the coach and the prodigal quarterback were much alike. "Look," said Ditka in happier times, "I don't pass judgment on Jim. He tries, works, leads, wins. He has the great admiration of his teammates. My job is to keep him healthy."

Of course, the normal quarterback—is that a contradiction in terms?—is usually content to exchange high fives with a teammate after a big play. McMahon and his linemen would butt helmets, sometimes knocking each other dingy, until Ditka put a stop to it.

For the better part of six years, Ditka never gave up trying to tame him. "You think about the quarterback position, O.K.?" said Ditka. "The guy with the cleanest uniform, the general, never really in the battle with his troops. Well, Jim's just the opposite of that. He thinks he's our best passer, our best runner, our best blocker. He'll do a lot of things other quarterbacks wouldn't, and they shouldn't. That's one position you can't afford to lose."

In November 1986, McMahon was the object of a cheap and nearly destructive play. He had thrown an interception against the Green Bay Packers and was watching the return when Charles Martin, the 285-pound defensive end, picked him up and bodily slammed him onto the artificial turf. The impact blew out what was left of an already ailing right shoulder.

Said Mad Mac: "It just reaffirmed my belief that there are some idiots out there who want to paralyze you."

Martin received a two-game suspension. McMahon landed in the hospital, underwent surgery, and missed the rest of the season and most of the next. His only consolation was that after the medical reports, no one questioned whether he had been playing hurt or making excuses.

It turned out he had been playing with a partially torn rotator cuff. Linebacker Dan Hampton openly, and Ditka indirectly, had questioned McMahon's dedication and his loyalty, implying that his off-the-field activities had dampened his fires. "I told them I was hurting, that I didn't want to throw in practice, I only had so many throws left in my arm. They thought I was loafing."

"It was the only time I thought we had a real bad relationship," admitted Ditka. "I can't listen to sixteen people. Our doctor said one thing; other people said another. He'd throw well before the games. I didn't know."

McMahon had taken painkillers before the six games he started in 1986. He was angry that no one defended him. He had played seven games in 1985 with a broken hand. Against the Raiders, he stayed on the field for fifteen minutes after he lacerated a kidney.

The defending Super Bowl champions were suddenly beatable; Payton was gone; the ballooning weight of Refrigerator Perry wasn't cute anymore; and Ditka made pointed threats: If any players were unhappy—hint, hint, you in the sunglasses—he would be pleased to trade them.

McMahon came off as petty and spoiled when the Bears brought in little Doug Flutie as a backup. The move didn't affect him; he was sidelined anyway, but he felt badly, he said, for the other quarterbacks. He questioned Ditka's loyalty to his players and he mocked the newcomer as "Tutti-Frutti."

Flutie came and went, and the Bears kept getting stopped in the playoffs. The verdict on McMahon begged to be written. He was still audacious, unpredictable, outrageous. "I don't watch film like a lot of quarterbacks," he says. "I knew what Mike wanted, but I got bored, distracted. I'm like a fan. I follow the ball. I look for my friends to see how they're doing."

McMahon may have been the most instinctive quarterback of his time. Ditka tried to meet him halfway: "He didn't have to spend as much time with film as others. When he sees something, he remembers it. When you tell him something, he remembers it. The only thing I wanted to see with Jim—which was not going to happen—I wanted to see him more serious. The ratio wasn't fifty-fifty and that can be a distraction."

Yes, he could be more serious, but then he wouldn't be Jim McMahon, who says: "Practice is practice. It's something you have to get through each week in order to get to Sunday. Sunday, that's show time. What's the use of having your best day on Tuesday? That's not gonna win the game.

"A good quarterback is a guy who won. Look at Terry Bradshaw. They said he'd never be great, but he won four Super Bowls. To me, he's probably the greatest just because of that. And Joe Willie. He didn't have the greatest stats, but he won the Super Bowl too."

If Chicago hoped that the departure of McMahon would end the team's bickering and controversy, management was in for the rudest of disappointments. The Bears saw their worst fears come true; they couldn't win with Mike Tomczak or Jim Harbaugh. Said McMahon in a bitter parting shot: "Ditka believes he can win with anybody. It's his coaching that gets it done. Now I don't have to deal with that anymore. I feel sorry for the guys who have got to put up with it."

Mad Mac made a mint out of being the punk rock quarterback, but he knows that winning makes the cash register ring, wherever the cash register happens to be. Mike Ditka was no piker either, with a popular restaurant and a string of radio and television commercials. In the end, there wasn't room in the City of the Big Shoulders for both McMahon and Ditka and that was a pity. At least in 1989, everyone wound up a loser.

☆4☆ THE PROUD AND THE PROFANE

The legend is so ingrained, the story so pure, that it seems most of the football fans of the 1960s attended Johnny U. Quite a few defensive backs took classes there too.

We constantly try to fit them into categories, these quarterbacks, according to arm or IQ or temperament. Johnny Unitas started his own school. He was rated by many as the best since Baugh, but the moral of his career can't be told through numbers. The message was: A lowercase nobody can become an Uppercase Somebody . . . if he has talent and the will to use it. They could reject Unitas, ignore him, release him, embarrass him, banish him to the semipro sandlot leagues. But they couldn't keep him down.

His story became a piece of Americana. It was a tale almost classical in character . . . the son of Lithuanian immigrants, busted, unrecognized, rising from total obscurity to the highest station in football. Before and since, the sport has produced some noteworthy performers, but Unitas had the good fortune to come into the game as it started to rise, and he rode it to the crest.

No one was ever a bigger underdog. Rated a fair high school prospect in Pittsburgh, he was scouted and rejected by Indiana and Notre Dame. When the University of Louisville offered a scholarship he quickly accepted.

He played both ways at Louisville, and against a bigger and classier Tennessee team he made so many tackles in a 59–6 loss he couldn't raise his arms after the game. His jersey and shoulder pads had to be cut off.

Unitas had been drafted in the ninth round by the Steelers in 1955 and signed to a contract worth five thousand dollars. The coach, Walt Kiesling, gave no real indication that he knew the rookie was in camp. If anyone else did, it was the result of the one puff of publicity that came his way. A photographer, who needed someone who wasn't busy, posed him with a Chinese nun, with Unitas demonstrating the correct passing grip. It is a scientific fact that no newspaper in America can resist a photograph of a Chinese nun looking at a football. Some of the captions even spelled the young man's name right.

The Steelers cut him in training camp without using him on a single play in five preseason games. Ahead of him were the likes of Jim Finks, Ted Marchibroda, and Vic Eaton. But the frugal Unitas still came away with a profit. He cashed in the bus ticket they gave him and hitchhiked home from camp. He made it on two rides.

He was married, soon to have a family, and his in-laws took in the young couple. Johnny got back his old job on a construction gang, as a pile driver, and signed on to play quarterback for a local semipro team, the Bloomfield Rams. Thus began a story that was to become pro football's "Gift of the Magi."

The Bloomfield Rams played every Thursday night at the Arsenal Street school in the Greater Pittsburgh League. They performed on a field with no grass, and the players had to walk around and sprinkle it with oil before every game to keep the dust down. Unitas was paid six bucks a game, in cash, and he collected it each week in the basement of a dairy on Liberty Avenue. He would take the money home and hand it over to his wife, Dorothy.

In the light of later and historic events, that experience seems the height of irony. But it was never a fit subject of humor to

Unitas, and it pained him whenever someone failed to understand what the money represented. "I was making a hundred
twenty-five a week on my job," he said, "and we were still living with my in-laws, so we weren't starving. What I needed was
a chance to prove that I could play football. The money I gave
to Dorothy every week was important, not because I needed it,
but because I had earned it playing football." Years later, by
then a star with the Colts, he was still wearing a jacket with the
logo of the Bloomfield Rams.

In 1956 the Colts were searching for a backup quarterback to
George Shaw. Weeb Ewbank had been hearing about Unitas from
Johnny's college coach, an old friend. He asked the team's gen-
eral manager, Don Kellett, to call and bring him in for a tryout.
John drove to the Baltimore training camp in a wheezy 1948
Oldsmobile. He was offered a contract for seven thousand dol-
lars, a fifteen-hundred-dollar raise over the salary the Steelers
never had to pay. Today that original Baltimore contract, calling
for seven big ones, hangs in a frame in pro football's Hall of
Fame in Canton, Ohio.

The Colts were to play their second or third preseason game
that summer against the Philadelphia Eagles in Louisville. John
Steadman, then the team's assistant general manager and later
the city's best known football writer, went to Unitas to tape a
radio interview to promote the game. "Sure, I'll make it," the
rookie replied, "but do you really think I'll still be with the club
by the time we get to Louisville?"

By midseason, all over the league, they knew that Johnny
Unitas was there to stay. Bob Waterfield, a classic quarterback
of another time, came out to see him play and marveled, "I've
never seen a quarterback 'look off' receivers the way he does."
This was quarterback language for the way Unitas would look
to one side of the field, pump his arm as if to throw there, and
suddenly fire the ball someplace else. No passer ever mastered
the deceptive delivery better.

To appreciate the impression he made, you had to know the
conditions under which he reported to the Colts. "He came in,"

recalled Weeb, "and we took pictures of him in practice. Not movies. *Still* pictures. In those days, we didn't have any film equipment. The only good stills did was, when you had a bunch of kids at a tryout, you could keep the pictures in front of you and it helped to remember which ones they were.

"We took pictures of John under center and again when he set up and right at the last when he followed through. That was the thing we noticed right away, the way he followed through. It was exceptional. The pictures showed it clearly. His arm went through so far that he turned his hand over like a baseball pitcher. I often wondered how he kept from injuring his arm, because it was like throwing a screwball, and all those guys ended up with crooked arms.

"I worried that he might get what they call a tennis elbow but, boy, I saw the way he could throw and I never bothered him about it. You knew right away. He was in camp no time at all and we knew that as soon as he learned the offense he would be our quarterback."

For the rest of his life, Unitas would represent a great sadness in the heart of Art Rooney, the unpretentious owner of the Steelers. It was Rooney who tipped off Carroll Rosenbloom about the jewel in his camp. Neither of them knew how to pronounce the name. "John had been in camp a few days," said Rosenbloom, "and Rooney called about something or other. He said, 'Carroll, you got that boy Uni-TASS. I want to tell you something. My sons tell me that guy was the best-looking quarterback we had in camp and my coach never let him *throw* the ball.'

"After that call, I watched John in practice. He was so relaxed, so loose, and a very likable kid. This whole time we were wondering if we needed to trade for another quarterback, or if Unitas could do the job backing up George Shaw. We went to Chicago and were leading the Bears by ten points, and in the middle of the second quarter, they ruined Shaw's career. The Bears hit him high and low and knocked out most of his teeth. They carried Shaw off the field, and Unitas had to come into the game. I must say he looked horrible, and we lost it, fifty-eight–twenty-seven. The first pass Unitas threw was intercepted for a touchdown.

"I went down to the locker room. John was never one to show his emotions, but he was sitting in front of his locker, still hadn't taken off his uniform, and had his head hanging so that all you could see was the top of that crew cut. I walked over and lifted his chin up. I said, 'Now look, John, that was not your fault. You haven't had an opportunity to play and no one is blaming you. You're not only going to be a good one in this league, you are going to be a *great* one.'

"Well, I was just trying to build him up, get him out of the dumps. I wasn't sure he'd even make the club. But many times over the years John would ask me how I could be so sure he'd make it. I'd tell him, 'What the hell, John. I'm an old jock. I know talent.' "

During Unitas's incumbency, he won praise for his skill, his coolness, and his stability. When camp opened he was there. He wasn't finishing a movie in Hollywood, completing a business deal in New York, or holding out for riches befitting the player judged the most important in the league.

Unitas gave little indication that he was aware of his status. Fame did not confuse him. He was a stoic, from the bristles on his scalp to the soles of his high-top shoes. He guarded his privacy and rarely complained about anything. For one in his position, he had a quality nearly as valuable as a powerful arm: He had an incredibly high pain threshold.

Few remember that Unitas had suffered what seemed to be season-ending injuries in the early weeks of the 1958 campaign. Late in a game the Colts were winning easily over the Packers, he dropped back to pass. His receivers were covered and he tucked the ball away and ran. He had a long, rather ungainly stride, but a big hole opened and he gained eight or nine yards before he was tripped up. He was already down and helpless when a defensive back came flying in with his knees in the middle of John's back.

He tried to get up but could not. It turned out that he had

three broken ribs and a punctured lung. The next day's papers reported that Unitas was lost for the year. Three Sundays later, wearing a special corset provided by trainer Eddie Block, Unitas was back in action. On the Colts' first play from scrimmage, he hit Lenny Moore with a high, arching pass down the sideline for a fifty-eight-yard touchdown.

In the press box that day, Tex Maule, whose service as the pro football writer at *Sports Illustrated* would parallel the Unitas years, spotted something else. After handing off on a reverse, Unitas doubled back and threw a block. In the locker room, Tex asked an assistant coach if it wasn't unwise giving Unitas a blocking assignment, in view of his recent injury.

"That wasn't his assignment," the coach answered. "That was his own idea."

Johnny Unitas knew he had arrived—knew he had it made—when he returned to New York two weeks after quarterbacking the Colts to that colossal victory over the Giants in the title game of 1958. The Colts had won in sudden death, in what was to become The Greatest Game Ever Told.

Certainly, no game in the history of the NFL had done more for the exploding popularity of what would become America's new national pastimes—the pro game and, specifically, watching it on television.

More than sixty thousand fans crowded Yankee Stadium for the third straight Sunday that December. The day was unseasonably warm, and toward the end of the day, the field was hazy with mist. The Colts dominated the first half, with Unitas showing for the first time in a championship game his genius at probing for small flaws. He flicked passes to Raymond Berry and Lenny Moore, and pounded inside against the Giants' line with Alan "the Horse" Ameche.

At halftime the Colts led, 14–3. Ameche had scored once and Unitas had found Berry with a fifteen-yard pass for another touchdown. The Giants looked like a tired, beaten team. They had needed a rousing emotional effort the week before to beat Cleveland, 10–0, for the Eastern title. The Colts had the benefit of an extra week's rest.

Late in the third quarter, Unitas went to the air with an assurance that seemed close to contempt. The Colts reached the Giants 3 yard line, first and goal. Now the New York defense, which had carried the club all season, stopped Unitas and his mates cold on four downs. The ball went over at the 1.

From the shadow of their own goal, the Giants proceeded to turn the game around. Two plays moved them to the 13, and the thirty-seven-year-old Charlie Conerly uncorked a weird, eighty-six-yard play. It began with a long pass caught at the Colts 40 by Kyle Rote, who fumbled at the 25 when he was scissored by two Baltimore defenders. The ball bounced crazily before Alex Webster scooped it up and rambled to the 1 yard line. When Mel Triplett scored, the noise was a solid wall of sound.

It grew even louder on the second play of the fourth quarter, when Conerly threw a fifteen-yard touchdown pass to Frank Gifford to send the Giants in front, 17–14.

The Colts still trailed by three points with less than three minutes to play, when Gifford was stopped inches short of a first down on third and four. Gino Marchetti, the all-pro defensive end, got one hand on Gifford and slowed him down. Big Daddy Lipscomb then piled on to complete the stop, breaking Marchetti's ankle in the process.

Gino watched the rest of the game propped up on a stretcher on the sideline, refusing to leave for treatment until the end of regulation play.

The Giants' Don Chandler punted to the 12 yard line, and Unitas had only two minutes and twenty-five seconds to move into position for the tying field goal. There he stood, a tall, thin, stooped figure in the swirling mist and the growing cold, calmly marching his team down the field. He passed once to Lenny Moore and three times for sixty-two yards to Raymond Berry, with his bad eyes and one leg shorter than another, but with hands that were the surest in football. With seven seconds to spare, Steve Myhra kicked a twenty-yard field goal to tie the score.

It was 17–17 at what should have been—and normally would have been—the final gun. But this was no normal day.

The teams moved into pro football's first overtime period. New York won the toss for sudden death, missed a first down by a foot, and punted. Unitas took over at the Baltimore 21 and brought the Colts downfield almost as if the Giants weren't there. He mixed sweeps and draws and slant-in passes to Berry. Once, on third and fifteen, after he had been sacked by Dick Modzelewski, he called a hook pass to Berry out of a formation the Colts had never before used. It worked for twenty yards and a first down.

He went to his fullback, Ameche, rumbling on a quick trap for twenty-three more. Now the Colts were on the Giants 20, needing a field goal to win. A pass to Berry and a short run reached the 8. Then came a daring and much questioned call— a sideline toss to Jim Mutscheller to the 1.

"No sweat," said Unitas later. "They were looking for a run. I threw it because I knew we would complete it."

On third down he faked one way and handed off to Ameche, who found himself hurtling into a hole "you could have driven a truck through." He scored and Baltimore won, 23–17, ending the first fifth quarter the sport had seen.

That became the game's enduring image: the floodlit stadium, Ameche smashing through from the 1 yard line, the clock that stopped forever at 8:15 of the extra period.

Small wonder that a mildly dazed Tex Maule stumbled into the offices at *Sports Illustrated* later that night and told an editor, "I think I have just seen the greatest game ever played." After some discussion, the editors settled on a slightly more modest headline over Maule's story: "THE BEST FOOTBALL GAME EVER PLAYED." Still, it was the other description that endured.

With a touch of irony, Unitas said, "I've always felt that it wasn't a real good football game until the last two minutes, and then the overtime. We played pretty well but we should have blown New York out of the stadium and we didn't. Then we had to come from behind in order to tie and then go on to win it. Just the fact that it was the first overtime in championship play, and it happened in Madison Avenue's backyard, that was enough to make people feel they had seen something fantastic.

"They always forget that the month before, in the game that clinched the division and put us into the playoff, San Francisco had us down, twenty-seven–seven, at the half and we came back to beat 'em, thirty-five–twenty-seven. That was a much better game."

Returning to New York two weeks after the overtime victory, Unitas and his wife wandered into what was then one of the city's most exclusive night spots, the Harwyn Club. The headwaiter recognized him, the hot new celebrity in town. "Right this way, Mr. Unitas," he sang out. They were led to a corner table, the most prominent in the joint.

It was at that very table, the headwaiter confided proudly, that Eddie Fisher and Elizabeth Taylor had their rendezvous the night before Eddie flew home to Hollywood to tell Debbie Reynolds he wanted a divorce.

It was not your ordinary table. But Johnny Unitas was not your ordinary quarterback. He was right for the times and perfect for pro football, which had begun to take off. The 1958 sudden-death encounter, more than any other single event, gave the game new visibility.

He clearly enjoyed analyzing a game, or a play, but for an independent thinker, Unitas kept his thoughts and emotions to himself. At one point, he and Weeb Ewbank disagreed completely on tactics and Ewbank began sending in more and more plays. John said nothing. When he felt strongly enough he simply ignored Weeb and called his own. The team was going poorly, but not once did he criticize his coach. Even after Ewbank had been fired and the Colts were on their way back under Don Shula, he refused to blame Weeb.

His last great years came during the Shula regime in Baltimore. Then Shula was gone to Miami. Unitas was near the end of his career when Don brought his Dolphins back to Baltimore, leading the Colts by a half game in the eastern division of the AFC.

Tex Maule went down to the dressing room to talk to John before the game. He was sitting in front of his locker, massaging a white analgesic cream into his shoulder with a vibrator. He looked relaxed, almost sleepy. Unitas was never an impressive physical specimen. His shoulders sloped, his skin was a marble white, and no one would describe him as muscular.

Maule asked him how he planned to attack the Miami zone.

"I don't know," he said. "I'll take what they give me. They got to give you something. All you got to do is find out what it is."

Then he went out and dismantled the Dolphins with two perfectly executed drives, each using up over nine minutes on the clock, and covering a total of thirty-four errorless plays. The Colts won, 14–3.

"Unitas was fitting the ball in between the defensive backs when we were in a three-man rush," said Shula. "He did everything right."

Tom Matte, the Baltimore running back, said, "Johnny called everything we have. He seemed to know just what was going to happen on every play . . ."

As usual, the explanation of Unitas was succinct: "The linebackers were dropping off fifteen yards and the defensive backs were dropping off fifteen behind them. You don't throw long into that kind of coverage unless you want to make a lot of tackles. So I threw under them, to my backs. That's what they gave us and that's what I took."

Years later Ewbank would be across the field, coaching the New York Jets, on what may have been the saddest Sunday of John Unitas's career—the day the Jets upset the Colts in Super Bowl III. Unitas spent most of the game as a spectator, coming off the bench late in the third quarter, trying to wake up the echoes one more time, rallying the Colts as he had done so often. And on the Jets bench a strange thing happened. Seeing the quarterback he had developed at Baltimore, Ewbank forgot himself. Weeb actually cupped his hands and shouted onto the field, and across the years, *"No interceptions now, John."*

Later when the game was over, a writer asked Unitas, "How good is Joe Namath?"

"Sixteen to seven," Unitas shot back, saying it all.

Even when he sparred with the press, he was direct, never coy. He didn't exactly *trust* the press, but he wasn't paranoid about them.

A moment that flashes to mind occurred during the week of Super Bowl V in January 1971, the Colts against the Dallas Cowboys. During a group interview, he was asked about the system then favored by Tom Landry, in which Craig Morton received all the plays from the bench.

John allowed that he could never tolerate such an arrangement. "If the coach sent in all the plays," he said, "you might as well have a dummy back there." Suddenly he sat up straight in his chair and his eyes narrowed. "Now, don't you guys go writing that I called Morton a dummy. I know you guys."

It took a while, but the guys got to know him too. They learned that he would not let you dig much below the surface. But his answers, far from being bland, had bite. And in all that he said or did, his enormous pride showed through.

He was utterly without pretension. You ask him how he feels about pro football today, what the game meant to him, and he tells you: "I'm not philosophical, one way or another. With me it has always been point blank—yes or no, can you or can't you? For me, the thrill wasn't only in winning. It was working with people who were as dedicated as you are, working at times like a big machine."

He was so secure in his values and discipline, Unitas for years refused to believe that his late teammate, Eugene "Big Daddy" Lipscomb, caused his own death from an overdose of heroin. John recalled how Big Daddy hated needles. He was suspicious of the fact that the fatal needle marks were on the right arm; Lipscomb was right-handed.

Unitas never changed, always the centurion. For not quite nineteen years he was about as emotional as a pet rock. But he was hardly humorless. His was a wry humor, the kind that worked for a slow grin, not a belly laugh. One's mind rolls back to the 1971 Super Bowl, and another ambitious effort to probe the innermost feelings of John Unitas.

The words and music went like this:

"How much sleep do you get at night?"

"Depends on what time I get to bed."

"Before any game in your entire career, have you ever been unable to sleep?"

"Nope. I always get my six to eight."

"Well, have you ever had any trouble staying awake?"

"Not exactly. But I can drop off in about five minutes if I want. In fact, before a game I always sleep for ten or fifteen minutes if I can find room to lie down."

Somehow it was reassuring to know that at a moment when the writers would be practicing their opening sentences, and thousands of fans would be trying to settle their nerves, Unitas would be taking a nap. He was the Perry Como of the quarterback lodge. He had the pulsebeat of a frozen haddock.

At one point, he said that he didn't believe in looking back and he added the familiar line. "Something might be gaining on you."

He was reminded that he had quoted a popular source, and he seemed honestly unaware. "Who said it?" he asked. "Paul Brown? Benjamin Franklin?"

"One of your contemporaries" came the answer, "Satchel Paige."

"Oh," said Unitas, at the time thirty-nine, "is he considered an old-timer?"

In the end, he had played eighteen seasons, one less than the number on his uniform. He was a winner. He was great. He brought us to the stadium and he made us cheer. He threw more passes and completed more for more yards and touchdowns than anyone else who ever played the game.

* * *

There aren't many cornball stories like it anymore. Getting cut by the Steelers. A season of semipro ball. The call from the Colts and, shazam, two championships before the 1950s had run out. He passed the test of greatness: He could beat the clock and bring his team from behind.

But he was much more than that. He may have been pro football's last hero. We have plenty of superstars, of course. Television and big money make them easy to find. But there are not many heroes left, of the kind little kids can admire and copy, and whose stories are the kind you once read with your breakfast cereal.

"That's what disturbs me about so much of what is written today," he said. "The derogatory things. I know, the newspaper people say, 'We've got to print it like it is.' But I'd hate for my kids to idolize someone who is into drugs, who treats others with contempt, who thinks his talent is a license to behave any way he wishes. I've busted my ass all my life to watch where I go, what I do, with whom I'm seen. I spent eighteen years in it and a few guys make headlines for smoking pot or snorting cocaine and now the public thinks all pro football players are dopeheads.

"Some of the fun has gone out of the game. The thing that was so irritating was that the players coming into the league today wouldn't take the time, or put forth the effort, of those of ten or twelve years back. They were more concerned then with the game and the team. Little else mattered. You don't have that now. They don't want to spend the time.

"That's one reason I wouldn't want to coach. I couldn't put up with a lot of the horse manure the coaches do now from some of the players. I wouldn't have any patience with the phoniness of some of 'em, and the lack of dedication. I'd probably end up with a squad of twenty-five. There are too many factions on the teams now. It's like one fellow said: He had been with a team a year and he got traded before he could learn all the handshakes."

The players had gone on strike that summer of 1975. It was

very much in character that Unitas had been the first veteran to cross the picket line when the Chargers opened camp. "Football has given me every opportunity I've ever had," he said simply. "No one else I know, from a poor section of Pittsburgh, from a poor family, has been able to sit down for lunch with three or four presidents of the United States."

And that is what was poignant about the leave-taking of Johnny U.

Unitas left football pretty much as he came into it—without ceremony. One day he was on the field, straining to recapture the rich talents of a spent career, and the next day he was sitting in front of a press conference, explaining dryly, "Your mind is willing but your body just wears out."

The scene was a little disjointed for a generation of fans. Pickets milled outside the front gate. And the field—the one Unitas had walked away from—was all wrong. It was catching a breeze off the blue Pacific, not the Chesapeake Bay. For most of his fans, the time to get sentimental had been a year and a few months before, when the Baltimore management decided the services of Johnny U. were no longer needed. The treatment was cold and a little mean, but no worse, when you get down to it, than England selling the London Bridge.

So Unitas, voted in one poll the greatest quarterback of pro football's first fifty years, ran out the string in San Diego, where the owner, Eugene Klein, called him "a living work of art." The dramatic gesture has always been alien to Unitas's character, and to his work. Everything about him—his style, dress, speech—suggested understatement, and this was the way he went.

He was on the practice field when the moment of truth arrived. "The legs just wouldn't respond," he said. "They were sore and swollen and I couldn't maneuver. I stepped in a hole and sprained the left knee and the ankle slightly. I was getting a message."

He limped off the field, went directly to Tommy Prothro, the new coach of the Chargers, and said he had decided to retire. Prothro offered a comment intended to be sympathetic. "I imagine it must be a little embarrassing to someone like yourself, who has been able to do the things you have done, to find that it has become an effort.''

''No,'' Unitas corrected, ''it's not embarrassing. It's just the fact that I can't do them anymore.''

And so it was done. No theatrics. No evasion. No cute exit line. Just Johnny Unitas, speaking with a directness that erased all doubt, the way a wet thumb wipes chalk from a blackboard. It was one of the qualities we came to know and enjoy.

''I came into the league without any fuss,'' he said. ''I'd just as soon leave it that way. There's no difference that I can see in retiring from pro football or quitting a job at the Pennsy Railroad. I did something I wanted to do and went as far as I could go.''

Of course, it was a job, and he was paid well for it, and maybe there is no need to romanticize what he did. But there is a suspicion that we will not see another like him. The urge was strong then, and now, not to let him get away unapplauded.

Once he described what it was like in the huddle: ''When the score is loose and you're way ahead, even the guards are offering you plays. When it gets nice and tight, you ask somebody for help and you don't hear a damned thing.''

He was summoned off a sandlot and he left as royalty. Somehow you find it hard to imagine Johnny Unitas asking for help.

A HERO FOR THE GERITOL GENERATION

Remember 1927? Calvin Coolidge was president. Lindbergh flew across the Atlantic. Babe Ruth hit sixty home runs. It was the year George Blanda was born.

Remember 1949? The musical comedy *Oklahoma* was playing on Broadway. Joe Louis was the heavyweight champion. Scientists were fooling around with something called the H-bomb. It was the year George Blanda joined the Chicago Bears.

Remember 1960? The Russians shot down an American U-2 spy plane, captured, tried, and sentenced the pilot, Francis Gary Powers. John F. Kennedy won the White House, promising to take America to the moon in that decade. It was the year George Blanda came out of retirement to play for the Houston Oilers of the new American Football League.

And remember 1970? A war was dragging on in Vietnam. College campuses were in turmoil. The economy was in trouble. Hot pants made a fashion statement. And George Blanda was winning football games for the Oakland Raiders.

In pro football, when you talk about the spirit of Christmases past, Blanda goes to the head of the line. He was tough enough to play linebacker for the Chicago Bears while he waited for his chance to throw the football. His chance was a long time in coming; ahead of him were Sid Luckman, Bobby Layne, and Johnny Lujack.

He spent ten mostly miserable years in Chicago, trying to prove to old George Halas that he was a winner, and fighting for every dollar at the contract table. One season he failed to beat out Ed Brown, and in the third quarter of a game when the Bears were losing badly the fans began to chant, "We want Blanda. We want Blanda."

Halas leaned forward and looked down the bench. "Blanda," he barked.

George jumped to his feet.

Halas jerked his thumb toward the stands. "Get up there. They're calling for you."

He was bitter when he left the Bears in 1959, picking up his off-season job with a Chicago trucking firm. Once, Halas had tried to explain to him why he wasn't playing, "We need Luckman for our Jewish fans," said the owner-coach, "and Lujack brings in all those Notre Dame people." Blanda sat down to think about his limited appeal. He came out of a mill town in Pennsylvania and played college football at Kentucky. Not much of a market there for the Bears.

In 1960 Blanda signed with the Oilers, who were getting a thirty-three-year-old quarterback with low mileage. He led them to the first championship the American Football League ever awarded. They repeated in 1961 and went to the finals the next year. If Blanda had been a lone wolf and a forgotten one in Chicago, he made up for it in Houston, where he was at the center of every drama.

"I was there seven years and we had eight coaches," he recalls. "We started off with Lou Rymkus, a nice guy and an excellent coach. We played real hard for him and won the title, but the next year Lou and Bud Adams couldn't get along and Adams fired him six weeks into the season."

The Oilers had opened the 1961 schedule by shutting out Oakland, 55–0. "Hurricane Carla was coming in," said Blanda, "and I threw a lot of long passes that night with a good strong wind to my back. But Lou was in a mean temper. He said it was the worst performance he had ever seen. All we had done was win by fifty-five points.

"We lost our next three games, and Lou gave us more hell. He benched me. He benched Billy Cannon. He benched five or six of our starters. Now we're getting ready to play Boston up there and we read in the papers that if we lose one more game, Adams is going to fire Rymkus. Man, we couldn't wait to get to Boston.

"Jacky Lee played quarterback and had a heckuva night, threw for over four-hundred yards. But we're behind by three points [31–28] and we had the ball at about the twenty-five yard line with just enough time for one play. Rymkus says, 'George, go in and kick a field goal.'

"W-e-l-l-l-l"—and no one since Jack Benny stretched out the word with more meaning—"I get in the huddle and Billy Cannon looks up and says, 'Miss it, George.' But, you know, my competitive instincts wouldn't let me. In my whole life, I had missed only one field goal in the last minute of a game. So I make the kick and we tie the score and Adams fired Rymkus anyway. Wally Lemm came in as the coach, we won our next nine in a row and win the conference by a half game. If I don't make that field goal, we finish second."

Blanda was his own man in Houston, but a somewhat crotchety one who warred with the press, snapped at certain of his teammates, and once refused to allow his substitute, Jacky Lee, onto the field. Lee was a bewildered figure, frozen in his tracks, his head swiveling as his coach, Pop Ivy, motioned him toward the huddle, and Blanda waved him back. George won.

Few quarterbacks delivered the ball more quickly than Blanda. He seldom took a sack, dedicated as he was to getting the pass away in three seconds. But he did throw a record forty-two interceptions in 1962 and that, along with the general decline of the Oilers, made him the target of the fans' disenchantment.

Benched against Kansas City, in 1965, he entered the game with the Oilers trailing by seventeen points and threw five touchdown passes in the second half to win the game. A crowd that had booed him all season, had booed him that day, now screamed his name.

Later in the locker room, a writer who felt genuinely pleased for him tried to offer his congratulations and began by saying, "Well, old man. . . ."

And Blanda, missing the softness of the tone, cut him off. "If you want to talk with me," he said, "knock off that old man shit."

By 1966, the coaching disarray and the team's inability to sign its draft choices had sent Houston into a tailspin. The rebuilding job, decided management, had to begin at quarterback. George had overstayed his time. He was thirty-nine, they said, and George didn't deny it.

For the second time his career should have been finished. But he wound up in Oakland and just went on and on, for another ten years. Some people thought he had made a pact with the devil, and no reference intended to Al Davis, the diabolical boss of the Raiders.

In 1970, in the space of five weeks, Blanda went on a rampage. No forty-three-year-old lad ever had a streak quite like this one. On October 25, with the Raiders and the Steelers tied at 7–7, Blanda entered the game, passed for three touchdowns, and kicked a field goal as the Raiders won, 31–14.

The next week he kicked a forty-eight-yard field goal with three seconds left to gain a tie with Kansas City, 17–17. (Sudden death had not been adopted for regular season games.)

The next week he threw a touchdown pass with a minute and thirty-four seconds to go, then kicked a fifty-two-yard field goal as time ran out to give Oakland a 23–20 win.

The fifth week he kicked a field goal with four seconds left as the Raiders edged San Diego, 20–17.

He had been responsible for three wins and a tie, with his arm and his foot, all in the last quarter, if not the last half minute. At forty-three, he would become the oldest quarterback ever to play in a championship game. The Raiders lost to the Colts that day, but Blanda accounted for all seventeen of their points.

He had become the darling of middle-aged America. The humorist Erma Bombeck hailed him as "the hero of the Geritol generation."

Saint George just kept slaying his dragons.

He wanted to play until he was fifty and he didn't miss it by much. And, of course, true to his character, George did not make it easy for the Raiders. He made them cut him. In the diplomatic corps one submits one's resignation when his services are no longer required. But nobody ever accused Blanda of being diplomatic.

In August 1976 the Raiders handed the last job George had, the job of kicking, to a rookie out of Boston College named Fred Steinfort. It was the biggest story in the Oakland camp and yet it was no story at all, because everyone already knew the ending. During one telecast the camera picked up a sideline shot of Steinfort, and Don Meredith, the ex-quarterback-turned-analyst, looked down from the booth and described him as "a flaxen-haired, side-winding, left-footed kicker from the Bavarian Alps, out after George Blanda's job."

One of the stories out of Oakland had Steinfort approaching Blanda on his first day in camp and trying to introduce himself. "I know who you are," replied Blanda. Those were just about the last words they spoke to each other.

So that was the way it would end, after a mere twenty-six years and 2,002 points. Of course, George was convinced he could still kick. He thought he could still play quarterback, and they took that away from him two or three years earlier. He looked no different at forty-nine than he had when he joined the Oilers or the Bears. If you hadn't known his age it would have been necessary to carbon-date his bones to find out.

He had started his last game in 1968, throwing four touchdown passes against Denver. He made the last field goal he ever attempted, a forty-two-yarder with eight seconds to go in a losing play-off game against the Steelers in 1975.

Blanda was a heavy smoker all during his career and enjoyed a drink, but in twenty-six years he never reported to camp out of shape. He would talk to himself as he ran two miles a day, repeating the phrases as his feet pounded the earth: "If you don't run, you can't make the team . . . you won't have all that excitement . . . you can't quit . . . somebody will take your job . . . you'll lose the thing you love." That was how Blanda killed the time, endured the aches and the boredom, by reminding himself where it all led.

Of course, the day came when the road no longer led there. He had been the Dorian Gray of pro football; no player in the history of the game had fought the calendar as effectively as Blanda had. He set records by completing thirty-six touchdowns one season, and seven in one game.

"Yet some people don't remember me playing quarterback," he laments. "They saw those dramatic and exciting finishes in 1970, and they think of me as a kicker, the guy who kicked four or five field goals to win those games. When I go around the country on speaking dates, I have to remind the fans that I was more than a kicker."

There must have been something in the soil of his part of Pennsylvania that stimulated the competitive glands. Within a range of twenty-five miles of Blanda's hometown, Youngwood, emerged such athletes as Unitas, Johnny Lujack, Stan Musial, Arnold Palmer, Chuck Knox, and Bill George.

Even in that company Blanda holds his own. His career spanned four decades, and he set the record for most times rescued from the scrap pile. Well after the Raiders turned him loose for the last time, he was asked if he had thought about coaching.

"The thing is," he said, "by the time I finished playing, I was too old to be starting out as a coach."

☆5☆ THE CONTROVERSY

George Allen always believed that absolutely the worst fate that could befall a coach, other than a one-year contract, was to have two quarterbacks of nearly equal ability. In which case, the fans and the press and, God forbid, the players themselves will choose up sides.

In Washington one year a newspaper poll invited the fans to vote on which quarterback should be the Redskins starter: Sonny Jurgensen or Billy Kilmer. The poll wound up in favor of Jurgensen. Whereupon Allen made Kilmer his starter.

"The one thing you never do," he said, "is let the fans pick your quarterback. A coach who listens to the fans and press won't even punt. He'll gamble for the yardage on fourth down."

The popular expression is a "quarterback controversy," and with the possible exception of where to put a toxic waste dump nothing will divide a town quicker. It runs through the league like a plague. Every team has endured at least one: the Bears, the Redskins, the Cowboys, the Rams, the Giants, are famous for them.

In Minnesota, Wade Wilson and Tommy Kramer traded the starting job back and forth through most of the eighties. No coach ever had a more vexing choice than old George Halas in Chicago

★111

back in the fifties. Papa Bear had to pick between Sid Luckman, Johnny Lujack, and Bobby Layne. Waiting in line were George Ratterman and a kid named Blanda, flat out of luck.

Halas broke the logjam by trading Layne. He counted on Luckman to attract the Jewish fans and Lujack to drum up the Notre Dame trade. There was nothing personal or ethnic about the decision, just business. Even with Layne on the roster, the Bears did not figure to sell tickets in Texas.

Forty years later the quarterback controversy is a tradition alive and well in Chicago.

The Redskins got wonderful mileage out of the rivalry of Jurgensen and Kilmer, then the two of them against Joe Theismann, followed by more recent contenders.

And leave it to the Dallas Cowboys to take an old yarn and give it a twist: They opened the 1989 season with two rookie quarterbacks. No one could recall any team going through an entire season with two rookies at the helm, and millionaires at that. Results of this experiment were somewhat mixed. Troy Aikman emerged as numero uno, broke a finger, and missed a month of Sundays. Steve Walsh started and finished the only game the Cowboys won. While the team lost a record fifteen times, the city was in an uproar. Half the fans feared the confidence of whichever youngster sat on the bench would be ruined, while the other half worried about the confidence of the one who played.

The new broom in Dallas swept so clean, a conflict over the quarterbacks was about the only part of the Cowboys' past the new management respected. To create such a swell opportunity for Aikman and Walsh, the Cowboys had to release Danny White, trade Steve Pelluer, and designate Babe Laufenberg as their emergency backup. No one wanted to guess what it took to qualify as an emergency.

Still, when it came to creating a quarterback controversy, no team did so with the style, the vigor, or the persistence of the Rams. Even one as admired as Bob Waterfield saw his career

complicated by his team's penchant for encouraging such competitions. In the 1950s the Rams were one of those teams that
always seemed to be making the best of a bad situation. They
got so used to it, some felt they went around creating bad situations so they could make the best of them.

A quiet genius, Waterfield was an emotional opposite of Bobby
Layne—slow to temper, serious, low-keyed, reserved. There was
a romantic quality about him, a California campus hero who
married a movie star—Jane Russell.

Waterfield had the committed athlete's craving for the open,
natural life, hunting and fishing, hours of solitude, the company
of other men under a high sun, sitting on a grassy bank. The
Hollywood scene was alien to him. He coped with publicity, his
own as well as Jane's, but he didn't require it and strangers
made him fidget.

It could not have been easy for him. Jane Russell was a sex
symbol, the heroine of a movie called *The Outlaw*, which sent
male temperatures soaring throughout the country. All through
the picture the buxom Jane was in danger of falling out of her
blouse. Bob let her continue acting, one gag went, because he
didn't want her bending over a hot stove and endangering her
career. Of course, boob jokes were a fifties kind of humor, crude
and sexist. Meaning just about right for today's locker rooms.

How Miss Russell felt about the marriage may have been reflected in her advice to the actress Marilyn Monroe, who was
planning to marry baseball's legendary Joe DiMaggio. "Well,"
counseled Miss Russell, "they're birds of a feather and you'll get
to know lots of other athletes. Otherwise, it's great."

Waterfield had everything going for him, the looks, the manners, the wife. None of it would have counted, of course, if he
had not performed. He was the ultimate triple threat, a storybook player who was the last quarterback to win both the NFL
title and the most valuable player award in his rookie year. That
was 1945, when the world was young and the Rams were still
playing football in Cleveland.

That year in the championship play-off in six below zero

weather, the Rams edged the Redskins, 15–14, on a Waterfield extra point that hit the crossbar and tumbled over. He had thrown two touchdown passes.

Waterfield was a pressure player who did things like that, fictional things, of a kind we once devoured in pure-at-heart sports novels by such writers as John R. Tunis, books young boys grew up with in the late forties and fifties.

In 1952, Waterfield brought the Rams from twenty-two points behind in the second half at Green Bay. Down by 28–6 at halftime, they had scored (28–13) and were moving again with eight minutes to play, at which point Waterfield kicked a field goal. In the press box, a Los Angeles writer named John Old leapt to his feet, threw down his pencil, and shouted, "How stupid can you be? That has got to be the dumbest call in the history of the game."

It was now 28–16, and the Packers fumbled. Again, Waterfield took them in to score. Now came another turnover, and in the last sixty seconds he did it again, throwing a perfect pass to Tom Fears to win it, 30–28.

In the dressing room, they asked Waterfield why in the world he had kicked a field goal with eight minutes left, when he needed so many points? "Well," he said, "I had to have a field goal sometime to win. I figured I might as well get it then."

Waterfield's ability to keep his turbines cool seemed to have a calming influence on his teammates. "He was great at sizing up the defense," assessed Tom Fears. "Cool as a deep freeze. He was the same one point ahead or fourteen behind. He'd look at me after the first couple of plays and say, 'Tom, anytime you got it, let me know.' That meant when I thought I could shake clear to tell him and he'd throw me one. And how he threw 'em. A country mile, and laid in your mitts so soft you'd never break stride."

His success established Waterfield as a celebrity, albeit a reluctant one, in a town where people wore sunglasses at night.

While appearing in a movie with Jane Russell, actor Vincent Price became a frequent visitor to the Waterfield home. He tried without success to befriend Bob. It became a challenge to him.

"This is silly," he told Mrs. Waterfield one day. "I've just got to get your old man to like me."

His efforts to amuse the quarterback were met with coolness, and one night Price ran out of patience. "I want you to know," he snapped, throwing in the towel, "that I don't know anything about football . . . and I loathe what I do know about it!"

A slow grin tugged at Waterfield's features. Warming up, Vincent Price proceeded to insult his host's manners, his vanity, his intelligence, letting out all the frustrations of the past weeks.

From that point on they were friends. "Bob liked honesty in people," Jane explained years later. "It was a passion with him. He'd talk football all night with someone who knew what he was talking about. He hated to yak with people who were just trying to make an impression."

The opinion of his teammates meant everything to him, and he tried consciously to reduce the gap between his salary (twenty thousand dollars) and status and theirs. When he arrived in camp in 1951, he tossed the keys to his new convertible on the dresser in his room. "When I'm not using it," he announced, "that's where the keys will be. Any of the guys want it, can have it."

You have to understand what this meant as a gesture. The two-car garage was still a novelty, a convenience for the rich folks. Not only did few players bring their wheels to camp, not all of them owned a car or could even afford one.

To an older generation of football men, Waterfield was the perfect quarterback, in a class with Sammy Baugh. Yet in all his years with the Rams, his job was never entirely, exclusively his own.

First there was Jim Hardy, a bronzed, happy-go-lucky Southern California product. There was no ill blood between them, but Hardy was popular and his friends on the team resented his lack of playing time.

After Hardy was traded away, the competition was a rookie who had more or less handpicked the Rams as his team of the future. He was Norman Van Brocklin, whose brilliant junior year at Oregon had led the school in 1948 to entertain Rose Bowl thoughts. But the young Dutchman had higher ambitions. He wrote to Dan Reeves, the president of the Rams, and informed him that he had the credits to graduate a year early—if the Rams were interested. They were, drafting him on the third round and laying a bonus of twenty-five hundred dollars on him for his thoughtfulness. The other NFL teams, not to mention the state of Oregon, greeted the move as though it were the reenactment of Pearl Harbor.

Van Brocklin played sparingly behind Waterfield as a rookie, until the last game of the season. On a hunch, Clark Shaughnessy let him do most of the quarterbacking against Washington, and Dutch threw four touchdown passes in a 53–27 rout.

That was the beginning. By 1950 Joe Stydahar had taken over as coach, with a plan to alternate his quarterbacks—Waterfield playing the first and third periods, and Van the second and fourth. The city, the team, and the press were split just as evenly.

The arrangement reached a climax, of sorts, when Van Brocklin refused a play that Stydahar sent in from the sideline in the final game of the 1951 season. The coach summarily benched him, and Waterfield finished the game as a soloist, brilliantly passing for five touchdowns and 256 yards. It was enough, by a fraction of a percentage point, for Waterfield to edge Van Brocklin for the league passing championship.

Later, Dutch and Stydahar engaged in a rather earthy cussing match, with the result that Waterfield quarterbacked the first fifty minutes of the championship game against Cleveland. The score was tied, 17–17, when Van Brocklin was finally summoned from the bench, and from the doghouse. He immediately passed for seventy-three yards and a touchdown to Tom Fears and the Rams won, 24–17, for their first world title since moving west.

To his dying day, Van Brocklin resented the two-quarterback concept and was bitter about being rotated in Los Angeles. It became a continuing news story. One writer, recalling the "foul" rumors of discord that plagued Waterfield and Jim Hardy, observed, "The same thing is now happening with a nice kid and a great quarterback, Norm Van Brocklin."

Nice Kid Norm was torn between ambition and his respect for Waterfield. When a columnist in Portland wrote that there was friction between them, and that Waterfield's attitude was holding back Van Brocklin, the two of them got together, sat down at a table, and composed a letter to the writer, telling him politely he was wrong and asking for a retraction.

The issue resolved itself after the 1952 season when Waterfield, weary of the constant battle, retired. Hampton Pool took over as the latest Rams' coach, their third in four seasons. Pool was to confide later that his association with Van Brocklin shortened his life span by at least eight years.

What happened next? Dutch was to alternate with Billy Wade, a nice young man out of Vanderbilt, whose NFL career was undistinguished (until he led Chicago to the NFL title in 1963). To share the position with Waterfield, one could tolerate. But Billy Wade? Dutch felt like a husband whose wife had brought another man home for dinner.

And so it went. Van Brocklin could do things like put forty-one points on the scoreboard in a *single* quarter—as he did against the Lions on October 29, 1950— and yet there was something about his skills that the fans disbelieved.

For one thing, he was slow at a time when quarterbacks were being looked upon as a third running back. One opposing coach said of him, "All he has is an arm. He runs like a girl with her girdle slipping." Added George Halas, in a withering judgment, "Van Brocklin can throw. Period. In the full sense of the word, he is not a professional player."

Van Brocklin sneered at his critics. He compared their complaints faulting a hockey goalie "for not rushing out of the cage and throwing body checks all over the rink. Or a pitcher who wins twenty games is a bum because he didn't hit .300. And Joe Louis wasn't a great fighter . . . all he could do was punch."

Still, the fans chanted for Wade at the Coliseum, and when Sid Gillman moved in as coach in 1955, he rotated them and won a division title. "Van Brocklin's speed," said Sidney, "was a terrible disadvantage in those years when a quarterback had to run on the rollout. But he had one thing that paid off in football—he threw the ball straight. There is no defense against a quarterback who can throw straight. That was Van's strong suit."

The Dutchman was a great passer because he always thought in terms of the receiver's problems. Once on a bet, he passed a football downfield, and then after it had stopped rolling, hit it with six of ten throws from thirty-five yards away. "The difference between a touchdown and an interception," he said, "is whether a ball drops over an end's right shoulder or his left."

His moods were volatile, his patience thin, and he loved a good argument, often taking either side. He was also a perfectionist, consumed by the game. His wife, Gloria, would wake up at odd hours, hearing her husband mumbling in his sleep, wordless noises punctuated by strange yips. "Even at three A.M."—she finally figured it out—"he was calling plays."

Van Brocklin was quite simply a man of conflicting natures. He had a wry side, and a flair for caricature. He came up with some of pro football's most colorful nicknames, i.e., Night Train Lane. He called Tank Younger "Bass Eyes," after he caught the rookie fullback tipping off the defense by rolling his eyes in the direction the play would go.

But Van Brocklin was also quite capable of meanness. He referred to Sid Gillman, the former University of Cincinnati coach who replaced Hampton Pool, as "the Rabbi." In later years Gillman insisted he did not take the reference as a slur. He did not regard Dutch as a bigot, but as one willing to test another's armor. There were not many Jewish coaches around. "I wanted to coach the team," admitted Van Brocklin, with the self-mockery of truth, "and Gillman wouldn't let me."

After he had become a coach, Dutch was asked what kind of quarterback he preferred. "A guy who comes in and throws three touchdown passes in his first game," he said. "Like me."

Based on the record, it was doubtful that Van Brocklin the coach would abide a quarterback as headstrong as himself—witness his run-ins with Fran Tarkenton.

Pool had been fired after a tumultous 1954 season. Gillman made a tactical move at the beginning of training camp to counter his college image. He called in Van Brocklin, Fears, and Don Paul, and made them an ex officio committee to represent the players' viewpoint. And then he went against the trend:

"The Giants preached that if you wanted to stop passing, the way to do it was man to man. As a consequence, everybody believed it—coaches are inclined to grab from the successful team, to this day. Well, perhaps the Giants could do it, but with us it was bombs away, and there was just no way the man-to-man was going to stop the bomb."

And the bombardier, the Dutchman, was a nonpareil. "Every time Van Brocklin threw the ball," said Gillman, "you could hear a little 'zzzt!' as it left his fingertips. We commented about it in practice. Zzzt! Zzzt! It was an oddity. Well, one week Van hurt his hand and he could hardly throw in practice. You no longer heard that sound. His velocity was down and the team slumped. For weeks we were depressed. And then one day he started throwing better and better, and suddenly we could hear it again. Everybody started laughing and yelling, 'The zzzt is back!' "

Those were halcyon days in Los Angeles. The Rams were *averaging* ninety thousand fans in the Coliseum—"wall-to-wall people," said Gillman. "The Brinks truck used to stop every fifteen minutes at the stadium and haul the money away in a wheelbarrow." The Rams won their conference and reached the championship game, losing to the Browns and Otto Graham.

In the locker room after the loss, there was still a certain amount of euphoria, and Tex Schramm, the general manager, cautioned his rookie coach; "Sid, just remember it isn't always going to be this easy."

It wasn't. The Rams struggled the next four seasons and Gillman was forced to resign at the end of 1959. The Rams spent those years becoming famous for ownership squabbles and massive trades. They packed off three quarterbacks who later won NFL titles elsewhere—Van Brocklin, Wade, and Frank Ryan.

WAITING FOR ROGER

Tex Schramm moved on to Dallas, where in 1960 he was the president and organizer of a new franchise, the expansion Cowboys. In Dallas the quarterback rivalry would be raised to the status of an art form.

Controversy is inevitable on a bad team, and the Cowboys were atrocious for five years. Eddie LeBaron, the glory tot from College of the Pacific, Amos Alonzo Stagg's last quarterback, was the team's original starter. The fans booed LeBaron and pleaded for Don Meredith, the laid-back, fun-loving character who had been a local favorite at Southern Methodist.

When Meredith won the position, the Dallas fans booed him more lustily than they had booed LeBaron, and they chanted for Craig Morton. In time Morton moved up and they demanded Roger Staubach.

All of which is fairly consistent fan reaction in the dance of the quarterbacks. Except that there was something personal and mean in the hammering of Meredith, the home boy. The Cowboys by 1965 were one rung below the league's top level. In Big D's boardrooms and barrooms, they were judged just a quarterback away. Dandy Don, they said, had a good arm, a good smile, and a good contract. And for five years none of the three improved.

It would be almost a test of faith, many years later, with the Cowboys absent from the Super Bowl since 1979, and the Landry era gone, to believe that they finally booed Staubach in Dallas and cried for Danny White. But they did.

To start for Dallas became an obsession for Danny White, who chased Roger Staubach with the intensity of Captain Ahab harpooning his great white whale. Of course, no one had observed

Roger at closer range, nor admired him more, but still there was an edge to the competition.

They even turned it into a game within a game. As they jogged their daily miles around the track of the team's California training camp at Thousand Oaks, they made up a game called Dateline. It was performed in a staccato, breathless, newscaster voice.

White was running out of patience, in 1979, when he opened the game: "Dateline! Dateline! Dallas, Texas . . . Tom Landry, at the age of eighty-eight, today announced his retirement as head coach of the Dallas Cowboys . . . seventy-year-old quarterback Roger Staubach said the entire team would miss him . . ."

Roger howled, the victim of a direct hit. Clearly his understudy had won that round. But Staubach had won more than his share. For four years they had competed at Ping-Pong, tennis, billiards, basketball, and one-upmanship. They even argued about who was taller. ("I am," insisted White, "by a quarter inch). In truth, they competed at everything but football. The job was Staubach's. He knew it. The Cowboys knew it. The fans knew it. Most of all, Danny White knew it.

For most of the 1970s, Staubach had been the very symbol of the Dallas Cowboys, and the Cowboys had been acclaimed "America's Team." They were J. R. Ewing's team. And IBM's team. In keeping with the general spirit of things, Staubach assured his understudy that White "was America's punter." Staubach's round.

He had earned the right to decide when he would no longer play. He was up there with Layne and Unitas when it came to taking over a game in the final two minutes. "I honestly used to feel sorry for the other team's defense sometimes," recalled a teammate, Cliff Harris, the Dallas safety, "watching Roger go to work in those last two minutes. You'd put yourself in their position and realize the feeling of utter helplessness. There was really nothing you could do to stop him when he was on."

"He can play until he's forty," Sonny Jurgensen once said of Staubach, "because he doesn't know what a hangover is."

Wholesome, straight-arrow Roger stepped down at thirty-eight.

Danny White's interest was equaled only by the enthusiasm of the rest of the National Football League. Of the ten super Bowls played in the 1970s, the Cowboys had appeared in five.

Now the problem that sooner or later engulfs every team stems from one fact: No quarterback is ever programmed to be number two. Staubach was number two once, and he didn't like it. For a brief period he was even number three. That was near the end of the 1960s, when he used his navy leaves to work out with the Cowboys.

Dandy Don Meredith was about to retire and turn the reins over to his pal Craig Morton in 1966. In what would be his last Dallas training camp, Meredith watched the rookie Staubach drive himself, hour after hour, improving with each snap. One day Meredith turned to Craig Morton, whose hair was thinning, and said, "Old Roger's gonna get your job, Curly."

Staubach was not quite sure what to make of his rivals. Watching the horseplay between Meredith and Morton, he asked a writer, "Do they always kid around like that?"

He was told that they often did. He shook his head. "I don't think I could be that friendly," he said, "with a guy whose job I was trying to take."

Push the fast-forward button and eleven years later you would hear Roger saying of Danny White: "He was very understanding of his role. We had a deep respect for each other as athletes. I told him I was not going to hang on until they had to drag me off the field. I knew what Danny was going through and knew he was important to the Dallas Cowboys.

"The bottom line is that we can both get the job done, in different ways. I've enjoyed being Danny's friend. He has a lot of depth. He may not be the overbearing competitor I am—he's more subtle—but he competes. It's in him and it's strong."

Once when White beat him at table tennis, Staubach flung his paddle against the wall in mock anger and it stuck in the paneling like a hatchet. White had the panel, with the paddle still in it, removed and framed and hung on the wall of his office. The story appeared in print without any disclaimer, a fact that nettled Staubach. "It made me look like a sore loser," he said. "I play hard. I lose hard. But I don't think anyone can say I'm a sore loser."

Between White and Staubach the affection was real. They had an almost big brother–kid brother relationship. But the frustrations of seldom taking a snap, and the feeling of being nearly invisible in the locker room and team meetings, forced White to bottle some strong emotions. "The worst part was waking up on Monday morning," he said, "and not aching anywhere. You felt like you hadn't done anything. I was never satisfied just to be a punter.

"We would be sitting in the meeting room, looking at a film, and it was as if I wasn't there. The coaches would say, 'Roger, look at this,' and, 'Roger, look at that.' Just once, I wanted them to say, 'Quarterbacks, look at this.'

"I remember one time the coach handed out this performance sheet. It graded us in different areas, cited things we had to improve. The first priority was to 'protect Roger.' Not 'protect the quarterbacks,' but 'protect Roger.' I cut it out and pasted it in my locker. I'd look up at it before practice and get all fired up."

With his dark hair, fair skin, and young face, White had the squeaky-clean look of a New Christy Minstrel bounding onto a stage in white trousers and picking at a banjo. In his early years he showed no temper, nor did he seem inclined to challenge his coach, Tom Landry. Pete Gent, the former Cowboy and best-selling author of *North Dallas Forty,* said of Danny: "The guy has a year's supply of dried food in his basement. He's got phone numbers to call when Armageddon arrives. Is that the kind of guy you want quarterbacking your team, down seventeen points with time running out? Hell no, man. Too logical. He knows you can't come back."

No question, Staubach had spoiled the fans—and many of the players. "Sure, at times I resented it," said White. "But only briefly. It was not as if Roger had politicked for the job. He earned it. He was a great quarterback, the best. I learned a lot just being around him. I saw Roger handle the media and the attention and my admiration just kept growing." While White was impatient, he was never mutinous.

The same could not be said of an earlier contender. The arrival of White in the summer of 1976 threatened the position of Clint Longley, who had been groomed by the Cowboys as Staubach's successor. Longley was not known for his control, on or off the field. Thrown into a game against Washington, a rookie without a down of NFL experience, Longley unleashed a fifty-yard pass with twenty-eight seconds left to beat the Redskins. The play became a precious memory in Dallas. In the Landry system, with its emphasis on precision, any spark of originality seemed to light up the team. "The triumph of the uncluttered mind," guard Blaine Nye described it.

But Longley was just as likely to have an errant pass bounce off Landry's tower, as happened one day in practice. "Clint had a great arm," recalled White, "but something in him turned sour. I guess it really had to do with my coming on the scene. He had backed up Roger for two years and had been the heir apparent. Now that was in doubt. It changed. He wouldn't even work out with us."

Longley's service in Dallas came to an end after he and Staubach traded blows. Well, they didn't exactly trade them. Roger gave and Clint received, knocked him down with one punch. White acted as a lookout, keeping an eye out for backfield coach Dan Reeves.

In midseason of 1979, after the Cowboys had lost three in a row, White decided to drop by Tom Landry's office. He did not ask to be traded. "That wasn't what I wanted," he said. "But I was afraid the coach had begun to think I was content to be a backup quarterback. I was not. Certainly not on a team that was losing. I wanted to play and I wanted him to know how I felt. He said he understood. Then Roger talked to me. He kind of hinted that he would not be back in 1980 and I should just hang in there and wait for my shot."

Hanging in there wasn't always easy. During games White stood on the fringe, a few feet away whenever Dallas gave up the ball and Roger trotted over to chat with Landry and Reeves. "My role on the sideline," he says, "was to be there when Roger had to let off steam. He'd walk over to me and pace around and say something like, 'Can you believe he called that play?' And I'd humor him."

Roger did retire before the 1980 season, and when Danny White's shot arrived he discovered, of course, that the Staubach comparisons would never end. The big question was whether he could duplicate Staubach's ability to bring the Cowboys back from seeming defeat.

"Over the years," reflected Landry, "we came to rely on Roger's ability to win the game in the last few minutes. We seldom played well enough to put it away early. If Roger had not had that ability, we might have done a lot more before the fourth quarter. But we always felt Roger would pull it out, no matter what was happening. You develop a mentality."

His hope was that White would not need to earn Roger's kind of reputation, that the Cowboys would learn to win a little earlier. "I think a quarterback reaches a point, as Danny White did, where he has to play. If Roger had said he wanted to play two more years, we'd have lost Danny. I think there is an obligation to a player like White, or a Craig Morton, to give him the chance to move on if he isn't going to fit in when he's ready."

The Cowboys went to the playoffs six straight years with White. But the string ended with a losing season in 1986, and through the rest of the decade. In Dallas the fans booed Danny White and called for Gary Hogeboom, and then Steve Pelluer. But in their hearts, really, they were calling for Roger Staubach.

Slowly, agonizingly, it all fell apart for America's Team. Clint Murchison went bankrupt and died. The ownership changed hands twice, and the second time Jerry Jones, an oilman and once a scrawny guard at Arkansas, blew into town from the Ozarks and did the unthinkable: He fired Tom Landry, The Only Coach the Cowboys Had Ever Had. The owner brought in his college roommate, Jimmy Johnson, who had won a national college championship at Miami, known throughout the land as Sunshine U.

The firing created a wave of sympathy for Landry, who had

been embattled in his last three seasons. It was, someone noted, like replacing Helen Hayes with Madonna as the First Lady of the American theater.

Jones declared he was going to run the team "from socks to jocks," whereupon the man who built the Cowboys, general manager Tex Schramm, retired. Gil Brandt, who had been the team's top talent sleuth since 1960, was fired, along with the ticket manager and the public relations director and a dozen others with twenty years of service. Then Jones went too far. The Cowboy cheerleaders threatened to resign over rumors that Jones planned to replace their traditional costumes with biking shorts and halter tops. He denied the reports, held a news conference to reassure them, and acknowledged their value as an asset to the team and the sport, calling them "the pick of the litter."

A Dallas business writer observed that Jones was "to public relations what the *Titanic* was to safety at sea."

After so tumultuous a start, it must have been a relief to have the fans arguing over the high draft picks, Troy Aikman, the UCLA product, and Steve Walsh, out of Jimmy Johnson's own Miami program.

Danny White had reported to camp believing, naïvely, that the team might need a veteran while the kids were maturing. Told by Johnson that he would probably never take a snap, White took the hint and retired.

CALIFORNIA DREAMIN'

Dante Pastorini had been something of a military secret in college at Santa Clara, which existed in the shadow of a school called Stanford. During those years Stanford was quarterbacked by a young man named Jim Plunkett, who would lead his team to a win in the Rose Bowl and walk off with the Heisman Trophy.

On a day when Plunkett was swiping all the headlines in the state of California with a good game against USC, Dan was down the road throwing seven or eight touchdown passes against Humboldt State, and nobody was watching.

His whole college career had gone like that. Which is why the 1971 college draft delighted him so much. On the morning that Houston picked him in the first round, a writer called to get his reaction, and it came in the form of a question.

"Did Boston take Plunkett?"

"Yes," the guy said.

"Great," replied Dan. "Now, for the first time, we are starting even."

The Oilers and the Patriots were then two of the sorriest teams in professional football. After three losing seasons, both teams finished 7–7 in 1974. Houston had won a total of six games up to that point, cranking them out at the rate of two a year. Boston more nearly achieved mediocrity, winning fourteen and losing twenty-eight.

The rivalry was reduced during this period to comparing the size of their lumps and measuring their capacities for tolerating pain. But while the Patriots were stagnant, the Oilers were developing into contenders. The link in the careers of these two interesting talents was all but forgotten until fate and Al Davis brought them together briefly as teammates—and competitors—in Oakland.

You have to remember what Plunkett had been. You have to remember the shining promise of the class of 1971. A dozen years would pass before the colleges would turn out a group to eclipse it. Three of the first four players drafted were quarterbacks: Plunkett, number one; Archie Manning of Ole Miss, taken by the Saints, second; and Pastorini, fourth. The Oilers also landed Lynn Dickey of Kansas in the third round.

Every year except his rookie year was a bad one for Plunkett in New England. In 1975 he underwent two shoulder surgeries—a pin was inserted to hold it together so he could play. When he ran onto the field in November for his first game back, he was drowned in boos and crushed by them.

"I saw him play in most of his eighty-four straight games for the Patriots, including the exhibitions," wrote Leigh Montville, in *The Boston Globe*, "and I watched his abilities chipped away in bits, here and there. Trying to learn about life in the National Football league was like trying to solve the Sunday *Times* crossword while sitting cross-legged in the fast lane of the Southeast Expressway . . ."

The next year Plunkett was gone, traded back to his native northern California, to the scene of his college glories. In a one-for-five swap, the Patriots sent him to San Francisco, home to the Bay Area, home to family and friends. There was only one sour note. The 49ers in 1976 and 1977 were even worse than the Patriots.

The week before the opener in 1978, the 49ers gave him his outright release. He cleared waivers, meaning that none of the other twenty-seven teams claimed him.

Splat. Jim was still waiting for the first good thing to happen to him in his pro career when he hit the pavement. His arm was sound, he thought, but his self-esteem was a mess. Then the Raiders hired him to stand on the sidelines and watch Ken Stabler. He didn't play a single down. In 1979 he threw a total of fifteen passes and then came the ultimate irony.

The Raiders traded Stabler for Dan Pastorini.

For the first time in his life, Jim Plunkett made a scene. He screamed. He stamped his feet. He demanded to be traded. The Raiders said no, they needed a veteran to back up the fellow the Oilers had fondly dubbed "the fancy-passing Dago."

"There's been a rivalry with Dan," said Plunkett, "no question in my mind." Although obvious to others, that was a major admission coming from one as reticent as Jim.

Pastorini had the more classic form, and a slight edge in power, but Plunkett had better control. Dan was a risk taker, a ladies' man, drop-dead handsome. Plunkett, a product of the Mexican barrios, liked his privacy. It took all of his nerve to audition for the part of Jim Thorpe in a movie about the Carlisle Indian. The project never got made.

Jim was a spectator for the first five games of the season while the Raiders stumbled to a 2–3 record. Tom Flores had succeeded the retired John Madden as coach, and there was a general restlessness in the Oakland offices. Pastorini, who had grown accustomed to an offense in Houston that featured the rushes of Earl Campbell, was adjusting slowly to the long ball game Al Davis wanted.

Plunkett, thirty-three, and fighting himself, tried not to give in to the idea of placidly accepting a permanent role as number two. In the second game of the season against San Diego, he had one play, one chance, to strut his stuff. Pastorini limped off the field with a bruised knee, with thirty-nine seconds left and the Raiders trailing by seven points.

Facing fourth and seventeen at the San Diego 23, Plunkett drew the Chargers offside on a snap count, then looped a pass to Raymond Chester for eighteen yards and a touchdown. That sent the game into overtime, and Pastorini, his knee heavily wrapped, returned to the game. The Raiders lost, 30–24.

Still, Plunkett had been reassured by his game-tying pass. So were his bosses. In the fifth game against Kansas City, Pastorini went down and out for the season with a broken leg. Plunkett stepped in, driven by nearly a decade of futility and disappointment.

The Raiders won nine of their next eleven, three more in the playoffs, and became the first wild card team to win the Super Bowl, beating the Philadelphia Eagles. Pastorini, whose leg had healed faster than expected, was physically able to play. The Raiders didn't bother to activate him.

Jim Plunkett was back, all the way back. For the last time in this tale of two California quarterbacks, one had prospered at the expense of the other.

NO TEA
OR SYMPATHY

All during the week of Super Bowl XXII, reporters kept pressing Doug Williams, who is a model of politeness, about whether he felt sorry for Jay Schroeder and his fall from grace. Doug was blunt: "No I don't have any sympathy for him. I think everybody goes through the feeling, at some time, that they should be in the ball game. If he feels that way, that's his opinion."

And Schroeder couldn't hide the fact that, yes, he thought he should be number one. But what he said was, "He's going to start the game, and we'll go from there." He didn't mean just the Super Bowl, of course, which Williams started and the Redskins won. He meant that game, and the next season, and the rest of their careers.

But a year later, Schroeder was with the Raiders . . . and in and out of the lineup there too. Meanwhile, Doug Williams was riding a familiar roller coaster—he missed half the 1989 season after shoulder surgery, then swapped starting assignments with Mark Rypien and, with a coldness that seemed stunning, was given his release by the Redskins.

Until the factory figures out a way to produce an unbreakable quarterback, these competitions will continue to intrigue us. Most coaches claim that the ideal situation would be to have two of equal ability. No coach, however, has found an ideal way to keep two quarterbacks happy.

☆6☆ ON THE BRINK

In the lifetime of fans of a certain age, the three most powerful photographs in sports have been:

Ralph Branca, the number 13 looming large on the back of his shirt, making the long walk to the clubhouse in centerfield in the Polo Grounds, after giving up the home run to Bobby Thomson.

Enos Slaughter, weeping in front of his locker after learning that he had been traded from St. Louis to the New York Yankees, protesting that he had always thought "they would have to tear this uniform off me . . ."

And Y. A. Tittle, on his knees, blood trickling down his bald head and streaking his face, his eyes dazed and unfocused. You didn't have to know the score to know that Tittle, and the Giants, had lost that day.

There are athletes who go through their careers always landing one ring below the bull's-eye, who tantalizingly reach the lip of the cup and stop. They are always next year's champions, which is a nice way of saying that they will never win it all. Which, to some critics, is a nicer way of saying they are losers.

Y. A. Tittle, with San Francisco and the New York Giants, was without argument the greatest quarterback who never won a championship. But for fifteen years he tried. And that photograph of Tittle, battered and beaten by the Bears in the final game of 1963, seemed as symbolic in its own way as the flag raising on Iwo Jima.

You could not dislike him. Even when he was beating *your* team, which he did so often in those games where the fate of the universe was not at stake, you could never hate him. Maybe it was that kindly farmer's face or that unlikely name, one of those names you never got tired of saying.

Phil Foster, a Brooklyn comic and genuine sports freak, worked it into his nightclub act in the fifties. "I used to love the tough guys in pro football," he would say. "In my day we had real he-men—Bronko Nagurski, Alex Wojciechowicz, Mel *Heinnnnn*. Now what have we got—names like Milton Plum . . . Y. A. Tittle . . . Y. A. Tittle?" And Foster would throw up his hands, as if to suggest that the next step would be to let girls play.

Yelberton Abraham Tittle was no loser. But his status was reduced by the fact that he could never nudge his team over the final barricade. He is remembered best, ironically, for a gimmick: the Alley-Oop play. Yet he was a tough, persistent operator whose thoughts were often original, and as a passer he was nearly an artist. When he retired he owned four career records, including most touchdown passes.

Y. A. Tittle won early recognition as the semihero of one of the classic stories of football lore. It happened in his college years, but no doubt helped build the character that sustained him through some of the trying times to come.

There is no way to put this gently. In 1947, playing for LSU against Ole Miss on his home field at Baton Rouge, in front of forty thousand fans including his fiancée, Miss Minnette De-Loach, Tittle lost his pants.

Y. A. was at left cornerback on defense when he intercepted a pass thrown in the flat. The Ole Miss receiver grabbed at him as he made his move, and in the process tore away his belt buckle. Football pants in those days were not the skintight stretch variety, they were loose-fitting and baggy. Tittle tucked the ball under his right arm and used his left hand to hold up his pants as he crossed the 50 yard line.

At the Ole Miss 20, hemmed in against the sideline by two Rebels, he tried to shift the ball from his right to his left, so he could stiff-arm one of the tacklers. When he made the switch, down came the pants and he fell flat on his face, twenty yards from what would have been the winning touchdown. Tittle staggered to his feet, trying to pull up his pants, and fell flat on his face, again.

There was a time when Hollywood could have made a full-length movie out of a scene like that, starring Jack Oakie.

Some doubted that Tittle, even if he kept his pants on, would make it in the pros. The entire NFL passed on him in its 1948 draft, and he signed with the Cleveland Browns of the All-America Football Conference for a ten thousand dollar salary and a bonus of two thousand dollars. Before he played a down, he was traded to the Baltimore Colts. There his passing philosophy was established by his coach, Cecil Isbell, who had thrown all those passes to Don Hutson at Green Bay: "Depend on yourself to complete the pass. Throw the damned ball. The only one you can count on for help is your receiver. Don't wait for a pass pattern to spring a guy open so you can lay it in his lap. Your mother-in-law can do that."

Tittle was traded to the 49ers in 1951 and spent the rest of the decade trying to shake off his feelings of insecurity. In training camp in 1951, he approached the veteran Frankie Albert and asked about some minor point on a play. Albert made a face and said, "Hey, Tittle, don't you know, you're after my job." The message: no help here.

The looseness of the game, the willingness to improvise on the field, made it possible for coaches like Buck Shaw to prepare their teams without a playbook. "The game was so different," says Tittle. "We didn't study two sets of films before each game; we didn't even have audibles. There was none of the preparation we know today. We did not have to face the great defensive stars who now play in the National Football League. In those days, the average life span of a pro was two or three years; today quarterbacks have to contend with defensive specialists who have seven, eight, nine years experience."

In fact, the only complicated part of the game were the signals, which then as now sounded like something out of a CIA codebook. Example: in 49ers terminology, left end was "port," right end was "rip," and the tight end was X or Y, depending on which side of the line he was positioned. So Tittle's call for the Alley-Oop in the huddle would go: "Fifty-one [pass pattern] . . . Y right . . . rip . . . Alley-Oop!" [R. C. Owens was the right end, "rip."]

The country wasn't as big, nor was football, and college wasn't yet available to all. So it does not seem odd that lives and careers overlapped and sometimes became a tangled ball of yarn. Born in Marshall, Texas, Tittle enrolled in the University of Texas but sized up the competition—another single-wing tailback named Bobby Layne—and transferred to Louisiana State. In 1947, Y. A.'s senior year, Bernie Moore put in the T formation at LSU, the same year Blair Cherry was introducing it to Layne at Texas.

Exactly what one coach would have done with two talents such as Layne and Tittle on the same team isn't known. But no doubt he would have smiled a lot and felt warm all over.

Every summer in San Francisco, Tittle had to defend his job in training camp against that season's rookie threat. The 49ers never finished below .500, but they never finished first either. They tied for the Western Division lead in 1957 but lost in a playoff to the Lions.

In 1961, Red Hickey decided to install the new Shotgun formation and he wanted young John Brodie to run it. Hickey could never bring himself to list Tittle among the great quarterbacks of his time. "He never won a championship," said Red. "That's what a great quarterback does: wins championships."

Meanwhile in New York, the new coach of the Giants, Allie Sherman, wanted to open up the offense. Charlie Conerly, pushing forty, could no longer throw deep, and the running backs, Frank Gifford and Alex Webster, were slowing down. In a preseason game Sherman spotted the younger quarterback he thought he needed: Y. A. Tittle, thirty-five years old, nearly bald, and asthmatic.

Just before the season opened, the 49ers traded Tittle to the Giants for a rookie guard named Lou Cordileone, whose reaction to news of the trade was a classic: *"Me?* For Y. A. Tittle? Just *me?"*

There were stirrings of a rebellion among the 49ers, but Tittle walked into the dressing room after the announcement and faced his former teammates: "I just heard that some of you guys are grumbling about me being traded. I've been here ten years and if anyone has a right to grumble, it's me. But I don't want to leave here with any of you feeling resentment toward the management. I owe them a lot for the many fine years I've had here. We all owe them a lot."

Although he was no debutant, Tittle could still run, and his versatility excited Sherman. Now the Giants added a missing ingredient: a speed burner. Del Shofner was a tall, slender receiver who had developed ulcers with the Rams.

Tittle was hobbling when the season opened and the Giants lost to the Cardinals, 21–10, behind Conerly and an erratic sophomore from Utah, Lee Grosscup. The next week they were struggling against the Steelers, and Tittle came off the bench to replace Conerly and complete his first eight passes. The Giants rallied and went on to win the Eastern Division title. What had been a storybook season was spoiled by Green Bay, and a 37–0 licking in the championship game.

After the season, Tittle was voted the team's most popular player, Conerly retired, and the club cut Grosscup, whose stay had been a strange one.

Lee had size and a powerful arm, and a kind of hip intellect the players and coaches distrusted. Which was a little curious right there; his braininess had given Allie Sherman his start in the pros, as a compact, left-handed quarterback in the early forties.

Grosscup had been an English major at Utah, and *Sports Illustrated* published a collection of letters he had written leading up to the College All-Star game. His impression of the Giants was limited to these observations, in shorthand: "Great bunch! Fine gentlemen, very spirited, close knit, good drinkers, great physical specimens." In an article more than three thousand words long, two words doomed his relationship with the Giants: "good drinkers." He was a rookie, he had overstepped some imaginary line, and in the retelling the comment seemed bigger and more damaging.

Grosscup was not exactly a pariah. They liked his raw potential, but the Giants rode him hard and rarely missed a chance to embarrass him. They were daring him to show the spine he needed to lead them. At the end of one road trip, Lee's wife and baby were waiting for the team bus. Lee kissed his wife and began wheeling the baby back to the car. Allie Sherman turned to Don Smith, the team's publicity director, and said; "Will you look at that? That's my quarterback . . . wheeling a baby carriage."

Grosscup failed to hang on with the Vikings, Jets, 49ers, or Raiders, and his innocent antics seemed to infuriate his coaches. In Minnesota, Van Brocklin blew up when he called a play and used the word "deuce" instead of "two." Explained Lee, "All I was trying to do was have some fun, and Van Brocklin said, 'We don't want any more of this Madison Avenue bullshit.' "

In his time with the Giants, there was one gesture of kindness, and one almost mystical moment when he made a connection with the fans. In the season's eighth game, with his team way ahead, he went in against Washington and had his first two passes intercepted. Then Tittle walked over and talked to him softly and suggested he throw some short percentage passes.

"So I got a little march going," recalled Lee, "and finally threw a touchdown pass to Shofner. And I got this standing ovation from sixty-five thousand people, and I went over to the bench and just sat there. And I was listening to this noise and I started to shake. And then I started crying, sobbing . . . it was . . . it was something. At least I can look back and say, 'Well, I had that. I know what it is to have a standing ovation in Yankee Stadium.' "

Y. A. Tittle would bring them to their feet over and over again.

He brought the "bomb" to New York, the long pass on fly patterns to the fluid Shofner.

After Conerly retired, Tittle for the first time found himself in the position of being a starter with no one waiting in the wings. He responded in 1962 by throwing thirty-three touchdown passes, breaking the old league record shared by Sonny Jurgensen of the Eagles and Johnny Unitas of the Colts. But once again the Giants ran into Green Bay in the championship game and lost, 16–7.

At midseason Tittle had put on one of the great passing shows of all time as the Giants outgunned an unbeaten Redskins team, 49–34. He completed twenty-seven of thirty-nine passes for 505 yards and seven touchdowns. Only two other quarterbacks, Sid Luckman of the Bears, and Adrian Burk of the Eagles, had ever passed for seven touchdowns in a game.

The 1963 season, in spite of Tittle's having a painful rib injury, followed the same scenario: He broke his own record with thirty-six touchdown passes; the Giants finished first in the east and then met the Bears for the title.

With the Giants leading, 10–7, the Bald Eagle injured his left knee in the second quarter. Although he was nearly immobile and grimacing with pain, he returned to play the second half. But the Bears won, 14–10, and New York's legacy was a photograph of Tittle, *bloodied by a blow* that knocked off his helmet, kneeling in the end zone.

"I'll remember what Y.A. did," said Frank Gifford, "long after I've forgotten the score."

In those years of finishing second, the fans of New York never seemed to blame Tittle. Instead, they suffered with him and gave him their empathy. And what was there to blame? Sherman called him "the best quarterback I have ever seen on the line of scrimmage." Maybe some of their affection had to do with the way he looked, with being bald. It was reassuring to a lot of middle-aged businessmen to see a bald guy out there, taking his licks and holding his own in the company of much younger studs. Y.A. was no painting. He had large ears and a big nose and blue-gray eyes—squinty, hunter's eyes—set deep in a bony

face. His voice was thinner than you expected, his speech reserved and polite.

He didn't smile much when he was working. He was intent,
nervous, taking everything in. Often on the sideline he would
squat down on his heels, cowboy style, and anyone who wanted
to talk to him had to squat too. Allie Sherman got to be pretty
good at it.

Tittle had no hang-up about showing his emotions. He was
not like Conerly, whose expression rarely changed whether he
had thrown the winning pass or an interception. Tittle would
slam his helmet to the ground if he missed a receiver.

People were usually surprised to meet him in person and discover that he was modest and often shy. At many points in his
career, he doubted his ability to be accepted as one of them by
the men with whom he played. There was this quality about
Tittle that made others want to explain, not criticize him. But
Y.A. knew there was one question he could never answer: He
was 0-for-5 in championship games, including three in a row
with the Giants.

He had not started the 1964 season with the intention of
making it his last. But he hurt himself running for a touchdown
in a win over the Colts, and the season quickly went downhill.
They were tied by Dallas, and Y.A. was benched briefly in a loss
to the Eagles. The Giants fumbled the ball away in the first minute and Tittle was booed when he left the field. Later he said he
hadn't noticed it.

The protection kept breaking down and the Eagles had his
feet in the air most of the day. "The traction is pretty bad up
there," he said in his laconic way, when the writers asked why
he had trouble setting up.

"I knew I wasn't playing well that season," he would say
years later. "I asked myself, 'How could I be so good in sixty-
three, and be washed up nine months later?' "

The three second-place finishes still rankle, but he doesn't try
to argue with the cold judgment of the record book. It was, he
reflects, a bittersweet time: "New York is really the most glam-

orous of all cities . . . if you win or have lots of money. The worst thing to be in New York is a loser or poor."

Tittle left New York in neither condition. He wound up as one of the game's respected names—and initials. He became half the answer to a terrific trivia question. What two all-American quarterbacks had the initials Y.A.T.?

(Answer: Y.A. [Yelberton Abraham] Tittle and Young Arnold Tucker of Army.)

THE URBAN
COWBOY

Don Meredith twice brought the Dallas Cowboys to a showdown with the Green Bay Packers, twice lost, and walked away with a view of pro football that was irreverent. Yet there was something touching and sad in Meredith's inability to (1) fulfill his potential, and (2) enjoy the success that he did have.

There have been few relationships more complicated than the one between Coach Tom Landry and Meredith. He had star quality from the moment he stepped off the campus of Southern Methodist University in 1960 and moved down the street to the practice field of the new team in town. Meredith was the first player ever drafted by the Cowboys. Landry's plan was to ease Meredith into his system slowly, and it was clear from the start that their philosophies clashed.

Meredith was glib and whimsical, with a magnetic personality. On occasion he would break into a song in the huddle (his favorite was "I Didn't Know God Made Honky-Tonk Angels"). This impulse drove his coach bananas, but Dandy Don recalled wistfully: "Back when the Cowboys were going bad, a lot of our guys used to sing in the huddle. Then we started winning, and one day I realized I was the only one still singing."

Landry wanted his young quarterback to be more serious and

dedicated. The differences were not drawn so sharply when the franchise was new and the fans expected so little. But by 1965 the Cowboys had turned a corner and were looking for an edge that would move them to the next level.

"We had many discussions," Meredith recalls, "but I wasn't listening."

Then one day Landry called him into his office and said: "Look, I don't care whether you like me or not. But I would crawl on my hands and knees through downtown Dallas to make you respect me." Dandy Don allowed later that he liked the mental image of the coach crawling through Dallas. He began to listen. He began to perform as his admirers had hoped. And the Cowboys were winning now, winning big.

Still, something stood between the Cowboys and the supremacy they craved. It was Green Bay in 1966 and 1967, and the Cleveland Browns in 1968. And then Meredith said adios, packing it in after eight seasons. In the end those close to the team believed that the inability of Meredith and Landry to operate on the same wavelength had cost the Cowboys.

Don had already acquired a certain independence as a schoolboy in the tiny Texas hamlet of Mt. Vernon. He made up his mind to accept a scholarship to SMU, but Abe Martin, the homespun coach at rival TCU, made one last pitch. "You don't want to go to SMU with all those city people and neckties," Abe told him. "Come on over with us, where you can wear old blue jeans and a T-shirt."

Meredith even then had visions of the cosmopolite swinger he was to become. "Coach, I've been wearing jeans and a T-shirt all my life," he answered. "That's what I'm going to college to escape."

Landry seemed genuinely fond of his prodigal quarterback and accepted as a personal failure Meredith's lack of motivation. But Don would complain to his friends that Landry lacked warmth, and implied that he might have fulfilled his potential under a more understanding mentor.

If Meredith left the game not quite on top, he didn't hold it against his chief tormentors, the Packers, or their coach, Vince Lombardi. "I often wondered if I could have played for him," he confided. "You know, it took a certain type of individual to play under Lombardi. We used to get into friendly arguments. His philosophy was basic. He would say to me, 'Wouldn't you like to know where all your people were going to be all the time?'

"And I 'd say, but if we did well what we were supposed to do, you couldn't touch us. On paper we could beat him every time. But it always came down to one thing. Execution."

In the early 1960s the Dallas offense was so complicated it looked like the invasion plans for Normandy. It was so complicated that for a long time only Tom Landry—and the other team's defense—could understand it. Meredith needed three years to get it down, but by the middle of the decade he thought the Cowboys were ready to conquer the world. Or at least Green Bay.

"That big game syndrome started in 1966," he said, "when we played what I thought was a super game against them. But the Packers had the better team. In 1967 I thought we were better, but that one was the ice bowl, and we were the victims of circumstances we couldn't control.

"Losing to Cleveland the next year was a more bitter disappointment in my book. We thought we had gotten it all together, and I still can't explain why we lost.

"Really, when we played Green Bay my feelings were those of delight. I liked Lombardi. I enjoyed his honesty, his frankness. It was a thrill to play against people that good."

Meredith had quick success as the third man on ABC's innovative Monday night television crew. He broke away to dabble in movies, then came back for a few seasons. But it was clear to anyone who knew him that his interest in football had ebbed, and in the 1980s he withdrew from the scene altogether.

But at least for a time, the public had a glimpse of the sweet nature that had once made the Cowboy huddles such an interesting place to be. There was so much to like about Meredith; he was slick and funny and without guile. He was cool when

Joe Namath was still wearing black football shoes and regula-
tion-length hair.

When ABC hired Meredith, his boothmate, the sardonic Howard Cosell, explained the move: "We have always been known
as the third network and we like losers." Cosell was half joking,
at least, and with Frank Gifford they captured a huge audience
and changed the way people looked at football on television.

Meredith's finest moment may have come on the night the
Oakland Raiders were shutting out Houston in the Astrodome,
and with the score 30–0 a camera zeroed in on a fan curled up
in his seat, apparently asleep. Sensing the camera, he opened
one eye and, in full view of millions, raised the middle finger of
his right hand.

There was an instant of perfect silence, broken quickly by
Meredith's Texas drawl: "That's all right, fans, he's just sayin',
'We're number one.' "

On the night Meredith made his debut as a football analyst,
ABC introduced him with a forty-second film clip containing
highlights of his previous career. You saw Meredith in a variety
of forced landings. There was Meredith on his back, on his face,
on his hip pads. Meredith with his head snapping like a rag doll.
Meredith being buried under tons of hostile beef. As he watched
his twenty-one-inch self being abused and smashed, Dandy Don,
ex-quarterback and blithe spirit, was struck by a thought: "That
was exactly the way I remembered it. And the film reminded
me of why I retired."

Don Meredith twice brought the Cowboys to a showdown with
the Green Bay Packers, twice lost, and walked away with a slightly
irreverent view of pro football that was in many ways attractive.

THE SCRAMBLER

When the New York Giants surrendered their top draft picks for
two years in exchange for quarterback Francis Tarkenton, there

were critics who argued it was Georgia's revenge against Sherman—Allie Sherman. The scramblin' man from Atlanta would now bring his brand of chaos and anguish to Yankee Stadium.

Indeed, Tarkenton seemed to be the classic right man in the wrong place at the wrong time. He had joined the Minnesota Vikings as they were coming out of the expansion chute and coached by a purist, Norm Van Brocklin, who considered it un-American for a quarterback to run out of the pocket.

And Francis was the original scrambler, a daring escape artist, a fun little guy sticking his tongue out at the big guys and living to tell the tale. What he lacked in artistry—the great arm—he made up for with energy and quick feet. He was like a tick; you had to set him on fire to kill him.

The Giants hoped the trade would strengthen them, but they needed Fran just as much for box office reasons. No longer contenders, they were losing the battle of New York to the brassy Jets. But while Tarkenton was trying to revive the Giants, a terrible thing happened to him. The Vikings were getting good.

In January 1970, the Vikings were preparing for their first Super Bowl appearance, against Kansas City, and their former quarterback traveled to New Orleans to see them play. Fran was uncertain that he wanted to be there, he said, but unable to stay away.

On the morning of the game, he visited with his old mates as they boarded the bus to the stadium. As he did, Joe Kapp, the quarterback who had taken his place, swept past him and swung aboard. The doors closed and the bus pulled away from the curb. "A great wave of feeling clogged my chest and throat," said Tarkenton, "some sorrow, pain, and, I guess, some anger and envy. I went off to a quiet place and I cried a little bit. For that was my team to quarterback and Minnesota was my place to play football."

He had been there in the lean years, including 1964, when Jim Marshall, the defensive end, landed himself in the Blooper Hall of Fame. He scooped up a fumble, fled sixty-sixty yards into the end zone, and then joyfully flung the ball toward the stands. It was the lineman's dream come true! Alas, he had landed in the wrong end zone for a safety. It was Columbus discovering China.

Marshall sensed something was wrong when the other team's players, the San Francisco 49ers, swarmed around to congratulate him. Tarkenton was the first to spell it out. "Jim," he shouted, "you ran the wrong way—the wrong way."

So the long run of Wrong Way Marshall captured the essence of the Minnesota franchise up to that point.

Francis Asbury Tarkenton would be traded from the Vikings to the Giants and back again before reaching the Super Bowl in his thirteenth season. Then he would lead his team to three Super Bowls in four years and lose them all.

Tarkenton didn't try to conceal the bitterness of that experience: "It is the ultimate humiliation. There is no consolation of any kind. People ridicule and abuse you. They look much more kindly on teams that don't get there than they do on a team that gets there . . . and loses."

There was no need to add that a special hell exists for teams that get there and lose three or four times.

Tarkenton came along when Meredith did, was compared to Tittle—for his heroic near-misses—and was judged against Namath. Yet what really made him interesting was the criticism he endured all his career, some of it for doing what no other quarterback did as well. "Tackling Tarkenton," said Fred Dryer of the Rams, "is like trying to pick up a watermelon seed."

You must understand the frame of mind of the man who pursues a scrambling quarterback. The pursuer will tolerate a dropback guy. He will even put up with one who rolls out. But the scrambler he cannot live with, because this man is making a fool out of him. However unwittingly, the scrambler is humiliating him and taunting him, reducing him to the part of the Keystone Kop engaged in some kind of absurd chase. It could be worse only if the pursuer got hit with a cream pie.

One of the original scramblers in pro football, Frankie Albert, advanced the theory that the greatest emotional blow the scrambler could deliver to his pursuer was to step discreetly out of bounds. The minds of the tacklers are primed to cream him.

They have chased him across the field, and there he is, vulner-able, trapped like a rat along the sideline. And at the last instant he jumps out of bounds!

A tackler watching Albert do this one day screamed in horror, "No!" He could have clobbered him anyway, but it would have cost him fifteen yards, and such a penalty offends the profes-sional dignity of any player.

Thus in the brain of the victim a large frustration develops. He prays for a shot at the scrambler. He wants to waffle him. And given the opportunity, he does.

So you sense the scope of the problem that confronted Fran Tarkenton every Sunday. As football's most productive scram-bler, he faced people even angrier than they usually were.

Of course, Francis did not fully agree with this appraisal. "I don't care what kind of quarterback you are," he said, "the tacklers hit you hard. A distressing feature of pro football is the fact that guys don't lay you down comfortably."

To compound matters, even those on his side did not wel-come Fran's improvisation. "A quarterback should run," in-sisted Van Brocklin, "only from sheer terror. When he is forced to run, you have taken away his effectiveness and made him play your game. He won't beat you running. He'll beat you throwing the ball. That's what he's paid to do."

Of course, when Fran did his dance his linemen rarely knew how long to hold their blocks for fear that he might double back. Tarkenton always maintained that he scrambled less as the years went on, and even then some of the scrambles were actually designed plays.

The Vikings, said wide receiver Ahmad Rashad, did not mind leaving the impression that they played a little sandlot ball. "In the huddle Fran would call a play," explained Ahmad, "maybe some combination of receivers, maybe a bomb. Then he'd add, 'Ahmad, you go ahead and do what we talked about on Tuesday.'

"I'll give you an example. He'd call one play that had three receivers going to the right side. I'd be on the left. He'd scramble to the right, but all that time I'd just stand there at the line of scrimmage. So he'd be scrambling all over the right side, and everybody in the stadium would be saying, 'Look at this guy improvise,' because, see, that's what he wanted them to think. The truth was, it was all planned, a planned scramble. He'd come running back to the left and there I'd be, all alone. He'd throw me a two-yard pass and I'd run for thirty."

To which Van Brocklin said, yeah, but . . .

"The first couple of years, Francis had to get out of there or get killed. And he was clever with it. But I think due to his youth and immaturity he got to thinking it was pretty cute. It was appealing and it was successful for a while."

The uneasy truce between Van Brocklin and Tarkenton was similar to the one between Landry and Meredith, but without the music. It went downhill in 1966 when the Vikings won only four games and Dutch started his backup quarterback, Bob Berry, in a meaningless, late-season game in Atlanta—in Tarkenton's home state.

Writers had heard Dutch say under his breath, "Fancy things make me puke." They thought they knew what he meant.

In a dizzying forty-eight-hour period in February 1967, Tarkenton wrote a letter to general manager Jim Finks, asking to be traded and indicating he would otherwise retire. And the next day Van Brocklin resigned.

Whatever his reasons, Tarkenton did not reconsider his request, and the Vikings accommodated him with the trade to New York. For most of his five seasons there, the Giants struggled to be a .500 team. But Francis was converting some of his critics with his smart and gutsy play. In 1968 he carried the ball a remarkable fifty-seven times for 301 yards and three touchdowns.

The picture of Tarkenton that survives is that of a quarterback in a competitive frenzy, dodging tacklers, buying time, making big plays out of nothing. With the Giants he used the multiple offense, and he flew it by the seat of his pants. Once he sent rookie halfback Rocky Thompson in motion, and Thompson went right instead of left. Tarkenton, leaning over the center, didn't call a time-out or risk a delay penalty. He just yelled, "Hey, Rock!

The other way!'' Thompson made a U-turn and Tarkenton went on with the snap count.

Fran never played with a full deck in the expansion years with Minnesota, or in New York, where to get Tarkenton the Giants had given up the draft picks they needed to rebuild the defense. "You've heard about the Rubber Band defense that bends but never breaks?'' described Don Smith, the former Giants' publicist. "Ours doesn't break either . . . it just stretches a hundred and one yards.''

Of course, his heart was still with the Vikings. And when he returned to them in 1972, the timing could not have been better. To begin with, Van Brocklin was long gone. "I have great respect for Van Brocklin as a coach,'' said Fran, "but not as my coach. I just have too many different ideas about football.''

Now the coach was Bud Grant, who had turned the team from the frozen tundra into a tough, steady, composed squad always in contention. They were the Purple People Eaters, with one of the game's fiercest front fours: Jim Marshall, Alan Page, Gary Larsen, and Carl Eller. And now they would be Francis and the Purple Gang, with Chuck Foreman getting the hard yards.

Grant shaped them into a thinking man's football team. Tarkenton, the son of a Methodist minister, and Marshall, sky diver, scuba diver, snowmobiler, were chess partners.

When Francis turned pro in 1961, an honor student from Georgia, he announced that he had two goals: "to win a National Football League championship and become a millionaire.''

One out of those two isn't bad. Even as a rookie he was delivering lectures on motivation to business groups. Soon he had his own firm, and tie-ins with such companies as Delta Airlines, Chrysler, and Coca-Cola. He was well groomed, God-fearing, straight-arrow, the athlete as Boy Scout.

In time he developed a philosophy about his profession: "You show me a quarterback and I'll show you a guy with a critic. You show me anybody who has done something in this world and I'll show you a critic of that person. The best way not to be criticized is to go in a closet and never come out. I didn't like to be criticized. I wanted everybody to love and respect me and think I was a great player. But that isn't possible—although all of us seem to get better after we retire.

"One week they call you the greatest and the next week some jerk says you never could run or throw. I think that's the biggest enemy of a quarterback—the extreme highs and lows of how you are appraised. It's very important to get through all that and you have to be somewhat arrogant and say, 'Screw the world. I've got a job to do and I know I can do it and I don't give a damn what anybody else thinks . . .' That's the most important ingredient a quarterback can have."

He lasted eighteen remarkable seasons, and his endurance surprised everyone. He grew sick of being described as a scrambler, but when coaches today talk about wanting a quarterback "who is mobile," they are paying a compliment to Fran Tarkenton.

When he retired, he had broken the records of Unitas and other immortals, passing for more yards and more touchdowns than anyone who had ever played the game. The three Super Bowl losses he would carry with him, and it would be like having nails on the inside of your shoe.

Still, not winning the Super Bowl didn't keep Fran Tarkenton out of the Hall of Fame. You wonder what he might have achieved if he had played in a system actually designed for him; say, the run-and-shoot that gained some converts in the late eighties.

The early perceptions—that he was self-centered, too much the corporate climber—may have delayed his receiving the credit he deserved. He hardly came across as humble, but Francis was grateful for the good and funny times.

He appreciated the fact that Bud Grant, once the NFL's most unusual coach, was never a slave to the clock. Grant's objective at game time on Sunday was to reach the stadium before the national anthem. One year in Detroit he didn't quite make it, drawing a five-thousand-dollar fine from the league office.

The Vikings were stalled—until fifteen minutes *after* the kick-off had been scheduled—in the heavy traffic outside the Silverdome. Tarkenton watched, mildly amused, curious, getting a little antsy, as Grant ordered an assistant coach out of the trapped bus and into the street to try and clear the traffic.

The assistant, walking between vehicles, shouted at the top of his voice, *"I've got the Vikings."*

And from a bus one lane over, a fan stuck his head out the window and shouted back, *"I've got Detroit and seven."*

☆ 7 ☆ HERE'S LOOKING UP AT YOU

This is the story of the Little Quarterback Who Could.

Once upon a time there was a little quarterback who yearned to play with the big boys. But the other players would laugh and say, "You are too small. You must be big to play football."

The Little Quarterback was very sad.

"I know I can," he said, and he practiced every day.

All his life he had been told he couldn't, and he kept repeating, "I know I can, I know I can." And when they let him, he always did.

But it meant nothing if he could not play with the big boys. The pros liked the Little Quarterback. They even gave him a uniform, and standing on the field with the other players, he looked like a Christmas Elf, or a mascot. He was so small that the uniform did not fit and you could only see part of the number on his back.

"I know I can," said the Little Quarterback when everyone laughed, "if they will only give me a chance."

But he wondered it he would ever play football with the varsity boys. Then came the day of a very important game. The big football players huffed and puffed and banged into one another. But the Little Quarterback only watched. He was too small.

150 ★

Then suddenly the big quarterback was hurt.

The coach looked at the bench and saw only the Little Quarterback. The coach sent him in.

The Little Quarterback ran onto the field, thinking, "I know I can, I know I can."

And he could. He became the hero of the game. And the season. And the city.

He thought, "I knew I could if they would let me."

The big football players said, "We will never make fun of you again. You can play football with us whenever you want."

The Little Quarterback only smiled and practiced that much harder.

And that, fairy-tale lovers, is the story more or less of Eddie LeBaron. It is also the story more or less of Doug Flutie, Pat Haden, Jeff Kemp, Jerry Rhome, and Kevin Sweeney—every Napoleon-sized fellow who ever played beyond his inches in the big man's world of professional football.

"There have been at least a dozen sub-six-footers who played quarterback in the NFL," says Seymour Siwoff of the Elias Sports Bureau, the official statisticians to the league. "I think Bob Griese and Billy Kilmer fit into the category. And others. But it's hard to tell because people lie. If a player is five feet ten or five feet eleven, the teams will list them at six feet."

Which brings us to LeBaron, the Little General of the Washington Redskins for a decade. The quarterback he succeeded was Sammy Baugh.

His was a long, splendid career and Eddie spent much of it listening to good-natured complaints about his size. In his twilight time, with the expansion Dallas Cowboys, Billy Howton described what it was like catching LeBaron's passes: "You run your deep pattern and look back and nobody's there. You can't see him. And suddenly it looks like the ball is coming at you out of a silo."

LeBaron, at five feet seven and 160 pounds, was one of the real miniatures of the National Football League. He earned his shot at the pros after leading the College All-Stars to a stunning upset of the NFL champion Philadelphia Eagles.

For reasons of his own, George Preston Marshall insisted on listing him at five feet nine and 180 pounds in the team's program. It may have been the beginning of all of those credibility problems in Washington. A popular photograph of the day shows LeBaron standing between two linemen, one six feet seven and the other six feet eight. He looks like a toy.

Eddie notes curiously that his size became more of an issue, more of a news item, as the years passed than it was when he reported to the pros in 1950. Maybe the players were getting larger. Maybe somebody finally noticed.

In 1956 Eddie LeBaron quarterbacked the East to a squeaky win over the West in the Pro Bowl, a game that meant three hundred dollars, cash, to each member of the winning team. In 1956, still years before the boom, a player would have killed for three hundred dollars.

As Eddie greeted his wife outside the locker room door, Big Daddy Lipscomb of the Baltimore Colts emerged from the other dressing room. "My wife hadn't been around football much," he recalled. "Big Daddy walked over. He was six-nine, three hundred pounds. He had a little beard and he wore a porkpie hat. He loomed over me and said, '*You little son of a bitch. I'll get you next year.*'

"Hell, my wife wanted me to quit on the spot."

For eleven years LeBaron was the smallest player in the National Football League. Nothing irritated the big boys more than to be done in by a guy who looked as though he should be delivering groceries. "I made it partly for mechanical reasons," he concludes now. "I had a higher release than people like Tittle. I threw completely overhand. I found one thing to be true. They either respect you or they don't. Size doesn't enter into it."

When his playing days had ended, LeBaron practiced law and returned to the sport as the general manager of the Atlanta Falcons.

LeBaron watched with a sympathetic interest as Haden and then, with greater fanfare, Flutie attempted to overcome the complaints against their size. "The only important qualities for a quarterback," he said, "are ability, movement, and intelligence. If a man has them, his height doesn't matter.

"Now if two guys have these qualities and one is six-three and the other is five-ten, you would prefer the big man, mainly for his physical durability. But to reject a good player because it is said he can't see over the rushers is silly. No one can see over the rushers, and in most cases, you don't have to. Even if you are six-three, defensive linemen are so big all you see are teeth when the rush comes."

LeBaron is amused by the fact that every time another shrimp steps into the spotlight, his phone rings in Atlanta. "When Flutie came out of college," he says, "my phone didn't stop ringing. And whenever he gets cut or traded, more calls come in. Then when the Cowboys decided to give Kevin Sweeney a chance, I heard from another wave of writers. I guess I'm the spokesmen for short quarterbacks.

"I repeat what I have always said. These fellows were winners in college. If they can move the team, if they can get the ball to the receivers, then they are tall enough. But to the extent that people need to be convinced, sure, their size will hold them back. It already has."

Pat Haden of USC, Oxford, and the Rams needs no reminder. And he was doubly cursed: a sub-six-footer and a Rhodes scholar as well. He knew the whole catalogue of complaints and studied them, searching for answers, looking for the tiny detail that might offset his disadvantage in height. Frequently, he admits, he didn't find any.

Sadly, short and smart will never replace tall and mean in the NFL.

Haden remembers playing cat and mouse with the Dallas Cowboys—you figure who was which—and their famous flex defense. "The best defensive lineman I ever faced," he says, "was Randy White. In fact, all the Cowboys front four played like gods—Too Tall Jones, Harvey Martin, John Dutton—and Dallas was the best team in the league at deflecting passes. It wasn't just a matter of me being a 'small' quarterback either. I watched films of the Cowboys, and every time a quarterback got set to throw they'd put their hands up. It's amazing how many teams are not coached to do that. I'd bet my house that the Cowboys led the league every year in tipped passes.

"White really beat me up in one preseason game, which at that time of year isn't supposed to happen to your starting quarterback. During the game one of our coaches must have said something to our guard who was responsible for White, because the guard came up to me and said, 'I can't block him.' You don't know how frightening that was. I looked at the guy and wanted to say, 'What do you want me to do? Do *you* want to throw the ball and let *me* try to block him?' "

Passing through the Rams' revolving door at quarterback, Haden knew he had to be alert and opportunistic. He learned to alter his cadence to slow down an overeager pass rush. During his second season, he came to the line against Green Bay and barked out the signals. It was a cold day and his voice, a trifle high to begin with, suddenly cracked. Jim Carter, Green Bay's middle linebacker, started laughing. "What's going on, Haden?" he shouted. "Haven't you reached puberty yet?"

The Rams always practiced a nonrhythmic count—*Hut!* . . . pause . . . hut! hut!—to make it more difficult for pass rushers to anticipate the snap. Haden's tendency was to go on a long count on third downs, and one day he saw a chance to set a booby trap. The booby he wanted to trap was with his old friends, the Dallas Cowboys.

"I played in the Pro Bowl after the 1971 season," he says, "and one day at practice Harvey Martin stood nearby and listened to me call the signals. He was trying to get my cadence down. I could tell that he thought he had mastered my three-count—'*Hut!* . . . pause . . . hut! hut!'—so I kept doing it that way and made a mental note of it.

"The next year when we played Dallas I varied my cadence and drew him offside on a third and two. I tried to save something like that for important situations. But if you set it up right, you could draw them offside all night."

That he is able to think at all is a testimony to any quarterback's poise and conditioning. At field level, frenzy rules. Linemen spring at one another. Pads slap. Players grunt and moan. And one man knows the microinstant when this havoc is going to be unleashed.

"It can get pretty noisy out there before a snap," says Haden. "If one of our linemen forgets the snap count, he'd ask out loud as I was calling my signals. You couldn't very well say, 'It's on one, Tom,' so we had a code. 'Able' meant one, 'Baker' was two, and so on. One time somebody asked, 'What's the count?' And Rich Saul, our center, said 'Able.' Then I heard somebody else go, 'No, no, it's on Baker!' and a third guy shouted, 'No, it's Castro.'

"By then I had forgotten the count myself, so I just stood there and waited for the ball to come up."

Riding the waves with the Rams, Haden did not always keep his footing, but he never lost his composure. He joined the club in 1976 and heard the merciless booing of James Harris and Ron Jaworski. He was the fair-haired boy then, a rookie, the quarterback in the wings.

In Los Angeles, as in most places, the most popular quarterback is always the one who isn't starting. Haden outlasted Harris and Jaworski, then Vince Ferragamo, and finally, Joe Namath. Then he heard his own clock ticking and after eight seasons, including a stint in the World Football League, Haden decided to retire. No more having to prove himself.

"I sound defensive about this," he says, "but I'm not. I just got tired of it more than anything else. Fran Tarkenton was the most prolific passer in NFL history, and he's no taller than I am. Bob Griese won two Super Bowls. He might have an inch on me. John Brodie was no giant. If it takes a big quarterback, how about Bobby Douglass—he was the biggest you'll ever see. What did he win?

"I'll concede this. If I had been taller, I could have carried more weight and perhaps avoided some injuries, but I'm not convinced of that. My injuries were all freakish. In the playoffs after the 1978 season I broke my thumb on Randy White's helmet when I followed through on a pass. I caught the little finger on my ring hand in the seam of the AstroTurf in Seattle and broke it in 1979. And in the opening game of 1980 I broke my right hand by catching it in one of my lineman's shoulder pads.''

It was the crowd reaction after that injury that led Haden to his decision to retire. From then on, he would plead his cases before smaller and, he hoped, less critical juries. "I walked off the field and the doctor bandaged my hand, and a couple of minutes later the news flashed on the scoreboard: PAT HADEN HAS BROKEN HIS HAND. And sixty-five thousand people, a majority of them anyway, cheered. That really blew me away. I felt like a gladiator in the Colosseum, with the fans up there giving the thumbs-down gesture.''

At least, Haden had his chances and he took them. In spite of all the commotion that swirled around him, he played on teams that won, if not always big enough to satisfy the owner or the fans. In training camp one year he roomed with Joe Namath, whose own storied career ended on the Rams' bench . . . backing up Pat Haden.

THE MAGIC
FLUTIE

Of course, singer-writer Randy Newman brought exposure to this sensitive subject with his novelty hit, "Short People," which included the sterling lyric, "Short people got no reason to live." Many disagree and are inspired by the success of countless Little Big Men. For the current generation the quarterback of choice is Flutie, the little wizard of Boston College. Flutie had clinched the Heisman Trophy in 1984 with one play, the miracle pass that brought down unbeaten Miami, and Bernie Kosar, 47–45. The pass traveled sixty-four yards in the air, and into football folklore . . . sailing on a high arc through the rainy twilight of the Orange Bowl and landing in the arms of his best friend, Gerard Phelan, as the clock ran out. He seemed to have everything going for him. The country had made a conservative turn, and here was a handsome, well-spoken, well-mannered young-ster with a flair for the dramatic moment.

In his hometown, the city fathers of Natick, a western suburb of Boston, named a street after him—Flutie Pass. And, no, it didn't take long to complete it.

But for all his amateur heroics, Flutie would have hell convincing the pros that he could play with the big boys.

And he still does. In the fourth game of the 1988 season, Flutie came off the bench to rally New England, running for the winning touchdown on the last play to beat the Colts, 21–17. When writers just happened to ask Jim McMahon, his onetime teammate and rival, what he thought of Flutie's comeback, the Bears quarterback replied:

"Who? Oh, Bambi. That was great, wasn't it? He's America's midget again."

Do we detect a slightly patronizing note here, mingled with a dash of affection? No doubt we do. Coaches, scouts, teammates, opponents, reporters, critics at large, all have experienced mixed feelings where Doug Flutie is involved. Trumpets and flourishes, doubts and disbelief, these have been the foods of Flutie's existence.

To begin with, no team in the National Football League wanted to risk a first-round pick on a minisized Merriwell, a hair over five feet nine and maybe 175 pounds. Nor did they want to meet the price that his agent, Bob Woolf, would be asking—in the million-dollar-a-year range. The Buffalo Bills, with the first pick in the NFL draft, refused to even acknowledge that they had an interest in him.

One NFL scout dared a writer: "Name a quarterback under six feet who ever won a championship. Super Bowl or before that, NFL or AFL. Name one."

The writer said, "Name a guy over six-three who ever won one."

The scout couldn't, and the point held until Doug Williams, six feet four, led the Redskins to victory in Super Bowl XXII.

Until then, going back to the arrival of the T formation, every team that won a championship had a signal caller who stood between six feet and six feet three. All of which proves whatever you want it to prove.

One might conclude that the height chart proves only this: A sub-six-footer is more likely to be given a chance by teams that are weak or hurting. The Redskins were hapless by the time Eddie LeBaron joined them, and the Cowboys were an expansion team. As a rookie for the Philadelphia Eagles in 1939, Davey O'Brien set the records for passes completed in a game and in a season. Davey was five feet seven. Two years later, he quit pro football to join the FBI.

They could play, and so can Flutie. He can think too. His whole mentality is geared to trying to figure out ways to win. Someday, he says, he would like to pull off a play that no one has seen in at least fifty years.

"There are two seconds left," he says, "and you're down by a point or two near midfield, out of field goal range. You have time for one play. Ninety-nine times out of a hundred, you'll see one of those Big Ben things. That play has little chance of success. What I'd do is throw to a receiver around the twenty-five or thirty, in the middle of the field, and then have him drop-kick a field goal on the run. It's legal. You can drop-kick the ball anytime."

And who could make such a play in these modern times? "I can," said Flutie. "Rich Camarillo, who used to punt for us [at Boston College], and I used to practice them. He could drop-kick it sixty yards. Find a guy who can do it and put him in as a wide receiver."

This is Doug Flutie, whose mind is always working, yet never claiming to be anything but a guy trying to prove that he belongs with the big boys.

It must have pained him to read the comments, among others, of O. J. Simpson, who played in Buffalo for nine seasons. "The kind of quarterback you want in Buffalo," said Simpson, "is the big, strong guy who can stand in the pocket and throw the ball through the wind. A scrambling type throws on the run . . .

Well, that wind [off Lake Erie] will take his ball and turn it upside down."

Yet his underdog stature, his choirboy looks, his popularity, and, not coincidentally, his record as a winner, made him that most appealing package, a franchise player, in the eyes of the United States Football League.

Remember them? With the NFL sitting on its hands, Woolf cooked up a deal with the high-rolling Donald Trump, whose New Jersey Generals already had the services of halfback Herschel Walker. The contract would pay Flutie $8.3 million over six years. It was a coup for Flutie's team, especially when you consider that there was no one bidding against the Generals. The only questions were (1) would the league last that long? and (2) would Flutie, playing behind the kinds of lines that one USFL owner compared to "untrained gerbils"?

Early in the negotiations as they looked down on Manhattan from the twenty-sixth floor of Trump Towers, Donald Trump lightly touched Flutie's arm and said, "This is your city, Doug. It's at your feet."

It was soon apparent that Trump had made the deal against the wishes of his coach, Walt Michaels, not to mention the team's number one quarterback, Brian Sipe. But Flutie soon won over Michaels and Sipe didn't matter, mainly because he was no longer there.

Three days after Trump had assured Bob Woolf that the Generals wouldn't rush his client, that they could afford to bring him along carefully because they had a veteran starter, Sipe was traded. The job was Flutie's.

Moving in one month from the campus to the pros, having missed most of the preseason, he took over the Generals' offense, started fifteen games and won ten of them. He won running and he won throwing and he won in the final seconds. But a curious thing happened at the Meadowlands—the fans began to boo him. The coaches let him improvise when they were losing and running out of time. Otherwise they kept the game plan simple, mostly handoffs to Herschel. Doug was usually limited to sixteen or seventeen passes a game.

Once against Baltimore, they were losing, 3–0, in the fourth quarter. The boos thundered down, and Donald Trump left the stadium. Meaning that he didn't see Flutie scramble and hit four of five passes and rally the Generals to a 10–3 win.

They met Baltimore again in the playoffs and lost, but this time Doug watched from the sideline. In his fifteenth game, Flutie had rolled out to his left and 280-pound Reggie White of the Memphis Showboats fell on him. His collarbone was broken. In June his season had ended.

For all his efforts, and all his charm, Flutie proved not to be the messiah the new league needed. He was not to be their Joe Namath. He didn't win the championship, or attract a network television contract, or save the spring league. His coach at Boston College, Jack Bicknell, felt for him: "He's twenty-two years old. He gets thrown into the big media thing, everybody wanting magic every game he plays. It was ridiculous."

Given his advance billing, he could have thrown for six touchdowns a game and turned Gatorade into wine at halftime and still not pleased everyone, much less Donald Trump.

And two clouds kept growing on the horizon. The USFL was drowning in red ink, and the NFL's snub still troubled Flutie, who believed that some would never accept his performance if they judged it by the standards of a lesser league.

The fickleness of Donald Trump, and the inevitability of the marketplace, in due time resolved all earthly matters. In August, preparing for a move to the autumn that would never happen, the New Jersey Generals announced that they had merged with the Houston Gamblers. They had acquired the rights to most of the Houston players, including Jim Kelly, described by Trump in the next day's papers as "The best quarterback in pro football. He's the quarterback and, right now, Doug is on the team."

Another paragraph or two and Trump added: "I have talked to Herschel about the merger and he's thrilled. I have also talked to Doug. Herschel is more thrilled than Doug."

As one writer noted, those words translated into a message for Flutie: The shuttle to Boston left every hour on the hour from LaGuardia Airport.

No matter. The league went into a holding pattern, then suspended its operation to concentrate on a billion-dollar antitrust suit it had filed against the NFL. (After a year of waiting and weeks of testimony, a jury awarded the league three dollars in damages.)

Doug Flutie was now in limbo while Woolf tried to settle his contract with Trump, and at the same time worked the phone lines around the NFL. Woolf, who practically created the role of sports attorney, soon found himself on a carousel. To negotiate with the NFL he needed a permission in writing from the Generals. To do so without it would expose those teams to charges of tampering. Although the Generals no longer had any use for Flutie, they resisted, offering instead their good word.

As they say, you trust your mother but you always cut the cards. Woolf insisted on and eventually received a letter. His priority now, in August 1985, was to get Flutie a crack at an NFL roster and give him a chance to prove himself—again. He was willing to make him available for a salary of around $130,000 a year—a fairly dramatic drop from the $1.3 million the Generals were paying. But he had to make him affordable.

Even at that price the interest around the NFL was tepid. Now it was September and the season was under way. Woolf was hearing it all over again: He's too short. He's too late; the season has started. We would have to change our offense for him, using play action, letting him throw on the run so he can see over the defenders.

The Rams, who owned his draft rights and were starting the legendary Dieter Brock at quarterback, didn't want to screw up their chemistry. The Cowboys were willing to talk about next year. Flutie's temperament, his mental health, would not tolerate sitting out a year. And with time running out, Woolf received a call he could scarcely believe. The Bears. Last year's Super Bowl champions. Those Bears.

When all the wrinkles were worked out, the Rams compensated, and the trading deadline met, Doug Flutie was on his way to Chicago. He was going to play for Mike Ditka and give the Bears some depth behind Jim McMahon.

Except that two weeks later, McMahon wrecked his shoulder and went out for the season, and Flutie finished the year as the Bears' starting quarterback. McMahon, feuding with his coach and unsettled by his injury, came off as testy when the Bears added Doug. But the other Chicago backups, Steve Fuller and Mike Tomczak, accepted him with a touch of humor.

When reporters asked if the Bears needed to design a special offense for Flutie, Fuller said, "Yeah. The sawed-off shotgun."

Doug was an instant favorite in Chicago, and by December two songs had been recorded celebrating his presence: "Flutie, Flutie," sung to the tune of an old Johnny Mercer hit ("Goody, Goody") and a novelty number called "If You Don't Like Doug Flutie . . ."

The latter was recorded by a group called Boss Dog's Big Bear Band, and the title echoed a famous remark by the late Mayor Richard Daley. Asked about some questionable business dealings involving two of his sons, Daley was quoted as saying, "If a man can't do something for his sons, you can kiss my ass." The composers took only a slight liberty with that sentiment to make it to apply to anyone who might not like Flutie. But what was there not to like?

So the love affair in Chicago lasted a long time, nearly half a season. What went wrong? Nothing, really, except Jim McMahon seemed healthy for a change—remember, he had never started eight straight games in his pro career. Meanwhile the Bears had drafted Jim Harbaugh from Michigan and were up to their eyeballs in quarterbacks. Suddenly Doug Flutie was looking small again.

The long and short of it was that, in the midst of the player strike of 1987, Flutie was traded to the New England Patriots. It should have been a joyful homecoming, but a few minor distractions intervened:

• In the last strike game, in the absence of the team's regular quarterbacks, Flutie led the Patriots to a 21–7 victory over Houston. The fans back in the commonwealth of Massachusetts

loved it, but to his teammates—former and future—Flutie was
a scab. A little scab, at that.
- His former companions were throwing darts from Chicago, and
  there would be more to come.
- Coach Raymond Berry announced that Flutie would be fourth
  on the depth chart when the other quarterbacks left the picket
  line, behind Steve Grogan, Tony Eason, and Tom Ramsey.
- Apparently the computers in New England had the same problem as the one in Chicago. Flutie's measurements wouldn't
  compute. He was fighting the same old stereotype. His critics
  were split down the middle: Some said he was too short and
  some said he wasn't tall enough.

All Doug Flutie wanted, all he had ever asked, was to get the
sideshow behind him. And let him in the game. He could do it
if they let him. He knew he could.

The Patriots were 2-and-4 after six games in 1988, and one of
the wins resulted from Flutie's Harry Houdini act against the
Colts. Finally with the season floating out there somewhere in
Boston Harbor, Berry made Flutie his starter. It was the stuff of
your boyhood fiction.

The Patriots won four of their next six, but a revitalized running game was the main reason for the turnaround, not Flutie.
"It's embarrassing," he said. "All I've done is hand the ball off
and watch our backs and offensive linemen do the work. This
isn't exactly the Doug Flutie Show."

Still, one of the wins was darned near poetic, a huge upset
over the Bears, who had been sounding off all week about what
they would do to Flutie.

Before the game, tight end Emery Moorehead said: "I think
everybody wants to squash him and eliminate him. We'd like to
put him down early and get someone else in the game. There
were some bad feelings between some people and him. He was
getting special treatment."

The reference was to the fact that Flutie had been invited to
Coach Mike Ditka's restaurant for Thanksgiving dinner, and Ditka

had been to Flutie's home. The lads were fairly subtle about it. "He was sucking up to the boss," said one.

But the Super Bowl champions did not squash little Doug. They did not pass go. They did not collect two hundred dollars. Flutie threw four touchdown passes and the Patriots rolled over them, 30–7.

He even received support from a higher source, the new owner of the Patriots, Victor Kiam, who made his fortune on Remington razors. He had been among the first to scold the Bears for the threatening tone of their remarks about Flutie. It was not the first time, one writer observed, that Mr. Kiam had taken up for a little shaver.

As if any additional irony was needed, Jim McMahon had to be helped off the field with a torn-up knee and wound up once again in a hospital. His streak of eight starts in a row, the longest period of sustained health in his pro career, was finished.

New England's upset win, and Pee Wee's big adventure, would not put an end to the questions or even the short jokes. Nothing would be settled in 1989, a year in which Coach Raymond Berry started four quarterbacks: Tony Eason, Steve Grogan, Marc Wilson, and Flutie. Playing quarterback for the Patriots was like taking a number at McDonald's.

Berry seemed fond of Flutie, but Doug didn't want to be adopted, he just wanted to run an offense. So far no team has let him. No one ever claimed that he lacked ability; he simply doesn't fit into the computer. Other quarterbacks make mistakes, get a pass knocked down at the line of scrimmage. When it happens to Flutie, the computer spits him out.

New England cut him, too, and Doug was looking once more for a chance to prove himself. He knew he could, if only they would let him.

The master mechanic, Otto Graham, took success to another dimension, leading Cleveland to ten straight title games. COURTESY *HOUSTON POST*

The pride of Peachtree Street, Steve Bartkowski was the number-one pick in the 1975 draft and led Atlanta to its first division title. COURTESY *HOUSTON POST*

Terry Bradshaw, who knew a touchdown when he saw one, collected four Super Bowl rings. COURTESY *HOUSTON POST*

Groomed for greatness: In Denver, fans described their team's hopes as John Elway or the highway.

PHOTO BY JOHN H. REID III/NFL PHOTOS

Most experts, including Unitas, call Sonny Jurgensen the best "pure passer" the game has known. PHOTO BY DICK RAPHAEL/ NFL PHOTOS

Below, Sammy Baugh, who defined throwing a football as an art form, also set records as a punter and defensive back. COURTESY *HOUSTON POST*

Dan Marino points the way for the Dolphins; he broke most of Dan Fouts's records. COURTESY *HOUSTON POST*

In the clutch, no one ever came up bigger; Joe Montana was the player of the 1980s on the team of the 1980s. In the all-around category, Golden Joe may be the best ever. COURTESY *HOUSTON POST*

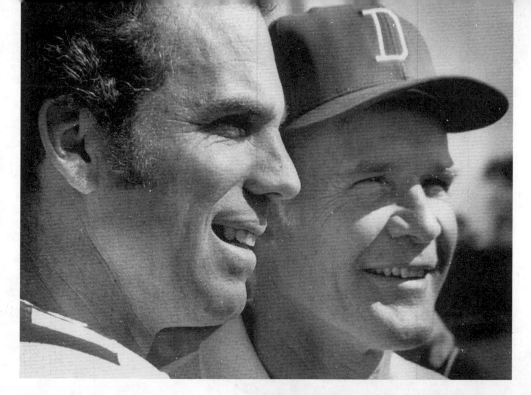

Above, a rare pair: smiling faces of Roger Staubach *(left)* and Tom Landry *(right)*. COURTESY ABC SPORTS

Danny White had no easy act, following a legend in Dallas. PHOTO BY LOU WITT

Washington's Doug Williams took his lumps along the way, but made a breakthrough as a winning Super Bowl quarterback. COURTESY *HOUSTON POST*

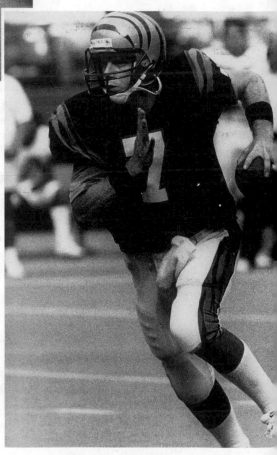

Even the other teams enjoyed watching Cincinnati's sunshine boy, Boomer Esiason, who led the ratings in 1988.

PHOTO BY MALCOLM EMMONS/NFL PHOTOS

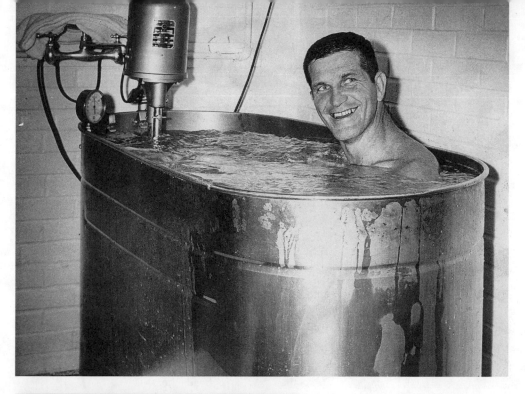

Above, George Blanda deserved an occasional dip in the whirlpool; he went on to play until he was forty-eight. COURTESY *HOUSTON POST*

Doug Flutie is a crowd pleaser, but has to keep proving himself to his coaches, who don't seem to notice that he plays tall. COURTESY *HOUSTON POST*

Rams' fans blew their horns over the powerful arm of Roman Gabriel in the late 1960s. COURTESY ABC SPORTS

Below, Oiler Warren Moon *(left)* empathizes with Jim McMahon *(right)* whose season in San Diego was one long headache. PHOTO BY LOU WITT

It was a stretch for Miami's Bob Griese, the first quarterback to wear glasses, to reach the Hall of Fame. COURTESY *HOUSTON POST*

Below, what Pat Haden lacked in length, he made up for with heart and brains. COURTESY *HOUSTON POST*

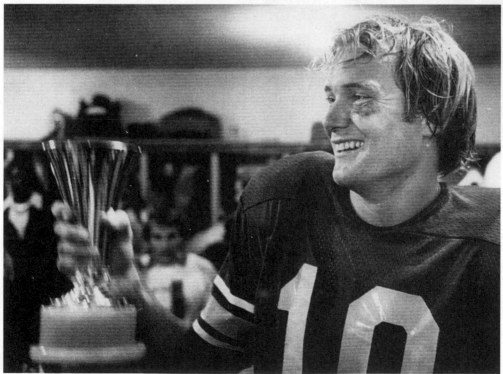

Ron Jaworski, the Polish Rifle, made a few stops in his NFL career, including the Super Bowl. COURTESY *HOUSTON POST*

In a rare pose, seldom-used Babe Laufenberg looks for a downfield receiver. COURTESY *HOUSTON POST*

When old-timers talk about the colorful field leaders, for some there was
only one: Bobby Layne. COURTESY WASHINGTON
TOUCHDOWN CLUB

Below, the Jets retired Joe Namath's
number 12, as Coach Weeb Ewbank
looked on, and the lights dimmed on
Broadway. COURTESY *HOUSTON POST*

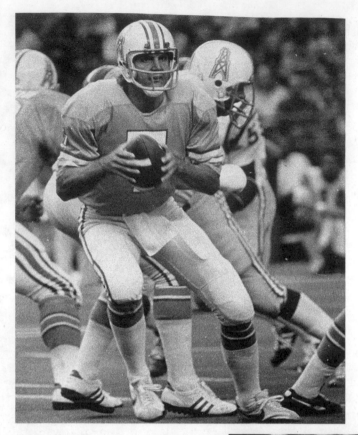

Above, some other quarterbacks en-
vied the arm of Dan Pastorini, but not
the amount of punishment he took.
COURTESY *HOUSTON POST*

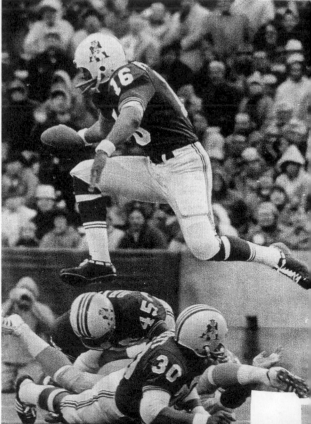

In one of pro football's notable come-
backs, Jim Plunkett went from the
junk pile to Super Bowl glory with
the Raiders. COURTESY *HOUSTON POST*

Frank Ryan shattered the stereotype; his idea of a good chalk talk was working a problem in physics.

COURTESY *HOUSTON POST*

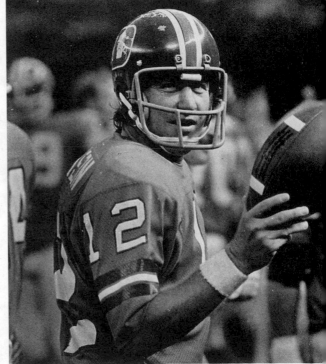

Playing with losing teams taught Charley Johnson, who went on to earn a doctorate, the value of a good education. COURTESY *HOUSTON POST*

The maverick Snake Stabler didn't mind studying his playbook by the light of a good jukebox. COURTESY *HOUSTON POST*

Bart Starr was Vince Lombardi's creation, a quarterback who could carry out what his coach was thinking.

COURTESY *HOUSTON POST*

Once the game began, no one was more awake or quicker-witted than Fran Tarkenton. COURTESY ABC SPORTS

No one ever accused the Redskins' Joe Theismann of taking things sitting down. COURTESY *HOUSTON POST*

Above, the volatile Dutch Van Brocklin battled with opposing players,
coaches, and his own teammates.

COURTESY *HOUSTON POST*

Unitas: Many a young quarterback
studied at Johnny U. COURTESY *HOUSTON POST*

☆8☆ SECOND BANANAS LAST LONGER

Weeb Ewbank remembers what it was like when the Baltimore Colts realized they had something special in Johnny Unitas. His first concern was for the feelings of his former starter, George Shaw. He went to him "like a father, not a coach" and urged Shaw to be satisfied as the number two man behind Unitas. "He might have lasted another ten years," said Weeb, "if only he had listened to me."

George Shaw—no, his middle name is not Bernard—had been the first player taken in the 1955 NFL draft, after putting up impressive stats at Oregon. He was a starter as a rookie for the Colts, but his injury a year later let Unitas into the lineup. And Shaw never got back in.

He begged to be traded and after the 1958 season, which ended with the sudden-death win over the Giants, the Colts obliged him. He went to New York, rode the bench, and in 1961 was traded to Minnesota. Never mind that the Vikings were an expansion team. This was a chance to start again, to be born again.

Alas, on opening day a rookie quarterback from the University of Georgia threw four touchdown passes to upset the Bears, and Shaw's days in the NFL were numbered. The rookie's name, of course, was Fran Tarkenton.

And there you have it. George Shaw, who wouldn't settle for being less than number one, lost his first and last jobs to Johnny Unitas and Fran Tarkenton, two of the most prolific passers in pro history.

There is no way to overstate the migraine caused when there is tension between the quarterback and his understudy, and the grief that awaits a coaching staff unable to choose between them. The backup is aware at all times that he is only one blitz, one concussion, removed from the most glorified position in sports. One with the right temperament has a value beyond his skill— he is a bearer of inner peace.

The young and ambitious are usually determined to go into business for themselves. Many coaches are partial to the elderly, who provide experience and will not disturb their digestion by threatening to go elsewhere.

Vince Lombardi, always a troubled man, was comfortable with Zeke Bratkowski. Don Shula favored Earl Morrall and Don Strock, a type described as the old pro, a man of steady habits. He will sit there with the pipe and slippers, rarely complaining, and he won't hurt you if he has to take over.

Perhaps a distinction needs to be made. There are backups destined by fate or nature to accept their role. The starter is entrenched, an indispensable man. The duty of the backup is clear; the promise is not of glory but boredom. In the absence of a calamity, his job is about as exciting as being a mattress tester. They are not waiting for number one to retire or land in a cast. They are sentries, as bored as a night watchman in a casket factory.

Of course, it happens, just often enough to keep the fantasy alive: The underdog has his day, the understudy steps into the spotlight and knocks the critics dead. The classic example is that of Earl Morrall, drafted by San Francisco in the first round after leading Michigan State to a Rose Bowl victory. He backed up

Y. A. Tittle for a year, then began his life as a vagabond, moving to Pittsburgh, Detroit, New York, Baltimore, and Miami.

Along the way he crossed some interesting paths. In 1958 the Lions gave up an aging Bobby Layne to obtain him from the Steelers, and he spent six and a half seasons as a stand-in for Milt Plum.

Shula was then an assistant coach in Detroit, and he filed away in the back of his mind a game Morrall started for the Lions at Baltimore, against Johnny Unitas. "John put on one of those late finishes," Shula said, "and Lenny Moore made a fantastic catch that put them up with about fifty seconds left. The Colt fans went wild and poured out of the stands, crowding the sidelines. Then Morrall started hitting passes. He crossed midfield with about ten seconds left, and Jim Gibbon came open down the middle and he hit him and we [the Lions] won it by a point. The crowd went dead silent."

Dealt to the Giants in 1965, Earl stayed three seasons, backing up Tarkenton the last one. By now Shula was the head coach in Baltimore, and to bring in Morrall he gave up a second-string end named Butch Wilson.

At thirty-four, he did not cherish the thought of joining the team whose incumbent, Unitas, was rated by many as the best ever to play the position. His prospects left Morrall so uninspired that he gave serious thought to retiring. They were sending him, he believed, to the graveyard where backup quarterbacks went to die.

What no one envisioned were two things: an injury to Unitas, who missed all of the 1968 season, and the emergence of Earl Morrall as a quarterback who could win twelve of thirteen games. He was named the league's Most Valuable Player and led the Colts to the third Super Bowl.

At the peak of Earl's success, somebody asked Unitas about the problem of getting his job back the following season. "Whaddya mean?" Unitas snapped. "I'm the quarterback on this club."

Morrall said nothing, nor did he respond before the Colts and the Jets collided, when Joe Namath went to gratuitous lengths to knock his mild-mannered rival. There were "five or six" quarterbacks in his league, the AFL, Joe said, who were better than Morrall.

Cruelest of all, Namath rubbed it in on the scoreboard. Near the end of the first half Earl failed to see a wide-open Jimmy Orr waving his arms in the end zone, and a pass that might have changed the outcome was picked off by the Jets' Jim Hudson. The Colts lost, 16–7. Later all Earl would say was: "He won. He gets to talk."

Morrall returned to his role as second banana for three more seasons. In 1971 when Dallas knocked an ineffective Unitas out of Super Bowl V, Earl once again replaced him and rallied the Colts to a 16–13 victory (in the game that became known as the Blooper Bowl).

A reporter once suggested that, human nature being what it was, his substitute's success might have stirred some resentment deep in John's Lithuanian soul. "Yeah," Unitas said, "if you're a horse's ass, it would."

The sequence that followed illustrates the stable nature of the profession. Released by the Colts one year later, Earl was picked up for the one-hundred-dollar-waiver price by Miami, where Don Shula had relocated in 1970.

Reunited with his longtime patron, Morrall would soon perform the same service for the Dolphins as a stand-in for Bob Griese. For Shula, it had to be reassuring to know that his hired gun would return to the bench like a model child when Griese came back, as he had in the Unitas years.

In the fifth week of the 1972 season, with the Dolphins moving in the first quarter against San Diego, Bob Griese left the field on a stretcher, after getting hit low by Ron East and high by Deacon Jones. He would be out at least two months with a leg broken four inches above the ankle.

And onto the field trotted their thirty-eight-year-old insurance policy, Earl Morrall. One of the running backs, Mercury Morris, had grown up in Pittsburgh and remembered seeing Earl play with the Steelers when he was eight or nine.

Morrall passed for two touchdowns and the No-Name defense scored another as Miami defeated San Diego, 24–10. (Few may remember that Tom Landry was responsible for one of football's most distinctive labels. "I can't recall the names of the players on the Miami defensive unit," he had said prior to Super Bowl VI, "but they're a big concern to me." From that quote, the No-Name defense was born.)

Ironies abounded when the unbeaten Dolphins prepared to play at Baltimore in mid-1972. The Colts had been projected as title contenders, but the team lost five of its first six games, Coach Don McCafferty had been fired and Unitas, healthy again, was on the bench. The Colts had gone to their backup, twenty-five-year-old Marty Domres.

While the teams went through their pregame exercises, Earl Morrall and Johnny Unitas made their way toward each other. It was another knot in the tangled rope of the two men's careers. Unitas greeted him with, "You're getting too old for this, aren't you?"

Morrall grinned and said, "Well, you're a pretty old buck yourself, John."

For four seasons before this one, the two had been teammates, roommates, and beer-drinking buddies, with an understanding deep enough to weather some wildly shifting fortune. But on this October day, on his home field, there had to be a moment of minor humiliation for Unitas, who had passed for twenty-three miles in the NFL and was never out of the lineup unless injured.

Now Earl Morrall, the perfect reserve, was at the helm of the Dolphins, 6–0 with another shot at getting to the Super Bowl. And Unitas was sidelined on orders of the new Colt general manager, Joe Thomas. "We need to test Domres," Thomas explained, "to see how much shopping we have to do for next season."

Unitas had described the difference between his style as a

quarterback and Morrall's: "I like to score in six seconds. Earl wants to take six minutes."

Which was pretty much how Morrall engineered a 23–0 shut-out, going eighty yards on ten plays on their first possession, picking his spots to throw, banging away on the ground with Larry Csonka and Mercury Morris.

No one really knew how good, no, how great a team Shula had assembled in Miami. The franchise had only existed since 1965. But the defense, small and quick, sparked by Nick Buoniconti at linebacker and Jake Scott at safety, had been under-rated all year. The backs were running behind an offensive line that would produce candidates for the Hall of Fame at nearly every position.

Yet no one suggested that the team had to overcome its re-placement quarterback to win. In truth, Griese was a brilliant play caller, but Morrall had been around, and the drop-off was slight.

In week ten, in a game that came close to ending their streak, the Dolphins trailed the Jets, and Joe Namath, by ten points in the first half and rallied to win it, 28–24. Morrall pulled off what may have been the play of the season by scrambling for thirty-one yards and a touchdown on a busted play in the third quarter.

Could anyone doubt that this game had down deep meanings for Earl? Did he feel any lingering bitterness, or did he under-stand that Namath's taunts in 1969 were part of a strategy to build up his team, to psych up his teammates?

Sure, he understood. Nevertheless, that week in 1972 Earl had been quoted as saying, "I wouldn't want my son to be like Joe Namath." All of which made for a less than jovial confrontation when the four Miami team captains, including Morrall, met the two from New York, Namath and Larry Grantham, in the middle of the field for the coin toss. Morrall said: "I knew Grantham from having played golf with him before. We shook hands. Then the official introduced me to Namath. Namath didn't put out his hand and he didn't even look at me. I don't know if any cam-eras were on us or not, but I thought it was kind of funny. I couldn't help laughing. I was still laughing when I ran off the field. Hell, there are a lot of people I didn't want my son to be like when he grew up."

His teammates were delighted for Morrall in the dressing room after the game. The touchdown run, not surprisingly, was his longest since his college days at Michigan State.

Week after week the Dolphins continued their winning streak. It would reach fourteen in the second game against the Colts, the last day of the regular season, and Shula would reveal a dramatic flair when he chose to bring Griese back from the injured list.

There was almost a subplot involving the "Back-Up Quarterbacks." Unitas came off the Colts bench briefly in the second quarter, after Marty Domres had been shaken up, and an Orange Bowl crowd of eighty thousand gave him a standing ovation. Unitas threw one completion, but his second and last pass of the day was intercepted.

Later Shula said: "The hand the crowd gave John gave me a lump in the throat. You know, I was a cornerback with the Colts when John threw his first NFL pass. That one was intercepted too." Shula seemed to be suggesting, and if so time would prove him right, that Unitas had thrown his last pass for Baltimore.

In the fourth quarter, with the Dolphins hugging a safe 16–0 lead, Shula decided it was time for Griese's return. The crowd saw number 12 strap on his helmet and another great roar filled the stadium. Griese grinned at Shula. "You should be writing for the movies."

Griese had returned just in time for the playoffs, but he had been idle for ten weeks and for now the job still belonged to Morrall. In five seasons with Baltimore and Miami, Earl had won thirty-six games in forty-two starts. Incredible.

Once again, the Old Quarterback had been rescued by fate from oblivion. Against Cleveland, the offense struggled and the Dolphins needed two Garo Yepremian field goals and a blocked punt for a touchdown to win, 20–14.

Morrall had gone all the way. The report on Griese was that the leg was stronger, he moved around better, but he was still putting the foot down flat—"pancaking it," said Shula. In two weeks, Griese thought, by Super Sunday, "I might be one hundred percent."

Of course, their presence in that one depended on their ability to dispose of the Steelers in Pittsburgh in the American Conference finals. The Steelers were still celebrating the touchdown that had beaten Oakland, when Terry Bradshaw's pass bounced off someone's shoulder and into the arms of Franco Harris—"the Feast of the Immaculate Reception."

With the score tied at the half, 7—7, and the offense sputtering again, Shula made his move. He walked over to Griese's locker and said, "Are you ready?"

Griese immediately started thinking of what plays he wanted to call. Shula stepped over to Morrall's locker and said simply, "I'm going with Bob in the second half, but stay ready."

The Dolphins scored twice on short runs by Jim Kiick in the second half, the first set up by Griese's fifty-two-yard pass to Paul Warfield. That was enough to hold off the Steelers, 21—17, for their sixteenth win in a row.

They were back in the Super Bowl, where Miami had lost once (to Dallas, 24—3) and Shula had lost twice. He wasted no time announcing that Griese would start at quarterback. Asked why he made the announcement so early, Shula replied, "Because you don't fool around with men the stature of Griese and Earl."

With cool efficiency, Griese and the Dolphins defeated the Washington Redskins, 14—7. It was one of those times when the score didn't fairly reflect the differences in the teams. Miami should have pitched a 17—0 shutout, a score that would have reflected their perfect season.

But leading by two touchdowns with the clock winding down to the final two minutes, the Redskins blocked a field goal attempt by Garo Yepremian, who then picked up the ball and—God forbid!—tried to pass it. The ball sort of rolled off the tips of his fingers and he tried to bat it out of bounds. Instead, the ball fell into the hands of Washington's Mike Bass, who raced giddily forty-nine yards for a touchdown.

That play added a zany footnote, but headlines belonged to

the first team in NFL history to finish 17–0. The *Los Angeles Times* bannered it: "WHO SAID NOBODY'S PERFECT?"

The name of Earl Morrall appeared in the column reserved for substitutions. But no one among the Dolphins doubted who had taken them that far.

When he retired in 1976, he had played twenty-one seasons and 255 games, second only to George Blanda. But he didn't exactly disappear from football. He wound up on the coaching staff at the University of Miami, working with quarterbacks named Jim Kelly, Bernie Kosar, and Vinny Testaverde.

THE TEAM
PLAYER

Whatever the desired traits are in a backup quarterback, you can be reasonably sure that no one goes into that line of work hoping to make it his career.

But for reasons that will soon be clear, this may turn out to be the case with Gary Kubiak of Denver. A record-setting passer for the Texas Aggies in his college days, Kubiak was drafted by the Broncos in the eighth round in 1983. He was jubilant. Denver's job was up for grabs. Then four days later, the team acquired John Elway in a trade with the Baltimore Colts.

Gary remembers his first encounter with the heralded artist from Stanford, who had been out in the world a year in the New York Yankees farm system. "It was at our rookie camp soon after the 1983 draft," said Kubiak. "I remember how intimidating it was. I'm human. I knew who John Elway was.

"It snowed that day in Denver, so they took us down to the Air Force Academy [in Colorado Springs] to throw. They had John throwing first, and I was throwing next. You have to remember it was my first impression of pro football. I looked at him and I thought about my chances and I said to myself, 'Hell, no way.' I didn't throw very well.

''I went back to my hotel room that night just devastated, and thinking, 'I can't play in this league; just look at this guy.'

''Then I came to realize there aren't many people around who could do the things that John can do. I mean, he makes throws most guys can't even attempt. What I had to do was learn to play within myself, and that's how I made it in the league.''

Initially Kubiak survived because Craig Morton retired and Denver sent Mark Herrmann to the Chargers. That left Steve DeBerg as the starter, Elway as the prince-in-waiting—not for long—and the pragmatic Texan as Elway's caddy.

He is an insightful young man, and that was part of what kept him alive in the NFL; his mental alertness overcame his physical limitations. ''My situation is a kind of catch-twenty-two,'' he says. ''You've got to handle it as best you can. There's no conflict in my mind. I root for John because I believe he is the best and that he deserves to be a champion.

''I don't think anybody who is a good person, a good competitor, would sit there and want somebody to get hurt. Yet he runs around so much that I catch myself looking to see if he gets up, instead of watching what the defense is doing. A guy like John keeps someone like me on the alert, all right.''

Most teams discourage their quarterbacks from leaving the pocket, from scrambling, feeling that this is an easy path to the emergency ward. They take the view that a few lousy yards are not worth losing your starter for a week, or a season.

Dan Reeves, the Denver coach, counters with the opinion that quarterbacks get hurt standing in the pocket too. Some, in fact, have been known to injure themselves walking back to the huddle. But those few lousy yards, points out Reeves, can be the difference between who goes to the playoffs and who stays home and shovels snow.

Says Kubiak: ''I've seen game plans where we had draw plays and things in there where John may be carrying the ball ten, twelve times a game—by design. Most guys . . . well, you've got a million-dollar guy back there, and you ordinarily wouldn't want him doing that. But this is when John is at his best.''

It is a fact that Kubiak, and the other Broncos, have followed

Elway's lead to three Super Bowls (losses to the Giants, Redskins, and 49ers). The record shows that Gary actually played in Super Bowl XXI and had a perfect game, completing all four of his passes for forty-eight yards. You might not have noticed. Not many did. The clock was winding down on Denver's 39–20 loss to New York.

"Most people were gone," he says. "I think my wife, Rhonda, was already on the bus. I had to come back [to the hotel] and tell her, 'Hey, I played.' "

Going into the 1988 season, Kubiak had spent most of his five seasons as a holder for kicker Rich Karlis. He had started a total of three games and Denver won them all. The highlight came in 1984: In front of ninety thousand fans in the Los Angeles Coliseum, Gary completed twenty-one of thirty-four passes, two of them for touchdowns, as Denver beat the Raiders in overtime, 22–19.

"That's what makes it tough being in this role," he said. "You remember how you felt after times like that, and what a big high it was for you as a player. I look at John and he's able to feel that type of thing twelve, thirteen weeks out of the season. The Raider game was a big thrill, and our football team played well, but . . ."

The sentence went unfinished, the moment uncaptured, but you knew what he meant. What's fair? In life everyone gets the same amount of ice. The rich get theirs in the summer, the poor get theirs in the winter.

"A lot of times," says Gary Kubiak, "my wife is mad at me because I take it out on her. But that's part of it. She understands my job. A lot of times we win big football games and everybody wants to go out and eat. I just want to go home. I get in certain moods from not being a part of the games.

"It's difficult for all of us. But at the same time it's exciting being in Denver, being a part of this. And I'm not ignored by my teammates. I'm not a cast-off."

Still, when you're young—twenty-seven—and proud and not essential, you search for answers. Kubiak said he sought out Miami's veteran quarterback, Don Strock, about how he handled their similiar predicaments. If anyone ever erects a Hall of Fame for backup quarterbacks, the statue of Don Strock would be at the front of the rotunda. Strock started five games in the decade of the eighties.

"Heck, he was doing this for thirteen or fourteen years in Miami," said Gary. "He reached a point where he was contented because he knew he was fixing to get out in the next few years."

When Denver lined up against Washington in Super Bowl XXII, Kubiak had been in the league five years and was still virtually unknown to the public. He refers to his playing time as "young years, because I haven't been out there taking a beating that a guy like John has. Each person, I guess, has to handle it in his own way. It's tough. I wish I could tell you how to do it. I just try to find a way, keep my head on my shoulders, and somehow keep a smile on my face."

They are the same age, Elway and Kubiak, and a strong empathy has developed between them. "Part of it is our ages, and the fact that we've been through things together," says Gary. "We've helped each other in that sense. But at this point John is running our football team. He's the leader, almost a coach out there. He does everything. This is *his* football team."

They run together on the road and Kubiak has a chance to see, literally, how the other half lives. "It's kind of funny," he says. "John has a great personality. He's outgoing. Then I see all the things he has to handle, and you have to remember that he is John Elway."

"We might be all set to go somewhere. Well, for me to walk down to the lobby is nothing. But John reminds me that we've got to go out the back door. You forget about who he is and the things he has to put up with. I get to see that side of him."

In Boston one night the two quarterbacks and a teammate, Keith Bishop, made reservations for dinner. "We had a car to use," recalls Kubiak, "but we didn't want to drive because we didn't know exactly how to get there. We asked the doorman to call a cab. Well, within two or three minutes there were so many people around John in front of that hotel we couldn't move.

Finally he said, 'Let's go get the car.' We couldn't wait for the cab, it was so uncomfortable for him.''

While his admiration for Elway is unrestricted, he sees him in his most human moments. ''The thing that is interesting to me,'' he says, ''is watching him change when we arrive at a hotel. On Saturday, say, he is one person. Then on Sunday, well, the change is like night and day. On game day the butterflies are jumping in him and it's time to play football.

''Usually, he is this pleasant, outgoing guy. Then all of a sudden it's like he cuts it off and a curtain drops. We might start looking at football tapes on a Sunday morning and the conversation just stops. The morning before the last Super Bowl, we could not have exchanged three words before we went to the stadium.

''The guy is simply a competitor. For instance, we play gin all the time. He'll be killing me, winning game after game, and then I might finally win a hand and John throws the danged cards against the wall. There's a competitive streak in everything he does.''

There is one in Gary Kubiak as well, but he isn't sure what to do with it. ''Catch-twenty-two again,'' he says with a soft smile. ''If you want to leave, people say, 'What's wrong with you? You have the best job in the world.' If you want to stay, people ask, 'Why the hell doesn't he want to play?' ''

The Broncos need no reminder why they keep him around. When an injury sidelined Elway in the middle of the 1988 season, Kubiak started on a night when his two-year-old daughter was in a hospital, fighting for her life. He wasn't as consistent as he usually would be, but he made the clutch plays and Denver won. In a year when all the teams in the AFC West were struggling to get over .500, he kept the Broncos in the running while Elway was recovering.

He doesn't have the height—he's six feet one—or the arm strength that coaches crave, but he has qualities they value. Many around the league believe Kubiak could be starting somewhere else. One who thinks so is Mike Shanahan, former coach of the Raiders and offensive coordinator in Denver. ''His teammates believe in him," says Shanahan. "Gary is a team player with a lot of class and intelligence, who can come in and win for you, and still give his support to the other guy."

That sounds more like the description for a saint, not a quarterback. The job seems to require an absence of ego, a huge supply of patience, and very little in the way of sympathy.

For a slightly different perspective, you need only to refer to the jockeying between Doug Williams and Jay Schroeder of the Redskins during the 1987 season. It is quite possible that both were sincere when they said they wished each other well when the other fellow was starting. And you get the impression that they made an honest effort to like each other.

But losing a job that once was yours isn't the same as riding the bench behind someone who is clearly superior.

YOU AND THEM, BABE

There was the original Babe, George Herman Ruth, so richly an American icon that Japanese jungle fighters in World War II taunted GIs with the cry, *"To hell with Babe Ruth."*

There was Babe Herman, a daffy but hard-hitting Brooklyn outfielder; Babe Didrikson Zaharias, once the world's greatest woman athlete; Babe Parilli, and Babe Laufenberg.

Laufenberg?

Chances are few fans have ever heard of Brandon "Babe" Laufenberg, unless they happened to be close observers of the Deals of the Week listings in their local newspaper. When last we looked in on him, Babe was the most experienced quarterback in the training camp of the nearly all-new 1989 Dallas Cowboys. He had started a grand total of six games in the National Football League . . . in six years.

He had been cut eight times by four teams and was not expected to beat out Cowboy rookies Troy Aikman from UCLA and Steve Walsh from the University of Miami. But Laufenberg, pro football's Happy Wanderer, doesn't discourage easily. He's like the barfly the bouncer just tossed through the swinging doors, and the next thing you know he's climbing in through a window.

"I know anything can happen," he says, "because everything has happened to me."

A son of Baja California, Laufenberg was heavily recruited as a schoolboy. He signed with Stanford after the coach, Bill Walsh, asked his friend Bart Starr to deliver a sales pitch. "The next year," recalled Laufenberg, "Starr gave the same speech to John Elway. I ran into Bart a few years later in Washington and told him I had never forgiven him.

"Even today, Elway is the kind of guy a lot of players just like to sit around and check out. He's so far above everybody else. It's almost unnatural how hard he throws. The ball just comes off on a line. I always felt like I had a pretty good arm. But when he showed up at Stanford, I looked like a girl throwing a softball. I started looking for the door."

He switched to Missouri, got homesick, and left after one semester. With mixed results, he started the next fall for a junior college five minutes from his house. "To this day," he says, "that was the worst pounding I've ever taken. There were games I'd get sacked ten times. Our offensive line averaged probably about one-eighty-five, one-ninety. We're up against guys two-thirty or two-forty. One day we're playing a team that's unbeaten, in the top five in the national ranking, and in the locker room the coaches are saying, 'They put on their pants one leg at a time, just like we do.'

"I didn't say it, but I was thinking, 'Yeah, but their pants take up a helluva lot more fabric than ours do.' "

The team's big road trip was to Bakersfield in the middle of the Mojave Desert. "We stopped for the big pregame meal," he recalled, "and it was one of those cheap, all-you-can-eat buffets. I said to myself, 'This isn't exactly where I wanted to be at that point in my career.' "

The Babe transferred to Indiana, where he broke several school records, beat Purdue 2 out of 2 in the Old Oaken Bucket rivalry, captained the team his senior year, and made it to the East-West Shrine game. There the opposing, and winning, quarterback was— you guessed it—John Elway.

In 1983, the Year the Quarterbacks Fell on the NFL, Elway was the first player taken in the draft. In the sixth round Washington selected Laufenberg, after 167 players had been picked. "I'm sure with all my moving around," said Babe, "the NFL people thought I was some sort of flake."

Out of his training thus far, a philosophy had begun to form: Take nothing for granted. At Indiana the coaches put in a razzle-dazzle play designed to break a long gain or even a quick six. It was a double reverse by two wide receivers lined up as tight ends. Regrettably, two instead of one went in motion—toward each other. "I hear this loud whack behind me," said Babe. "I turn around and they're both on the ground."

In 1983 he made the Redskins' forty-nine-man roster but never played. He established a curious pattern, passing well in one or more preseason games, but getting cut in 1984 and 1985. The fans adopted him, drawn by his persistence and his quirkiness. "Love the Babe" banners began to wave at RFK Stadium. He was hailed as the most popular Redskin never to play a down in the regular season.

The San Diego Chargers picked him up for two weeks in 1985 and let him go, unused, after Dan Fouts recovered from an injury. Then he drove to a fishing camp in Mexico, Caba San Lucas, where he met one of his two heroes, singer Bruce Springsteen. There are pictures of Bruce and the Babe in Babe's apartment.

Laufenberg was in a bar called The Giggling Marlin in the village of Caba San Lucas the night Joe Theismann suffered his gruesome, career-ending broken leg. Instantly he started looking for a phone and within forty-eight hours he was back in Washington. Of course, he never got to play, but he did warm up once on the sidelines.

His other hero is Joe Namath, which is why Laufenberg is partial to wearing number 12. In 1985 Namath came to Redskin

Park in his new role as a television analyst and Babe planned to introduce himself. But that turned out to be one of those days when the Babe got cut, and when he saw Namath he didn't feel like talking.

His best year by far was 1986; the Redskins released him twice. So did the Saints. No one in Washington ever said he performed poorly. He was simply stuck in the middle of a parade, consisting of Theismann, Jay Schroeder, Doug Williams, and Mark Rypien.

Coach Joe Gibbs called the Babe into his office and offered what amounted to an apology: "If you were my son, I'd be in an uproar right now. I'd be wanting to tear my head off."

And the Babe replied, "It's not my father you need to worry about, it's my mother." He walked out the front door of the Redskins' offices, wearing a scraggly beard and a pin-striped suit and with his head high. "I had nothing to be ashamed of," he said. "I didn't want to let someone else's perception of what I can do affect the way I feel about myself."

A few days, later the Saints called. He made a reservation on the first flight the next morning—and his plane was canceled. He arrived on a Thursday afternoon and by Saturday night was wearing a New Orleans uniform, feeling strange, almost foolish, "like you're stealing someone else's equipment." He didn't play.

On Monday morning he was told to see Coach Jim Mora. "They would have said, 'Bring your playbook,' except I didn't have one yet." Mora told him, "I think you can play," but the Saints had other moves they needed to make and wished him luck.

He caught the next plane back to his home near Los Angeles in Canoga Park. "It wasn't as devastating as being cut by the Redskins," he said. "But it hurt. There was a young guy on the plane, I think he was in the navy. He says, 'Are you a football player?' I didn't want to start talking football. I said, 'No, I'm not.'

"He says, 'Boy, you look an awful lot like a guy on the Saints. They just picked up a quarterback.'

"I wanted to say, 'Yeah, they just let him go too.' Then he

asked me, 'What do you do?' I said, 'Nothing, right now.' He started pumping me to join the navy.''

There are, understand, hundreds of Babe Laufenbergs out there every year, the last half dozen or so cut by each of the pro teams; failing with one, catching on with another for the chance to relive the experience. They find themselves seldom straying very far from a phone, hoping in some kind of remote, subconscious hope that the enormous error that had been made might be suddenly discovered and corrected.

Why? What could possibly keep a fellow going with so little to show for the effort, the pain, the futility, the self-doubt? Babe thought about getting a job. Thought about it when the weeks passed and the phone didn't ring and the restlessness nagged at him.

There was just this one obstacle: "I can't go down to IBM and say, 'I want to start marketing for you, I want to work for you.' They say, 'Great.' I say, 'There's only one small detail. If a team calls, I'll be gone tomorrow.' They say, 'Good, that's just the kind of guy we're looking for.' "

At home Laufenberg worked out with his older brother, Jeff, who is also his agent and years ago dubbed him Babe. Jeff has broken three fingers catching Babe's passes and says proudly, "No other agent is out there breaking fingers for his client."

One year Babe kept in shape playing with the intramural team his younger brother, John, played on at Loyola Marymount. The team was called Sigma Phi Nothing.

In September 1986 an injury in New Orleans led to a second chance with the Saints. He was flying back from the West Coast when the pilot picked up the intercom: "The weather in New York is sixty-two and partly cloudy . . ." Laufenberg shifted impatiently in his seat. "Who the hell cares about how the weather in New York is?" he remembers thinking. Then a light bulb went on and he slapped a hand to his forehead: "Ah, Babe, you didn't do what I think you just did?" Yes, he had.

New Orleans turned out to be just another short stroll down Bourbon Street. Briefly, always briefly, he bounced back with the Redskins in 1987; to find a relationship like this one you had to go back to Nelson Eddy and Jeanette MacDonald, warbling "Indian Love Song" across a lake.

Hitting the free agency lists once more, Laufenberg caught on with the Chargers in 1988. He became a part-time starter for the first time in his pro career, on a woeful team, under an uncertain coach, Al Saunders, who was going to be fired and coached like it.

Babe started six games, two of them wins, and passed for four touchdowns and five interceptions, as the Chargers finished with a 6–10 record. The club brought in a relay team of quarterbacks, finally turning the job over to Mark Malone, the Steelers' castoff.

Meanwhile the Dallas Cowboys were cleaning house. New coach Jimmy Johnson told Danny White to retire; Steve Pelluer was holding out for more money. The Cowboys signed their high-priced rookies, Aikman and Walsh, and gave every indication that they were prepared to go into the season without a quarterback who had ever started a game in the NFL. In no one's memory had a team attempted such a stunt.

During the winter the Cowboys signed Babe Laufenberg, and there he was in camp, competing with the baby boomers. Dallas decided to keep a third passer, one with experience and a little gypsy in his soul. "I've been thinking about Babe and what he's gone through all these years," John Elway was saying. "He's the epitome of a guy who keeps going no matter how tough things get."

After next season, maybe sooner, the Babe will give more thought to looking for a job. At twenty-nine, he has been in more hotel rooms than the Gideon Bible. But, no, he was not yet ready to admit defeat. In his heart he doesn't really feel that he ever received a fair chance, which is what keeps him going. Then there is the business of not belonging. If he can't play, could he bear to watch?

"Have you ever tried to find some place on a Sunday afternoon," asks the Babe, "that didn't have a television set tuned to a football game?"

☆9☆ A LONG AND WINDING ROAD

After ten years of struggle, of knocking down barriers, of having to prove himself, Doug Williams finally chased away the demons that had dogged his career. In the grand tradition of show business, he became an overnight success.

The hero of the 1988 Super Bowl was a thirty-two-year-old son of Louisiana and Grambling College—dark hair and eyes, bats right, throws right, scars on both knees . . . no other distinguishing marks. There. As part of our national therapy, we just made it through an entire paragraph without the obligatory reference to what "kind" of quarterback he is.

Be assured that in the days leading up to Washington's 42–10 rout of Denver, the media did not let any fragment of that angle go unspared. Do you want to know how thin the line is between fame and obscurity? Not until the morning of the game did the press learn that Williams had seen a dentist on Saturday to have an abscessed molar treated. If this news had broken earlier in the week, before the players were off limits, his dentist might have been the most interviewed man in America. Some two thousand reporters would have been trying to squeeze through the transom of his office, straining for a glimpse of his patient, shouting down to those trapped below: *"He's rinsing with Listermint."*

Still, it is usually true that the fans get the Super Bowl they deserve. They are the ones with the insatiable appetite, who, like the carnivorous plant in *The Little Shop of Horrors*, devour everything and beg for more, more words and pictures, so that we have to go around asking Dexter Manley what kind of tree he would be if he had it to do all over.

Whatever the outcome, Doug Williams, an astute fellow, had concluded that he would not have to wrestle with the pressures of fame. "If we win," he predicted, "the press will just write that Elway had a bad game."

He was wrong, of course. But not as wrong as the rest of us.

Williams had been set up to play the Indian to John Elway's cowboy. Instead, he threw four touchdown passes in the second quarter alone as Washington scored a record thirty-five points in fifteen minutes. And he did it on a gimpy knee that had forced him to leave the game for two plays. What could the press say then?

That Doug Williams had made it to the mountaintop? That he had leapt out of the shadows of a haunted career? That he was the first black quarterback to start in the Super Bowl, and to lead his team to victory . . . after a root canal?

Actually, Williams received almost as much publicity before the game as John Elway. The difference was that Elway's press clippings hailed him as a one-man band. Williams's had to do with his skin pigment. At one point Doug had been asked what even the media agreed was the dumbest question of an excessive week: "How long have you been a black quarterback?"

But Williams knew what the fellow meant, and his answer was not the quip many took it to be: "I wasn't a black quarterback until I got out of Grambling."

Up to then, he was saying, his blackness didn't identify him. He was like everyone else on his college campus, except that he was the quarterback. Now he was the quarterback again, after an uphill climb at Washington and a roller coaster ride in Tampa.

Exactly what had he done, and what did it mean? For openers, he had fulfilled a dream that was not his alone. He had laid to rest a myth and a stereotype. For, he wasn't really the first black quarterback to appear at the Super Bowl. There were literally dozens before him, except that they came disguised as wide receivers and running backs and defensive backs. A few, of another generation, got into the stadium as ushers or vendors.

To make matters more interesting, the Doug Williams show opened in an atmosphere charged and heightened by recent controversies. Buzzy Bavasi had been forced to resign as general manager of the Dodgers after saying on national television that blacks "lacked the necessities" to hold high management positions in professional sports.

And barely a month before Super Bowl XXII, Jimmy "the Greek" Snyder had been fired as a CBS football analyst for offering some decidedly novel theories to explain the success of black athletes. They were bred for size and strength, he said, in the days of slavery. While many observers were still undecided whether to laugh or cry over this statement, the Greek struck again, adding that blacks have "large thighs that run up into their backs."

While a fairly general uproar greeted these disclosures, most black athletes reacted with a giggle. Asked one: "Where did Jimmy the Greek take his anatomy class?"

It was maddening and frustrating, but in twenty-one years, all the Super Bowl quarterbacks had come in one color. No pastels. Joe Gilliam had suited up once for the Steelers but never entered the game.

Now, on the last day of January 1988 in the San Diego twilight—prime time in the East—Doug Williams was the story. Not the whole story, of course, but surely the warmest part of it. What a road he had traveled to get there, nudged along by the love of a brother and the obsession of an old coach named Eddie Robinson. Just coming into his own as a pro, Doug was kicked in the heart by the tragic death of a young wife. Then he was penalized half the distance to his goals after a bitter contract dispute with his original team, Tampa Bay. Finally, signing on as a spare part, an insurance policy, with the Redskins. Slow curtain.

That was the backdrop as Willliams pulled millions of Americans into the act with him. The publicity overload was so high that a television interviewer asked Denver's Vance Johnson, who happens to be black, if he would be happy for Doug Williams if the Redskins won.

Johnson, one of the wide receivers known as the Three Amigos, seemed stunned by the question. He blinked and said patiently, as if giving directions to a man who had just arrived from Mongolia, "I'm with Denver. I want Doug Williams to lose."

The lesson of that exchange was clear: The Super Bowl is not the time or place to get sentimental.

Lord knows, the Broncos tried. They didn't turn conservative on us. John Elway tossed a fifty-six-yard bomb to Ricky Nattiel on his first play from scrimmage. On their next series Elway caught a pass from his halfback for twenty-three yards. With the game five minutes old, Denver led by ten points and all of Washington's worst fears seemed to be coming true. They had let Elway get up a head of steam.

Meanwhile, Doug Williams, known as a streak passer, had seen two of his throws dropped and another batted down out of his first four attempts. To make the Redskins' prospects even grimmer, late in the first quarter Williams was sacked by Rulon Jones, twisted his knee, and had to limp off the field.

Eddie Robinson was on hand for the emancipation, sitting in the press box, looking down on the 50 yard line, a guest of the National Football League. If Doug Williams felt as little pressure as he claimed before the game, then let the record show that his old coach picked up the slack. He was sixty-eight years old, had spent forty-seven of them at one school, and had waited nearly that long for this moment. A quarterback whose skin happened to be black was starting for one of the Super Bowl teams. Other human issues aside, he wanted him to be from Grambling.

"At my age," he said, "if Doug didn't make it I might not have had another chance." One can only guess at the anguish he felt as the Redskins fell ten points behind and Williams limped off the field late in the first quarter.

"I died a thousand deaths," said Robinson. "All my dreams were going down the drain. I prayed that he wasn't hurt. And I know Doug was praying. He told me in the locker room, he said to the Deity, 'Oh no, not now . . . don't do this to me now.' But you know, if he had gone out then and hadn't come back, there would have been no excuses. People get hurt in football games and that's the way it is."

On the next play the Broncos sacked his replacement, Jay Schroeder, proving they had an equal-opportunity pass rush.

Williams reentered the game for Washington's first offensive series of the second quarter, and on first down hit Ricky Sanders streaking down the sideline for eighty yards and a touchdown. On their next possession, Williams found Gary Clark on a 27-yarder and the Redskins led, 14–10. The teams were moving in opposite directions, one bound for the record books and the other going south to Tijuana.

Williams, the runaway pick for most valuable player, had tied in one quarter the record for most touchdown passes in a Super Bowl. "He was cool as a cucumber in the huddle," said Gary Clark. "He was hitting us in the numbers. When we started scoring, we just got pumped. We were breaking quick from the huddle, yelling, 'One more time, one more time.' We thought we had to keep scoring because we feared Elway. We saw what he could do to you with one quick strike. But the more you score the more energy you get, and good things kept happening to us."

Mainly Doug Williams happened to them. And he answered those who doubted and those who were merely curious. His arrival had raised again the question that for so long had puzzled pro football aficionados: Why were there so few black quarterbacks? Why had it taken so long to bring one to this exalted status?

The list isn't long: Before Williams a total of eleven blacks had taken snaps in the NFL, beginning with Willie Thrower in 1953. In 1987, the season of the deliverance, two others were starting, both extremely talented and mobile, Warren Moon in Houston and Randall Cunningham in Philadelphia. "Their turns will come," insists the fellow who got there first.

When extraordinary things happened to him, Doug always asked himself a fairly universal question: "Why me?" And the answer always came back: "Why not me?"

Even as the 1978 NFL draft approached, no one had to tell him to read a trend. He belonged to a fairly exclusive club and the ranks were thinning fast. When pro scouts wanted to time him in the 40 he refused. "Quarterbacks don't run," he told them, "if they can avoid it."

He knew what had happened in his time, and before it: Eldridge Dickey and Marlin Briscoe. He saw what went on at other campuses. "Look at Ohio State," he said. "Rod Gerald was moved for Art Schlichter. At LSU, Nicky Evans went to defensive end." Stephen Starring, who once quarterbacked against him at McNeese State, was moved to wide receiver by New England. In 1986 the Redskins drafted Alfred Jenkins, six feet four and 230, who broke passing records at Arizona, as a tight end.

It was the system, believed Doug, not bigotry. "They were great athletes," he says. "If I had been a great athlete it might have happened to me. But I wasn't."

On the other hand, the system on occasion sucks. "The way it has always been with black quarterbacks," says Williams, "is 'put up or shut up.' For example, Vinny Testaverde gets eight million dollars at Tampa Bay, and they tell him he's not ready to play. They want him to learn and develop. I got five hundred and seventy-five thousand over four years and I had to play the very first down. Give us time to develop too."

In 1978 Tampa Bay made him the first black quarterback ever chosen in the first round of the NFL draft—for the purpose of playing that position. He was the first quarterback from a black college to be named to the Associated Press All-America team. He was selected over Gifford Nielsen of Brigham Young, and Guy Benjamin of Stanford, whose pro careers fizzled. "My whole life," he said, "whatever I was, I was 'the first of.' "

Before the Buccaneers drafted Williams, they sent their offensive coordinator, a fellow named Joe Gibbs, to Grambling. There he spent most of two days with Doug, chalking plays on a blackboard and quizzing him on offensive strategy. What Gibbs saw and heard he liked, and his report was a favorable one.

Everyone pretended that there was nothing unusual about the interview, that it had little to do with stereotypes or whether a black could meet the intellectual challenge of playing quarterback in the NFL. Nor did Williams care that Tampa Bay, coached by a salty, wisecracking veteran, John McKay, who had won national championships at Southern Cal, was the most forlorn team in the league, an expansion franchise that lost its first twenty-six games.

It isn't likely that the major universities knew much about Doug Williams, whose high school had a graduating class of twenty-five. He received only two scholarship offers, both from schools within seventeen miles of his home. But Doug knew about USC. Under John McKay the Trojans were playing a black quarterback, Jimmy Jones, and after Grambling they were his favorite team. When Tampa Bay drafted him, he was eager to meet his new coach. "I liked his attitude right off," he says. "Because he'd tell you where to get on and when to get off, and he doesn't bite his tongue."

At the Super Bowl, Williams had shown a fine instinct for saying just the right thing: "My being a black quarterback is not going to win it. We're going to win it together or lose it together. I know an awful lot of people here want me to do well. Black, white, green, and yellow. At the same time I can't go around saying I'm playing for black America when Joe Gibbs, Bobby Beathard, and Jack Kent Cooke gave me my contract. And when I got a whole bunch of white guys—as well as black guys—protecting my case. I don't think Joe Jacoby or Jeff Bostic or R. C. Thielemann, or Raleigh McKenzie or Mark May, thought of me as black or white. They thought of me as their quarterback."

If that was the diplomatic answer, it was also the one Williams truly believed. He had learned to temper his answers after getting burned in Tampa, as a rookie, when he remarked innocently that "every black kid in America is rooting for me to make good." He was criticized in print and on the air and in local taverns for promoting "reverse racism." Doug was baffled. "I thought I was just telling the simple truth," he said. "And the Lord loves the simple truth."

Williams is no extrovert. But you needn't be in his company long to sense the depth of his character, his dignity and honesty. There were cross burnings in his hometown, Zachary, when he was growing up, but he loves the town and the people and heads there like a shot after each season. He has Louisiana in his soul and in his voice. He remembers people making fun of his speech after he turned pro; he said "ax" instead of "ask" and his nouns and verbs don't always agree.

"Maybe they think I'm dumb because my grammar isn't perfect," he said. "But I think I talk O.K. I mean, people can understand what I'm trying to say." Gibbs can recall how Williams once astonished him by instantly recalling a variety of formations and schemes, player for player, several minutes after the coach had erased them from the blackboard.

At Tampa, McKay drove them hard. After one sloppy defeat he was asked how he felt about his team's execution. "I'm in favor of it," he said, dryly.

What Williams remembers about those years was living with the certain knowledge that he would get hit on every play. When he went deep, his receivers lacked the speed to outrun his arm, and on even the short throws his ball sailed in the swirling bay winds. With the hostage crisis in Iran dominating the political news, he became the punch line to a joke that spread across the country. Mike Tierney, a sportswriter in St. Petersburg, suggested that the State Department should send "Doug Williams to the Middle East, because he was one American who could overthrow the Ayatollah."

The Bucs went 5-and-11 his rookie year, but there were good times to come: friendships with Jimmie Giles, Greg Roberts, and the late Ricky Bell, and turning the team into a winner. His second season they were a Cinderella story, reaching the NFC championship game, before losing to the Rams in a driving rainstorm, 9–0.

He drew raves from such people as Tom Bass, then the Tampa Bay defensive coordinator: "Doug is probably the most mentally tough quarterback I've been around in my life. He got the heck knocked out of him every week, yet he hung in there and never complained."

If he was anything, Doug Williams was a survivor. Put aside for the moment the bounces of his football career. His personal and private shocks would have flattened a person of lesser mettle. His wife, Janice, died of a brain tumor in March 1983, just ten days short of their first wedding anniversary, and ten weeks after the birth of their daughter, Ashley Monique. They had been college sweethearts. "It seemed so unfair," he says. "We had dated since our freshman year at Grambling when we didn't have anything. We dreamed. We made plans. We had just bought the land where the house is now. And then right when she was really going to start enjoying life, she died. Her death taught me that no matter who you are, or how much money you make, it doesn't matter. You can't buy off death. You can't pay it to go away."

He remarried in June 1987, and a difficult year and a half later went through a bitter divorce. Whatever the additional problems, Doug had struggled with less than total success to put the past behind him. In his dreams, he confided, Janice would appear and ask him, 'Doug, why did you get married?' "

At other moments, he said, he would be driving along, lost in thought, with Ashley, then six, in the car. "And she'd say, 'My mommy's up there. My mommy's in heaven. God's up there. The devil's down there. My mommy's up there with God.' I don't know how, but she knows."

After Janice's funeral, Williams had spent a week driving aimlessly around Texas with Greg Roberts. When he returned home to Zachary, there was the matter of a new contract to be resolved with the team. It never was. The world Doug Williams lived in must have seemed a barren place. He had played what would turn out to be his last season in Tampa, working for $125,000, a salary that put him below forty-five other quarterbacks in the NFL.

If Janice had not died, if Joe Gibbs had not moved on to another coaching job, he might have been less inclined to make a stand. But Doug had been knocked down hard, and he had a powerful need to feel that his team was not pushing him around. His teammates lined up behind him. "The negotiations were going back and forth," recalled Jimmie Giles, "at what was a crisis time for him. He felt the Bucs should have cut through all that."

He had led them to the playoffs in three of his five seasons, while taking a fearful pounding. Now he wanted to be paid on a par with other established quarterbacks. His agent asked for a multiyear deal that would average six hundred thousand dollars a season. Tampa Bay offered four hundred thousand dollars and never budged. "Their attitude," he says, "was 'take it or leave it.'" He didn't air his complaints in the press. He simply left and sat out the season. No other NFL team even made him an offer. Football, he decided, "didn't seem so important."

Then the Oklahoma Outlaws called and met his price, three million dollars over five years, and he signed with the spring league. At the time, of course, he seemed to be signing away any chance he had of becoming the first black quarterback to start in the Super Bowl.

In the summer of 1986 the USFL folded and Williams was once more an unemployed quarterback. "I didn't think my career was over," he says. "I didn't think I was that bad. I thought I was better than at least half of the quarterbacks that were playing in the NFL. There are twenty-eight teams and I didn't consider myself the twenty-ninth best quarterback."

Again he went home to Zachary and pulled the town around him like a parka. He is fond of saying that you can't really know Doug Williams without knowing Zachary, Louisiana. But it is a safe bet that one can get to know the town a lot faster than one can the quarterback.

* * *

To reach Zachary (population 7,747), you follow a two-lane road north out of Baton Rouge, winding through fields dotted with dairy cows, horses, and chickens. Just over the town line is a store called The Fishen Hole. The sign advertises live catfish from the pond out back. A placard next door reads SAWS SHARPENS.

"Zachary is a place you've got to be going to, to get there," says Williams.

The Williams house, five rooms behind a grocery on Plank Road, had no indoor plumbing. The kids took turns drawing water from a well in the backyard. Today Doug's parents live in a new four-bedroom brick house on Lemon Road. From their back door they can see Doug's new two-story house. In fact, the dwellings of the Williams clan are visible in whatever direction one looks. Within the triangle formed by three roads live thirty of Doug's kin.

His mother, Laura, helped support the family by working twelve hours a day as a cook and food server in the school cafeterias. His father, Robert Williams, Sr., was an army veteran disabled by a back injury and later crippled by rheumatoid arthritis. In 1983 his left leg was amputated just above the knee. Pride and pain and inconvenience kept him from making the trip to San Diego to see his son play in the Super Bowl. "He's the type of guy who for years has been able to do so much on his own," said Doug. "He hates the idea of being rolled around on a wheelchair amongst so many other people."

Over the years Doug never lacked for heroes. One of his first was Don Drysdale, the strong-armed Dodger pitcher. Baseball, not football, was his game then. Later his role models were James Harris and Joe Namath and, always, his older brother, Robert Jr.

Robert was the eldest of the eight Williams children and paved Doug's way to Grambling. Recruited for baseball, he had been the first Zachary resident to earn a scholarship and graduate from college. He pitched for three years in the Cleveland Indians farm system before a torn rotator cuff ended his career.

Robert returned to his hometown to coach junior high football and varsity basketball, and he forced a reluctant Doug to try out for quarterback as an eighth grader. Showing a high degree of intelligence even then, Doug hated the roughness and dreaded the idea of getting hit. Robert lined up his brother at middle linebacker and had the offense run right at him until, in self-defense, he fought back.

"I was never good enough for Robert," he says. "He was my toughest coach." On the eve of the Super Bowl, he called Robert "the greatest influence on my life. If it weren't for him, I wouldn't be where I am today. I don't know if I'd be in San Quentin. But I wouldn't be in San Diego."

Jackie Robinson once said that he had no heroes as a boy. Black kids didn't have heroes, he said, didn't hero-worship the way white kids did. [I wasn't convinced that he really believed it; the blacks I grew up with had heroes and Robinson, who had broken baseball's color line, was foremost among them. Jackie was going through political changes in his life at the time and the trivial side of sports annoyed him. But now, many years later, listening to Doug Williams talk about his older brother, the point no longer seemed obscure.]

Doug's nature was made secure by family love and toughened by years of racial testing. "Segregation was a way of life for us in the South," says Robert. "From an early age, Doug was faced with adversity. He knew how to stand up to it, to not let it stand in the way of success."

When integration came to American Legion ball in Baton Rouge in 1971, Doug was the ace pitcher of the Central Sealtest team, one of five blacks playing under his brother Robert, the league's only black coach. League officials rigged the opening schedule to send Sealtest against the defending champion, clearly hoping to embarrass the racially mixed upstarts.

Heckled and harassed throughout the game, Doug struck out fourteen and drove in four runs as Sealtest won. "The more they called him nigger, the harder he threw the ball," said another brother Manzie, who also played in the game. "Our father always told us, 'When people call you nigger, be so good at what you're doing they'll have to call you Mr. Nigger.' "

Now, when Doug was thirty-one, with two weak knees, and an entire league shot out from under him, no one was calling him much of anything. No one called, period. He had begun to think about a new career as a coach when the phone rang and an old friend was on the line—Joe Gibbs. The Redskins wanted to sign him as a backup for Jay Schroeder, but Gibbs wondered if that was a role Williams's ego could handle. It did not take Doug long to consider his options.

"There were no starting jobs available in the NFL," he noted. "No other team had even called. What else was I going to do?"

In all of 1986 he appeared in one game, for four snaps, attempting one pass, an incompletion. He said he could accept his fate and he had. He was prepared for more of the same in 1987, especially after a deal that would have sent him to the Raiders fell through. Talks broke off six days before the season began and Williams was crushed. "At the time," he said, "I felt that going to the Raiders was the only chance I'd get again to start."

In Washington, Schroeder's luck began to run out. On the fourth play of the 1987 opener he separated a shoulder, and Williams rallied the team to a 34–24 win over the Eagles. The players strike hit a week later, after a one-point loss to Atlanta, in Williams's first start for the Redskins. Everyone retired to the sideline and some to the picket line.

When the strike ended four weeks later, Schroeder was healed and back in command. But control problems plagued him. He was a horrid 16-for-46 in a loss to the Eagles and had an erratic start against the Detroit Lions. He kept missing open receivers. Gibbs yanked him, and Williams again came off the bench to pass for two touchdowns and a 20–13 victory. For most of the game, Schroeder stood on the sidelines, his hands on his hips.

It was mid-November, and for the first time in his seven years as a head coach, Joe Gibbs had voluntarily replaced his starting quarterback. His earlier resistance could be traced to a trauma he experienced as a young assistant at USC in 1970. He scouted a UCLA—Oregon game in which the Bruins pulled their starter, Dennis Dummit, with a twenty-point lead in the third period. A gunner named Dan Fouts and a wide receiver named Bobby Moore (later known as Ahmad Rashad) rallied Oregon to a 41—40 victory.

In what might be viewed as a slight overreaction, considering that it was not even his team, Gibbs described UCLA's blown lead as "tragic," adding somewhat unnecessarily, "It made a lasting impression me." And thereafter, he committed himself to one quarterback at a time. His starter would be number one, and number two would be just that, not a one-A or one and a half. Even in practice, his starter received most of the work. "The backup doesn't like it," he says of the system, "until he gets to be number one."

So the significance could not have been clearer when Williams started the next week against the Rams, on *Monday Night Football.* Art Monk dropped two touchdown passes and the Redskins lost, but Doug had earned the job.

Then in practice on Thanksgiving Day, he twisted his back and sprained a ligament. Schroeder returned to the starting lineup against the Giants and had one of the best days of his career, passing for 331 yards and three touchdowns and producing a come-from-behind win. Gibbs announced to the press the next day that Schroeder had reestablished himself as the first-string quarterback.

Then an unusual and poignant thing occurred. When he was asked his reaction by a television reporter, Doug Williams's voice cracked on camera and tears filled his eyes. "Not because I wasn't starting," he explained. "It was all the things that had happened . . . a lifetime of frustrations."

Understand, the lifetime we are talking about is not Doug Williams's alone. It belongs as well to Eddie Robinson and Robert Williams, Jr., and Willie Thrower and countless others who have been a part of this continuing drama. The year would twist its way to the most improbable of all endings, a Super Bowl victory, but Doug Williams didn't know that on the day the tears fell.

In sports, nothing wipes the slate quite so clean as success.

The odyssey began with Willie Thrower, who, on October 18, 1953, in Wrigley Field in Chicago, became the first black to quarterback an NFL team. He completed three of eight passes for twenty-seven yards in a substitute's role for the Bears in a losing effort at San Francisco. That year and those figures represent his only line in the player's register. He pretty well knew what to expect in the preseason, when old George Halas subbed him for George Blanda with the Bears trailing the Redskins, 35–21. The rookie moved them down the field, sixty yards, to a first and goal at the 5. He walked back to the huddle to call the play. Surprise. There was no room for him. Blanda was back in the game.

"The coach didn't think I could finish it," Willie would say thirty-five years later. "He wanted George to take them in. He wanted George to do it."

Later that year George Taliaferro, a halfback for the Baltimore Colts, took a few snaps from center to become the second black quarterback. Two years later Green Bay used Charlie Brackins in a reserve role. He was the third. Thirteen more years were to go by before another black quarterback, Marlin Briscoe, appeared in an NFL game for the Denver Broncos. In 1969 James Harris, another Grambling product, then with the Buffalo Bills, became the first black to start at quarterback.

Between Willie Thrower and Doug Williams, twenty-five years had passed. Put it this way: Where black quarterbacks were concerned, time was about the only thing allowed to pass. Thrower had been a virtually forgotten man when the Redskins and Williams made him a footnote to this piece of history. In a curious way, he was not much remembered even as he played.

"Nobody ever gave it a thought," swears Frank Kush, the former college and pro coach who was his teammate at Michigan State. "Believe me, it was not an issue. Nobody ever thought about it. He was a football player and he played."

Willie Thrower—who could invent a more perfect name for a quarterback?—knew he was not just another player. He competed in 1953 with George Blanda for a chance to quarterback the Bears and recalls without judgment that George was none too helpful. "But I didn't expect him to be."

Blanda went on to play twenty-six years for three teams and land in the Hall of Fame. "Willie was a great football player," he says today, "a great prospect. But you have to remember that there were not a lot of spots in those days. There were fewer teams and only thirty-three men on a team. Back then, one and a half years was a long time to spend on a prospect. He was raw and there was no time to develop him."

Another future coach was among Thrower's teammates at Michigan State, Chuck Fairbanks. "Our offenses were not very sophisticated," said Fairbanks. "We did not attack out of good passing formations. It was geared to the run more. But Willie could throw the ball any way he wanted. Where I came from, I had never seen anyone who could throw a football like that. He could throw it hard; he could throw with finesse."

Thrower's arm earned him a free-agent contract, but that was about all. The Bears drafted Zeke Bratkowski the next year and had Ed Brown returning from the army. "It was not a black-white issue," says Blanda. "He was just at the wrong place at the wrong time. I was there and pretty soon I was gone too."

Thrower always suspected that there were deeper currents at work. "With the Bears," he says, "I could always feel the electricity. Not with their fans. The fans loved me. They loved Michigan State players in Chicago. They accepted me. Nobody had to say anything, but being black you could feel, you could sense it. But it never came from George Halas. You never had it with him."

After the Bears released Thrower in 1954, he played three seasons in Canada. "There has always been that 'intelligence' thing," he said. "No one ever said it to me directly, but it's there. You have to understand that the majority of offensive linemen come from Southern colleges and always have. For years whites and blacks were not allowed to even play against each other. It was really something to walk into a huddle filled with players like that and call plays. You could sense the lack of confidence."

The reference to white Southern linemen is interesting. This is not a theory widely circulated, but a check of rosters in the late 1940s and early 1950s does indeed reflect a preference for linemen from such outposts as Texas, Oklahoma, Ole Miss, Tennessee, and throughout Dixie. Those schools in that era recruited big, beefy farmboys and taught them how to pass-block in the wide-open aerial games that had swept through the South and Southwest—part of the Sammy Baugh legacy.

Now in his late fifties, Willie Thrower lives in the Pittsburgh area and has kept track of the black quarterbacks who came after him. Joe Gilliam, then competing with Terry Bradshaw as the starter for the Steelers, visited Thrower once and received some coaching tips. Gilliam might have played in a Super Bowl a dozen years before Williams, of course, but his off-the-field problems kept him from fulfilling his immense promise. "He got more or less what he deserved," said Thrower. "I could never see mixing playing and drugs. I'm against all that."

Thrower enjoyed his rediscovery by the press, answering questions, hearing himself described as a pioneer, a kind of football Jackie Robinson. But he surveys the game today, and the huge sums commanded by the talent out there, and he says wistfully: "I know I definitely played in the wrong time. I was w-a-a-ay ahead of my time. I look at a Mark Malone . . . I could've thrown that well falling backward."

Down through the years the question echoed and endured and perplexed as no other: Could anyone explain why were there so few black quarterbacks? For so many years why were they automatically diverted to wide receivers and safeties?

Willie Thrower attributed the shortage to a lack of black drop-back passers in college . . . and high school, for that matter. "Most black quarterbacks operate out of the wishbone or run mostly option offenses," he said. "The bad thing about playing the Wishbone and Split T is the pros don't have time to teach them how to be drop-back passers. Schools like Brigham Young and San Jose State that feature the drop-back passer rarely have black quarterbacks."

* * *

Another longtimer—Eddie Robinson of Grambling—troubled by the Question, reached a similar conclusion in the early 1960s. The difference is that Robinson was in a unique position to do something about it. And he did.

No one can begin to appreciate how far Doug Williams traveled without knowing Grambling and the irrepressible man his ex-players often call Coach Rob. The school is located in the town of the same name, sixty-one miles east of Shreveport in the red clay country. In 1941 all Grambling had was a college, and all the college had was six frame shacks and a football team. The sawmill had closed and the town had no industry, no office buildings, no motels. The population was less than four thousand and the trains didn't stop there unless somebody stood in the tracks and flagged one down.

In 1941 Eddie Robinson was hired as the school's head football coach and Grambling lost all but three of its eight games. That was a good year, 1941, if you were in the scrap metal business. The Japanese bombed Pearl Harbor in December and the world went to war. The next season the Tigers were undefeated and Coach Rob might have felt terrific, except that they dropped the sport until the world recovered its temper.

For Eddie Robinson, coaching would become not so much a career as a quiet crusade. When he flew into San Diego to watch Doug Williams perform in the Super Bowl, he had completed his forty-seventh season. He had won 341 games, more than Alabama's Bear Bryant had won, more than any coach in any class of ball. He had turned Grambling into the black Notre Dame. His team played in a new stadium that bore his name, almost on the spot where he had plowed the field back in 1941 and put down the yard markers so the Tigers could practice.

It hasn't been that many cotton crops ago that schools such as Alabama didn't recruit black athletes. The WHITES ONLY signs came down in 1967 and although this was seen as a social breakthrough, it didn't make Coach Robinson's job any easier. Now he not only had to compete with the Big Ten and the Pacific Coast and the Eastern independents to keep his talent at home, he had to hold off his Southern neighbors as well.

It was surely a simpler world when Eddie Robinson started. Not all black and white, but close. People forget that pro football had no color line as such. In the 1920s Duke Slater starred at Iowa, Fritz Pollard at Brown, and Paul Robeson at Rutgers. All went on to play in what passed for pro football. Robeson won more renown as a classical singer.

Somehow, though, the black stars got lost. Then in 1949 a newspaper clipping reached a scout with the Los Angeles Rams. It told about a fullback at a little school in Louisiana called Grambling. His name was Tank Younger and he had scored twenty-five touchdowns in one season. The scout had never heard of Tank Younger and he had never heard of Grambling, but he knew how many points twenty-five touchdowns were worth. He caught a plane and rented a car and found Grambling. For the first time, the pros were going to offer a kid from an all-black college a chance to play football for a living.

Eddie Robinson and the president of the school, Dr. Ralph Waldo Emerson Jones, haggled over the terms until Younger was offered a fair contract for the times: six thousand dollars in salary and another thousand in bonuses. "Dr. Jones," Robinson said, "could talk the horns off a billy goat."

Over the years some two hundred players followed Tank Younger out of Grambling and into the pros. A bunch of them are in the Pro Football Hall of Fame now: Younger, Willie Davis, Willie Brown, Buck Buchanan. You figure an NFL game doesn't count unless at least one Grambling product is on the field.

And it wasn't by accident that one of their own made it to the Super Bowl as the first black starting quarterback. It was part of a plan, a quest, that really picked up steam when Coach Robinson was interviewed by the relentless Howard Cosell in the late 1960s—he can't exactly pinpoint the date. Howard peppered him with questions: Why was there no black quarterback in the NFL. Could he, Eddie Robinson, develop one? Was he trying? How long would it take? And the bitter truth was that he didn't have any answers, but he made it his objective to find them.

As he crossed the country, attending coaching clinics, he looked for the speakers who knew something about what it took to play quarterback in the NFL. He made sure that players from Grambling who were making it in the pros came back in the spring to work with the team "and pay their dues." He became a regular visitor to NFL locker rooms.

On the recruiting trail he sought out athletes who had the size (at least six feet four) and potential to win a championship. James Harris was the first, in Buffalo, starting just three games in three seasons before the Bills cut him in 1972. Then he signed with the Rams, whose director of personnel was none other than Tank Younger. Tiny Grambling was working on a network. Harris beat out John Hadl as the starter and led the Rams to within a couple yards of the Super Bowl in 1975. But his stay in Los Angeles was a controversial one, with some of the players, the fans, and the media choosing sides along racial lines. He finished his career with the Chargers.

Matthew Reed—"a great specimen, he could throw the ball farther than anybody"—was the next black knight to attempt to pull the sword from the rock. He signed with the World Football League, moved on to good years in Canada, and faded from view.

And then along came Doug Williams. Eddie Robinson had turned a corner. His young men were being given a chance.

The Grambling coach had begun to tailor his efforts to that goal: "A chance isn't much good to you if, when it comes, you're not ready to take advantage of it. We wanted them to graduate, and we worked on that, but on the field everything we did was aimed at making them good enough to play in the league. From the beginning, when Younger made it with the Rams, we were using the Rams offense. When the NFL scouts came by our place, I'd ask them not to leave, and after practice I'd take them under the stadium and ask what our quarterbacks needed to work on to make it in the NFL. We worked on the drops, the three-step, and the five and the seven.

"We started to stress that our receivers needed to run precise patterns. We had Dub Jones, who lived in Ruston, and had been a great receiver with the Browns, helping us, and so with the people passing through we were finding out what it would take.

"I even got up at our meetings and talked to the coaches in our conference about being sure that all our quarterbacks were up on the latest techniques. And when they had one leave and go to the pros, be sure they came back to tell the younger ones what to expect.

"When James Harris was with the Chargers, and they had those great passing schemes under Don Coryell, he'd give me some of their pass plays over the phone in the middle of the week and on Saturday we'd get two or three touchdowns out of them. They'd be wide open.

"Every guy who had success was expected to come back and help. Younger was the first, and after a couple summers he predicted that Willie Davis was going to be a great pro. Then Willie started coming back, and each one would pass on what he had learned."

If you ask Eddie Robinson what took so long, and who is there better to ask, he won't give you any heavy social commentary. Nor does he talk about racial prejudice, a subject he seldom lectured on even to his players. "Coach Rob believes in America," said Williams. "If you live in America, he said, you will get opportunities like everybody else. He never tells you what you can't do or what they won't let you do."

If anything, Robinson's answer excuses everyone but himself. "It starts with coaching," he says. "I wanted to know if we as coaches were doing what we were supposed to be doing? Could our players read the defense? Change plays at the line? Did they understand the terminology? I had to learn these things so I could pass it on to them.

"I remember when Tommy McDonald, the great receiver, played with the Eagles, and they were playing the college all-stars in Chicago. The quarterback called a couple running plays and then a couple passes in the flat to the left, and then on the fifth play he went to McDonald deep down the right side and it was a touchdown. I was fascinated by how they could do this.

"I went into the locker room and asked McDonald to describe

what he was doing. He said on each of the first four plays he ran the same pattern on his mind, trying to lull him to sleep. He'd go down and cut to the outside. The last time his man got careless, and he faked to the outside and broke for the post and he was open.

"I wasn't embarrassed to go to people like this, to other coaches and quarterbacks, and ask them how they did things. I had to do my homework if I was going to be able to get it across to our players. That's what we did. We tailored our game to give them a chance in the NFL. I can't say that it took too long or it should have come sooner. I only know it wasn't going to get done with screaming and hollering. But it did get done, and that's what matters."

☆ 10 ☆ THE EGGHEADS AND THEM

The definitive comment on an opposing quarterback's intellect came from Thomas "Hollywood" Henderson, then with the Dallas Cowboys, appraising Pittsburgh's Terry Bradshaw: "He couldn't spell 'cat' if you spotted him *a* and *t*."

Leaving aside the merit of that judgment, the importance of braininess in a quarterback has long been a matter of debate. "It depends on what you mean," says Sid Gillman. "He needs to think quick, not deep. He needs to be able to react. You judge his arm, his size, mobility, toughness. Is he a leader? If he checks out on those, yeah, you'd like him to be smart."

You can argue who the heavy thinkers are, but beyond any question the most educated quarterbacks ever to play the game were Frank Ryan and Charley Johnson, both of whom earned their doctorates during their NFL careers. Give the bronze medal to Pat Haden, the Rhodes scholar.

Dr. Frank Ryan won a championship with the Cleveland Browns in 1964, when that *was* the Super Bowl, only without the hype and TV ratings. The games were played outdoors, on organic grass, never at night, and the goalpost was shaped like the letter *H*.

Dr. Charles Johnson played fifteen seasons with St. Louis, Houston, and Denver and never took a snap for a championship team. The Oilers were losers and the Broncos not much better, but they taught him the value of a good education. If he makes it into the Hall of Fame it will be in the medical wing, a tribute to his twelve surgeries, eight on his knees. He also suffered six or eight concussions, he can't remember exactly, which may be understandable.

Ryan needed seven years to get his Ph.D. in mathematics; Johnson spent ten years of off-seasons getting his in chemical engineering. This and the pain are what their careers had in common.

In a sense they represented the ideal of the student-athlete. Their records were the answer to all those Neanderthal stories you have heard about football players. You know, the dumb clod who is happy with a cream pie. There may be little point at this late stage in trying to convince the world that most athletes are smarter than the average fish. But then you pause to think about someone like Frank Ryan.

He retired from pro football in 1974 to become director of information services for that esteemed body, the House of Representatives. It was Ryan who put in their computer systems. So even as he moved to another plateau, Ryan remained a rare fellow, a doctor still willing to make a House call.

Later he went to Yale as athletic director and taught a few math classes, as he had done before at such universities as Rice and Case. There is no question but what his academic status caused problems for Frank as a jock. Not many years ago, athletes had an intuitive distrust of teammates who read books, and they viewed with panic those who would write one. So what could they make of a fellow who described himself as a geometric function theorist and whose doctoral thesis was entitled ''A Characterization of the Set of Asymptotic Values of a Function Holomorphic in the Unit Disc.'' There is simply no way that the average human can begin to grasp what Frank's work was about. You had to be a bloody wizard just to understand the title.

Of course, it is exactly this kind of dwelling on his mental prowess that hounded and irritated him all of his football days. He seemed to feel that it was an affront to those very real scholars—on the faculties at Rice and Yale, for example—whose knowledge and achievement so clearly exceeded his own.

To be sure, the subject was overblown and worn thin as a wafer. If Frank had spent his life as a professor, no one outside his family would have known he existed. But that's the point. He happened to be a football player, and a fine one, who led another life in a world few of us understood. In jock circles, it was easy to think of him as strange or, worse, a genius.

''I don't like words like 'genius,' '' he said. ''It's a bad label. I worked hard to avoid that sort of image and I drank a lot of beer with the boys. And had fun doing it. There is something quite wonderful about sports people, their humor, their gregarious nature. We got along famously. They did think of me as flaky, but all quarterbacks are flaky. I was just a different variety.''

That Ryan went on to a football career of any distinction is in itself a triumph and a curious one. To begin with, he was the first Ryan in three generations not to attend Yale. He was recruited out of Fort Worth to play football at Rice when that school was still a factor in Southwest Conference championships.

But he had to convince the coaches that he was serious about majoring in physics. That was a pretty stiff course, they felt, for an athlete. Unlike most schools, Rice did not offer degrees in physical education but when necessary steered their players into creative but not taxing classes, such as chiropractic criminology, which is the science of discouraging crime by breaking the criminal's back.

Ryan insisted and was allowed to go his own way, but he spent most of his college career on the second string, playing behind King Hill. In 1957 Hill made the all-America team and was the first pick in the draft—the bonus pick—by the Philadelphia Eagles. Flown to New York, he startled reporters by announcing that there was a quarterback better than he on the Rice team who might have been there instead of him, "except that he had to miss practice a lot on account of his labs."

Of course, the reference was to Frank Ryan.

That was decent of King Hill, all the more because it might have been true. Ryan remembers his college years as a gentler time. "When I was an undergraduate at Rice," he says, "athletic life was relatively simple. There were five sports: football, basketball, baseball, tennis, and track. Good athletes were recruited for all five and given a kind of 'B-track' education. When I told them at Rice I wanted to take an engineering course, they said it wouldn't work out. After a time they agreed to let me major in physics. They needed quarterbacks, and in those days I could throw a football ninety-five yards.

"I took the free ride—room, board, and the rest. It's struck me since that when the coach said, 'We'll meet at ten o'clock on Monday night,' I had to be there, whether that interfered with physics homework or not. I was being paid to be there."

Frank was amazed when the Los Angeles Rams drafted him. As luck would have it, he had been accepted for graduate studies at UCLA. The arrangement seemed not only sensible, but perfect.

The Rams were then coached by ex-quarterback Bob Waterfield, but the team's style seemed to be influenced by Hollywood. One mistake and you were back on the bench. Observed Joan Ryan: "It was click, click, razzle-dazzle. Make it big or out you go. Our third year in Los Angeles, we knew it wasn't working out. By then we had children and we had moved to Burbank, where we lived in a big apartment complex with a lanai. We had a view of the Burbank Flood Control. That is California for 'ditch.' "

The Rams, the team that once boasted of the glories of Waterfield and Van Brocklin, now needed a turnstile for quarterbacks.

They brought in Billy Wade, Zeke Bratkowski, Buddy Humphrey. They had traded off their entire offensive line for Ollie Matson, who couldn't learn the plays. While Ryan's confidence was flirting with zero, inquiring minds wanted to know: What was wrong? Was it Frank? Was it the team? Was it the coach? Was the stadium facing the wrong direction?

Traded to Cleveland in 1962, Ryan was reduced to an instrument—a robot with a voice—by Paul Brown, who had invented the team in the heady days that followed World War II. Brown insisted on calling all the plays. All of them. No audibles. As a condition of employment, you ran the play that Paul Brown sent in from the sideline.

The quarterback who was arguably the smartest ever to play the game could not call his own plays. Not that it mattered at first. Ryan had been hired neither to think nor to play. He was there to relieve Jim Ninowski, who had more talent than he needed, since Cleveland's offense consisted largely of giving the ball to Jim Brown.

Only when Ninowski broke his shoulder halfway through the 1962 season did Ryan start for the Browns. He was twenty-six years old, and it was the first time since high school that he had been a first-string quarterback. Soon afterward, pressing, he threw an interception and with great effort made the tackle himself near the goal line to avoid a touchdown.

When Frank trotted off the field, Paul Brown grabbed him. "Why?" Brown screamed. "Why, why, why?"

"Why what?" asked Ryan.

"Why did you throw that interception at a time like this?"

The next year, with Jim Brown leading a player revolt, the owner, Arthur Modell, fired the most famous coach in the game. Under Blanton Collier, Ryan was installed as the starter. Now he had only his fullback to harass him.

There were vague racial tensions at large in Cleveland, revolving around Brown, the best ball carrier since the dawn of football. When he looked at Ryan, Brown saw a white intellectual with a slight Texas drawl who was his rival for team leadership.

Ryan aggravated the matter by wanting to open up the passing game.

Jim responded by refusing to block. Publicly he said that he had to conserve his strength for carrying the ball. In private he is said to have regarded blocking for a drawling white passer to be "an act of servility."

With a veteran team, and Collier a fatherly figure, the posturing of their star back was a nuisance, nothing more. The Browns made a run at the title in 1963, Ryan's first full year at the helm, but fell short.

It was his nature to love exactitude and Collier gave it to him. "I remember going to Bob Waterfield my last year with the Rams," he said, "and telling him about a problem—a thing of getting tense in the pocket. The more time I had to throw, the more nervous I got. Waterfield told me to forget it. Blanton would have had an answer. He would have told me to concentrate on my key. The point is, he gave me specific answers and I'm a man who needs specific answers, even if they are wrong. I need something to think about. Otherwise, I flounder."

Ryan had acquired a reputation as nervous and erratic, but 1964 would be the season he erased the doubts. He threw five touchdown passes to beat the Giants, 52–20, and Cleveland's first conference title in a decade was assured.

The championship game, against Johnny Unitas and Baltimore, was to be a classic collision of theories: the Colts' short-fused-bomb offense against Cleveland's conservative, containing defense. Almost the reverse turned out to be the case. "Our defense went in with the idea of playing the receivers real tight," recalled Frank. "Don't give them any room and hope the rush can get to Unitas. There's nothing that bothers a quarterback more than seeing a defensive back play just a few yards off his receivers. It worked. By the time Unitas took a second look our defense was on him."

Ryan made it seem simple. For the first half he sent Jim Brown into the line, forcing Baltimore to close its defenses. The half ended scoreless. Then Ryan passed over and around the defenses and Cleveland won, 27–0.

* * *

Six months after he had passed the Browns to the title, Frank Ryan walked across a stage on the Rice University campus and kept an appointment that had been seven years in the making. At the appropriate moment, he ducked his head and allowed to be slipped about his neck the academic hood that identified him as a doctor of philosophy in mathematics.

His dark hair, always salt and peppered, was turning solid gray. At six feet three he had the right length for a quarterback, but otherwise he hardly fit the mold. At twenty-eight, Ryan had the ascetic face of a priest.

Frank Ryan had emerged as an egghead in a world that prefers its eggs scrambled. "I am sure Ryan will be glad to talk to you," the Cleveland publicist would tell visiting sportswriters. "But that doesn't mean you'll know what he's talking about." And a local scribe cautioned an out-of-towner: "You will find him a little far-out. I mean, like one time it was picture day at the Browns' training camp, and we had our photographers out there. Ryan threw left-handed all day. What a damned time we had at the office. We thought every negative had been reversed."

"Oh that," says Ryan with a grin. "Actually, it was Ninowski who started throwing left-handed, but I kept it up and all the pictures were wrong. But that isn't the point. Wouldn't you think the photographers would have noticed? The point is that a professional photographer, assigned to spend a day taking pictures, should make it his business to prepare himself to find out whether his subject throws right or left."

His image as a nonconformist was helped along by his choice of the number 13 when he joined the Browns. "They [the press] really made something out of that," he says. "It's this simple: I wanted number eleven but Jim Ninowski had it. The only other number they had was eighteen and I didn't want that because it had belonged to Len Dawson, who up to then had been thought of as a perennial second-string quarterback. We had a rookie on the squad, John Furman, and when he got cut I grabbed his number. It was thirteen."

It was true that Ryan took a mad delight in an occasional

practical joke. He put a dead seagull in Lou Groza's kicking shoe, after carefully spreading a story about people dropping dead of parrot fever. "I thought it was pretty funny at the time," says Frank, "but Groza was very upset. He had to have his shoe disinfected. I wasn't there when he found it, and they told me I was lucky . . . he would have killed me."

At other times he might call a teammate, disguising his voice, announce himself as a reporter, and ask how he felt about being traded. "Anyone can recognize Frank's voice," testifies Joan, "after a minute."

As a writer herself, Joan Ryan understood how the repetition of such stories created an image. To the extent that he indulged in them, she believed, he did so to counter the genius thing. "He is mild-mannered," says Joan, "and every bit the gentleman. He is interested in challenges of the mind; that's what football is to him, although he can't stand to hear me say it. It burns me up when stories make him sound like some kind of nut."

Ryan preferred to think of himself as "serendipitous," an obscure word coined by Walpole. It relates to a talent for finding valuable things you have not sought. Said Ryan: "The ideal quarterback must have serendipity. Why does he make good plays constantly? By accident? By coincidence? Or is it a sixth sense? The times I have felt best on the field, then my mind was following no logical, conscious thinking pattern. There was no effort to analyze, to evaluate, to review, to study patterns or tendencies. Something just came to me and it worked . . . not once or twice, but time after time."

He felt it in the championship game, his finest day, but an incident near the end of it changed his career. With a few minutes left, the Browns were driving for another touchdown. Ryan wanted to throw a scoring pass to John Brewer, whose morale might ride for a year on one touchdown in the playoff. But with time counting down, the fans poured onto the field, and the referee picked up the ball.

"All right, boys," he said to the players, "that's enough."

"No," Ryan cried out, "I want one more score."

At least one Baltimore lineman believed Ryan was trying to

embarrass them. And a couple of Colts tucked that memory away and saved it for the Pro Bowl, and for an unguarded moment. "When you get hit," explained Ryan, "the impact jars, but it's often overrated. You're padded. You tuck your elbows in and you go down." In the Pro Bowl, Ryan was knocked unconscious while he was *upright*. He fell, elbows wide, under a pile and separated his passing shoulder. At the bottom of the pile was a Baltimore player.

Ryan would rarely again throw without pain. The next year Cleveland lost to the Packers in the title game. In 1966 he needed surgery on his elbow and a year later he sprained both ankles. The Browns were less and less able to protect him. The team was slipping. Jim Brown had retired so he could make movies and talk about the world.

Ryan was now their undisputed leader. He identified with the city and bought a rambling house on four acres in the suburbs. Joan, who had majored in English at Rice, was writing a sports column for the *Plain Dealer*.

She was, in fact, the only writer who could be sure of his approval. One disadvantage of the brilliant mind is that it sees all the more clearly the indignities of sport. When one of his injuries kept him out of a game the Browns won in 1967, he was dressing quietly in front of his locker when a reporter approached. "How did it feel to sit one out?" he asked.

It had not felt very good, but what was the use of saying so? Ryan elected not to answer. He turned away.

"Just because you've gone to school five years longer than the rest of us," the reporter said, "don't think you're too good to talk to me."

"Get your face out of mine," Dr. Frank Ryan screamed as if in pain. "Get your face out of mine and get away from me." His voice carried over the buzz of a winning clubhouse and the sound of it embarrassed him. The scene embarrassed him, too, for a long time afterward. He had let a boor wound him in front of everyone.

Flattery, compromise, mixing with strangers, did not come easily to him. It would upset him when writers misstated his work in mathematics. It surprised him that scholars allowed themselves to show their envy of his football career. He felt blessed that he never had to choose one world over the other. He could talk about a math equation as though it were a beautiful poem.

He could see the beauty in a well-thrown pass too, and in Cleveland he really cared about the franchise. Never a reticent soul, he seized an opportunity to share his thoughts during dinner at Art Modell's home. He listed some things he felt were wrong, and even put in a plug for better public relations, citing the Dallas Cowboys as an example. The networks and national magazines loved the Cowboys, and the players noticed such things. They got a boost from them.

Modell reddened and raised his voice. He was not going to listen to Frank Ryan on PR—he had been an advertising man himself. And speaking of public relations, he went on, one thing he could live without was Joan Ryan's column. He considered it terrible.

"Joan ," Frank said tightly. "We'd better go."

At the door the Ryans heard at their backs a forced chuckle and Modell calling after them, "Not that she isn't better than the other sportswriters in this town."

As a curtain line it was only slightly premature. Ryan was replaced as the starting quarterback a season later and released the one after in 1969.

Whatever came along—the years of study, football, their four sons, the moves from Houston to Los Angeles to Cleveland to Washington to New Haven—they were in it together. Joan once attracted the wrath of the fans of Dallas when she wrote that the Cowboys wouldn't win the big games with Don Meredith. Sacks of hateful mail spilled across her desk, but Joan was miserable mainly because Frank caught some of the overflow, and they booed the hell out of him when the Browns played in Dallas.

At his ease, Frank was nearly always gracious, sensitive, and modest. On game days he could be difficult, intense, and angry. In a lab or a classroom, he was precise and patient, a superb teacher, his students said. He even taught himself chess to make himself even more patient. You wondered how he did it, how he alternated between his two worlds.

"It it hadn't been for pro football," he said, "I doubt that I would have finished my studies. I'd have quit along the way and found myself a career. But you can't hold down a good job working only half a year. So pro football gave me the excuse to continue my education. I see nothing strange about it."

For years Joan had threatened to shoot him in the foot if he didn't retire. But when he did and could devote his time to science and the academic life, he was like a boy whose dog had died. "I hated seeing him in the backyard," Joan told a friend, "really grieving because he couldn't throw another Z-out."

"Well," countered Frank, "I love to throw Z-outs. I love to throw a football."

His mourning was interrupted by a call from Vince Lombardi in Washington. Lombardi wanted Ryan to play backup for the Redskins team he was then trying to rebuild. "And so that we all feel right about this," the coach said, "we'll pay you the same salary you were getting as a starter in Cleveland."

"I grew ten feet in two minutes," said Ryan. "I had not thrown my last Z-out. That accounted for five feet. The rest was because of the man who made the call."

Coaches were often confused by Ryan. They seemed to think that he spent his spare moments in his cellar, reconstructing the Frankenstein monster or something. The one who might have understood him, who might have gotten the best of what was left in him, died of cancer a year later. He stayed on a year after Lombardi's death, and when he retired in the spring of 1974 the news stories mentioned that he had thrown a total of seven passes in three years.

Not included in that figure was a meaningless pass in a pre-season game against the Boston Patriots. The Redskins were leading by four touchdowns when Ryan went in for the starter, Sonny Jurgensen. On his second series he hit a pass over the middle, then moved out of the pocket and had blockers in front of him if he wanted to take the first down. Instead he stopped.

The long arm whipped. A spiral rose high over the top of the grandstand, carrying until sixty yards away. A running back named Henry Dyer, wearing 32, Jim Brown's old number, caught it in full stride. But Dyer, no Brown, was caught from behind at the 3 yard line.

A running play failed, and another, and Ryan went to his tight end Mack Alston for the score.

After the game Joan was waiting for him with shiny eyes. "What a beautiful pass," she said. "That long one was the most beautiful pass of the day."

"I read the wind," said Frank with a smile. "I had help from a twenty-mile tail wind."

Ryan is in many respects a purist. The Astrodome and other indoor stadiums angered him long before other players began looking for plastic worms in the plastic carpet. He resented what it would take away from him, from a quarterback: the shifting winds, the muddy field, the wet football, the factors that create strategy and enlarge the drama and allow a man to *think.*

It is true that the most glorified quarterbacks are not necessarily the most interesting. Frank Ryan had integrity and he had an attitude and these are often seen as unconventional. He stayed on as athletic director at Yale for ten years, teaching math classes on the side, before going into business for himself.

A COLLEGE
OF ONE

Like Ryan, Dr. Charley Johnson did not believe that football should interfere with getting an education. This is a provocative theory and many are still waiting to see if it catches on.

Charley Johnson came out of Big Spring, Texas, with so little reputation that he went to New Mexico State on a basketball scholarship. There he attracted the notice of Warren Woodson, who was in the process of building a Border Conference football power. They played a throttle-open game in the desert, with Charley throwing and a stable of fleet backs, including Pervis Atkins and Bobby Gaiters, running a streak.

He finished second in the nation in total offense in 1959, led New Mexico State to an unbeaten season in 1960, appeared in the Sun Bowl twice, and was drafted in the tenth round as a future pick by the St. Louis Cardinals.

Charley never expected to stick. You might not believe it of anyone else, but he swears that he reported to camp in 1961 figuring he would last a few days, then he could go home and tell his buddies what the pros were like. Or maybe he would hang on through a preseason game or two and get a glimpse of Tittle or Unitas or Jim Brown.

Instead he made the team, and in the process he messed up his own game plan, which was to return to New Mexico State, finish his graduate studies, coach, and teach. He never imagined he would hang around for fifteen seasons, or that he would be able to combine his doctoral work with football. Of course, he did a lot of studying in his hospital labs.

Johnson had an edge even over Frank Ryan. Forget the years of classroom labor, the long hours in a white smock bent over test tubes simmering with exotic potions. Charley's education included a full year of study—as a kind of College of One—under professor Bobby Layne, the noted lecturer on human behavior, handoffs, and the science of third and long. This wasn't F. Scott Fitzgerald showing Sheila Graham which fork to use, or even Yogi Berra with Bill Dickey "learning me all his experiences." But it was close.

The year was 1965, and what a dramatic contrast they must have made, the two Texans from overlapping eras. There was Layne, a legend: flamboyant, fiercely competitive, impulsive, always living for the moment. And Johnson: studious, sensitive, methodical, thinking years ahead.

The Cardinals the year before had lost the Eastern Conference title to Ryan's Cleveland team by a half game. Charley Johnson looked around and noted that no one on the club, or the coaching staff, knew more about playing quarterback than he did—and he had been a starter for roughly two seasons.

"I decided," he said, "that my lack of experience had hurt our ball club, that we were not getting the quality of play that might be available. There were things I could do well. We moved the ball. But I felt I was ready to learn from someone who had played a lot of years, someone who had been successful. I went to our coach, Wally Lemm, and asked if he knew of anybody who could come in and spend a year with us, who had actually been there. A lot of things had happened to me on the field that I was reacting to without knowing why. I didn't know what I should have been doing and no one on our coaching staff even understood what I meant."

Lemm was not the kind of coach who resented a player showing an interest in the team. He immediately placed a call to Lubbock, Texas, and a few weeks later Charley was shaking hands with Bobby Layne. If he had entertained any worries about how they would mix—the volatile old pro and the modest young scholar—Layne soon dispelled them.

"He was so happy to be there," says Johnson, "he floored me. He won me over completely. I knew I could talk to him. I had played against him at the end of his career. The safety blitzes had just come in, and some of the other blitzes were new and had really gotten to him. But he knew the thought processes you ought to go through and we could talk about those things."

Whenever Charley wasn't in class or in the chemistry lab at Washington University, he was with Layne. They talked, they diagramed, they compared. Bobby drilled into him the importance of establishing a running game, of setting up the pass, of creating a rhythm. If a quarterback throws three consecutive incompletions, he pointed out, he may have used only twenty seconds on the clock. "Now—boom—your defense has to go right back in there again, their tongues hanging out."

One of Johnson's problems had been not knowing how to reduce the pressure when the team was tense and the air seemed to have been sucked out of the ballpark [a common problem and one Ryan had mentioned]. "Bobby would tell me, 'Just give it to the fullback up the middle.' And I learned the value of doing something like that to release the tensions." Layne also drilled into him that one wrong call can lead to a series of bad ones, and if you are not sure what to do, "Throw the ball to your grandmother in the fifteenth row."

It was an ideal arrangement, of course, not unlike a young law student sharing Bernard Baruch's park bench. It would have been a terrific story if the Cardinals had gone on to win the championship, with Charley Johnson performing wondrous deeds while Bobby Layne looked on from the sideline, a small puddle forming in his baby-blue eyes.

It didn't quite work that way. The Cardinals had won four in a row and the writers were hailing Layne as a kind of Svengali, when the team fell through the trapdoor. Johnson separated a shoulder in the fifth game, tried to come back a week later against the Giants, and ruined himself for the season. They lost the game, 14–10.

"I've got some fond memories of Bobby and me bawling in New York that night," he says. "I stayed over for a speech and Bobby decided to stay behind too. We just couldn't believe that everything we had talked about and worked for had been wiped out. But we both knew it was. It was pretty frustrating. I remember Bobby hired a limousine and flashed a pocketful of money and had his main man drive us around. We went to a bunch of places and that's about all I remember."

If any one word could characterize the career of Charley Johnson, the word would be frustration. He ranks among a handful of quarterbacks who passed for more than twenty thousand yards. Yet he never played in a game where a title was on the line. His career was interrupted not only by his many operations, but by a hitch in the U.S. Army, just when his skills had begun to mature.

Charley was one of those athletes about whom writers lost their critical faculties. There was no temper or malice or meanness in him. He had a disarming way of making football sound as though it were still played by real people, not robots, a sport in which personal feelings counted.

No one ever doubted his desire. In 1970 he injured a knee, broke a collarbone, and played with five metal screws in his left shoulder, wearing a linebacker's shoulder pads. You ask him why he put up with it, why he came back from all those operations, why he persisted in playing a boys' game when he had all that knowledge in his skull, and he replied: "Each time it was the chance to be a part of something. In 1965, when I hurt my shoulder, I thought we had a chance to be real good. In 1966, after my first knee operation, we had the same guys and, I thought, the same potential."

Soon the Cardinals were going downhill, and then Wally Lemm quit and went back to the Houston Oilers. Johnson could never get comfortable with the new coach, Charley Winner, and when Lemm swung a trade that brought him to Houston he was elated. "I really felt I was hurting the club in St. Louis. The trade to Houston kept me going. A desire to play again for Wally and help him turn it around there. That kept me going through 1971, through the two surgeries on my right knee.

"By 1972 I had accepted in my own mind a backup role to Dan Pastorini and Lynn Dickey. It made sense for the Oilers to go with the young quarterbacks and I felt I could pass on to them the things I had learned from Layne. I was looking forward to it . . . and then I got traded to Denver."

John Ralston was building the foundation for a Super Bowl contender in Denver, but not many realized it at the time. He would not be around to take any bows. Neither would Charley. Craig Morton would be the quarterback in the heyday of the Orange Crush, followed by the electrifying John Elway.

The relationship between Ralston and the new fellow was a wary one at first. Ralston had to weed out some veterans when Charley arrived, ones who had grown complacent, or couldn't take seriously an emotional coach who made his rep at Stanford. And here was an aging quarterback with bad knees and an IQ that was out there where the meter didn't register.

"The players accepted me before John did," recalls Johnson.

"It took about three weeks. I went out and did everything he asked me to do. He knew about my knees but I didn't ask for any special treatment. I think he decided then that I wasn't around just to pick up a check."

Johnson liked Ralston's style. He liked it when the Broncos hit a big one, and you looked up, and the coach had raced from midfield to the end zone to greet the guy who scored. Something else impressed him: "He was a rare individual in one respect. He could make a decision, and if it turned out badly, he had the capacity to come back and face the guys and say, 'I made a poor decision,' and not be any lesser a man for it."

For Denver, 1973 was the millennium, the first winning season the Broncos had ever experienced. They finished 7–5–2 and tied with Kansas City for second place in the AFC West. "We went right to the last game of the season in Oakland, down to the last few minutes, with a chance to win our division. It was an exciting thing to get that close, to be right there, battling the Raiders."

If it really doesn't matter whether you won or lost—and it doesn't, according to the One Great Scorer—then Charley Johnson deserves to be remembered as one of the able quarterbacks of his time. Certainly he would receive high marks under the how-you-played-the-game clause. What can't be computed is the point spread between his years of classroom grind and that Sunday kind of love.

This is a fellow who for five years in St. Louis was up at dawn for a seven-thirty class at the Washington University graduate school, then hurried to the football field for daily practices from eleven to three, and then back to the campus for evening labs. Five years of it. All of which earned him a doctorate in chemical engineering, specializing in something called polymer plastics and the science of rheology, which has to do with the behavior and flow of plastics.

Do you remember the deathless scene from the movie *The Graduate* where Benjamin is milling around looking lost at a party in his honor? A drunken guest corners him and says confidentially, "I have just one word for you. Plastics."

Remember? Well, Charley Johnson had heard the word and had gone a few dimensions beyond it. He did his Ph.D. research on *polyimidazopryolene,* which, as you no doubt know, is the name for a family of plastics developed by scientists at NASA. And no one knew what to do with the stuff. During his two-year hitch in the army, Charley was an artillery officer assigned to Langley Research Center in Houston. They gave him a budget and laboratory and asked him to find an application for the plastic—a bomb, maybe, or a better football helmet.

"I found a way," he said, "to make it melt and to mold it. NASA pursued it and got a patent on the process. Like so much of the research that goes on, it turned out not to be very practical. It's the next generation of plastics after Teflon, but there was no way to use it then. For one thing, it cost up to two thousand dollars a pound. It was too expensive even to use it in the nose cone of the reentry vehicles for the space flights."

Moving easily from one glamour industry to another, from plastics to pro football, Charley Johnson must have had a notion that success was a mighty elusive quality. To look at him, with his country good looks and west Texas twang and wheat-colored hair, you would not suspect that after his name he was entitled to use the initials B.S., Ch.E.; M.S., D.Sc. (translation: bachelor of science, chemical engineering; master of science, doctor of science).

What he really needed was a great offensive line to block for him. "As a player," he said, "I never considered myself an intellectual. I don't know if there is even room for an intellectual on a football team. Any help I've gained in football from the education I've had is from the discipline of learning and remembering."

At an even six feet, he was never as tall or as bulletproof as his coaches wanted. But he could pick at a defense as few others could, and he had a fine, quick arm. He wouldn't bring the fans to their feet with a 70-yarder, but that was never his style. He didn't thrill a crowd, he charmed it.

Some football people wondered how Charley might have fared if he had not led two lives. As it was, the best he could do was take two teams, the Cardinals and the Broncos, to the brink of winning. But Charley doesn't wonder. "I like to think," he says, "that hard work is the harassment you have to take to get into society. To join the fraternity. I started graduate school in 1961 and I finished in 1971. But you don't think about how long it takes. It was more like learning a new offense, and staying with it until you get it right."

Of course, the coach has not yet been born who will tolerate a quarterback who needs ten years to master the system. But Charley recalls with amusement that he endured more wise-cracks in the classroom than in the locker room. To his profes-sors and the other doctoral candidates, he was their "token jock."

After he left football, he started two companies with other partners, one of which grew into a twenty-million-dollar-a-year operation. Now he runs his own, a company that leases natural gas compressors.

Irresistibly you return to the question of why? What com-pelled him to maintain two schedules—which is at least one more than most of us—for a decade of his life? Where did he get the drive, the energy, the ambition, the time?

Dr. Charley Johnson laughed. "I started working when I was pretty young," he says, "at summer jobs . . . sacking groceries, delivering laundry, picking up trash, all those things. My home-town was in the middle of a big oil field, in the Permian basin, in west Texas. The guy that wore the tin hat and walked around with a clipboard under his arm, he was called the engineer, and I wanted to be one of those because he didn't have to push a shovel. So I had some inspiration, first of all, to be an engineer and to be educated."

You don't have to hear him say so to know that Charley Johnson is the type who believes that everything happens for the best. The wins, the losses, the trades, the injuries. Yes, even the twelve operations. And when he left the hospital he remem-bered to thank everybody, including the guy who brought in the bedpan.

Once he was explaining to a writer why he spent the time to answer, personally, the letters he received from little kids. It had to do with growing up in Big Spring, in that vast ocean of sand known as west Texas, growing up poor and never seeing a sports star.

And then he caught himself . . . he had used the word "star," and for the next several minutes he apologized and explained that, of course, he wasn't referring to himself. "It's the position," he said, "being a pro quarterback, that's what they look up to."

He said it in the kind of voice people once used when they talked about the presidency.

☆ 11 ☆ THE ALTER EGOS

Pro football doesn't lend itself to Ruthian heroes; it depends too much on the group so that often the one who orchestrates the effort—the coach—commands the attention.

And that brings us to Otto Graham, whose career may be said to have defined greatness for pro quarterbacks. He was the finest mechanic of his time. He led his team to the championship game *every* season he played, which doesn't sound quite legal. He was not flamboyant, but he had style, a quality that is beyond talent.

Otto didn't smoke or drink—that made him 0–2, Sonny Jurgensen once said—and his values were right out of the Eagle Scout handbook.

When Graham was at Cleveland, one coach he most admired of Cleveland's rival teams was Buck Shaw, then of the 49ers. One day Graham started against the 49ers despite a heavily taped knee that should have kept him on the bench. On Cleveland's first series he threw a touchdown pass to Dante Lavelli and the Browns won easily. The 49ers sacked him at times during the day—he couldn't maneuver—but no one hit him unnecessarily hard. Later, he learned that Shaw had warned his team in the locker room, "The first guy who roughs up Graham gets fired."

His decent instincts did not prevent Shaw himself from being fired at the end of that season. But Graham recalls the incident warmly because it suggests that there was still room in the game for the gentlemanly gesture. As the game moves into the 1990s, it is hard, if not impossible, to picture a coach asking his defensive players to go easy on the other team's quarterback.

The old Browns, says Graham, "had two things going for them. We had one of the greatest coaches who ever lived, Paul Brown, and we had something else, an esprit de corps you find very seldom on a football team today. We didn't have the petty jealousies. It didn't matter who got the credit . . . who made the headlines . . . who scored. The important thing was, did you do a good job?

"The Browns stayed together. Paul Brown believed—he insisted—that we be a big, happy family. We'd bring our wives to camp, we'd hang out together, we had picnics, for heaven's sake. It worked because, for one thing, we didn't make the kind of money that allowed us to live like playboys."

Paul Brown set the standards of excellence for the NFL. He showed them how to scout, how to organize, how to demand more than a player thinks he has to give. Aside from the technical innovations Brown introduced—the draw play, the sideline pass, the face bar—he had a puritanical approach to coaching and winning. In training camp, players were not allowed in the dining room in a T-shirt. Some prospects were cut from the team simply because Brown found them obnoxious to eat with.

A man of cool reserve, in perfect control, icily calm on the sidelines—this was the picture of Paul Brown. And his always dapper attire reinforced the impression: trousers with a knife-edge crease, camel hair coat neatly buttoned up, a snap-brim felt hat squared away on his head.

Otto Graham subscribed as a player and later as a coach to what Brown called "eternal truths." These were rules spelled out in a speech he gave at the beginning of every training camp. When he spoke, he required his players to take notes. One year Brown traded a player who was talking during his speech.

"We're going to be as good a football team as the class of people you are," he would tell them. "We intend to have good people because they're the kind that win the big ones. If you're a drinker or a chaser, you'll weaken the team and we don't want you. If you think about football only when you step on the field, we'll peddle you . . .

"I like to think that the Cleveland Browns are different from the average professional team. I want to see exuberance in your play, some sign that you play for the sheer joy of licking somebody. We're the Ben Hogans, the Joe Louises, the New York Yankees of our game, and that's the way we want to keep it.

"I expect you to watch your language, your dress, your deportment, and especially, I expect you to watch the company you keep. That pleasant guy who invites you to dinner may be a gambler."

Otto Graham was the quintessence of Brown's vision of a quarterback. Paul chose him as his T formation leader on the basis of one play as a collegian. "When I was coach of Ohio State," says Brown, now eighty and still active in the ownership of the Cincinnati Bengals, "the only Big Ten game we lost was to Northwestern in 1941, fourteen–seven, and we lost it on a play where Graham ran left from the single wing, then threw back to his right to a man going lickety-split away from him, right on target, for the winning touchdown. I asked myself, 'What kind of player is this?' And he was the first man I picked for my Cleveland team."

Graham remembers it well: "My first year with Cleveland, Paul Brown signed me to a two-year contract for seventy-five hundred dollars a year. I was an air cadet at Glenville Naval Base at Evanston, Illinois, and Paul was at Great Lakes. I was making seventy-five dollars a month as a cadet and he offered me this two-year package, plus a bonus of one thousand dollars. But the big payoff was, if I signed right then, he'd pay me two hundred fifty dollars a month for as long as the war lasted. I signed. The war lasted only a few more months.

"After we won the championship my rookie season, he tore up the contract and gave me a new one for twelve thousand dollars a year. In 1955, my last year, my tenth, I was the highest-paid player in pro football at twenty-five thousand dollars. I suppose I could have gotten even more money out of Paul by becoming a holdout, but it never really occurred to me. What he offered always seemed fair and so I signed.

"Of course, we played for the title every year for ten straight years. They were great years, carefree years. When you went in to talk contract with Paul he always used the championship money as part of your salary. He would just add it on like interest on a note. We always got it and you could hardly negotiate against it.

"I suppose athletes then were more naïve. Certainly we still talked about things like sportsmanship and we didn't question everything. We accepted some things simply because they *were*. There weren't many prima donnas in the league. They got weeded out early because it just wasn't worth it to them to stick."

Brown's idea that "class people" were essential to a championship team was never more dramatically demonstrated than in his first year as a pro coach. Jim Daniell, a starting defensive tackle who had played for Brown at Ohio State before the war, was arrested for being disorderly and punching out a policeman the night before the Browns played San Francisco for the All-America Conference title. Brown kicked Daniell off the team and he never played another down of pro football. For years to come the Daniell example lived with the Browns to discourage curfew violators.

Of course, discipline wasn't difficult to enforce when the athletes were a special breed. "The players then," said Brown, "were not many years away from the hardship of war. This sort of transcended the way you played football."

Otto Graham agreed. "We didn't put a price tag on everything. When we were dominating the old All-America Conference for four years, the NFL kept knocking us. Well, when we played them for the first time, against the Eagles in Philadelphia in 1950, we had been looking forward to it for four years. We'd have played those guys anywhere, anytime, for a barrel of beer or a milk shake, just to prove we were a good football team.

Paul Brown didn't have to do anything to get us up for that game. If anything, he had to tone us down."

The war between the NFL and the All-America Conference, in a time of small parks and scarce dollars and little or no television, was the forerunner of the conflicts that would come with prosperity, fought by new leagues eager to share in the growth of the game.

The early Browns had as much to do with that expansion as any single team. They came into being in 1946, midwifed by a famous sports editor, Arch Ward, of the *Chicago Tribune*, who conceived baseball's All-Star game, then the College All-Star game, and finally, the All-America Football Conference.

The fellow who grabbed the Cleveland franchise was Mickey McBride, the owner of a taxicab company, a fanatic smitten with football because his sons went to Notre Dame. Later when Paul Brown insisted on keeping more players than the allowable limit of thirty-three, McBride circumvented the league rules by putting the extra players on his company payroll—thus originating the term "taxi squad" for handy reserves.

McBride, always promotion-minded, staged a contest to choose a name for his new team. The winning entry was actually the Brown Bombers, in honor of heavyweight champion Joe Louis, a Cleveland native. Soon the name was shortened to the Browns, which was clearly influenced by the admiration McBride and most of Ohio held for Paul Brown.

The first "official" season had a perfect denouement in matching the Browns in the 1950 title game against the Los Angeles Rams in Cleveland, the town the Rams had deserted after winning the NFL title in 1945. The Rams had assembled a team that many considered awesome. "They were like a Who's Who of pro football," said Brown, "with Glen Davis and Elroy Hirsch and Tom Fears, Waterfield and Van Brocklin." The Browns won a classic game, 30–28. To put it in a more modern context, it was as if the Kansas City Chiefs had edged the Green Bay Packers in the inaugural Super Bowl.

At the end of his career, Graham was to say, "I never played in a greater game than that one. It had everything." What it had mainly was a passing duel between Graham and Bob Waterfield. The Rams' opening strike on the first play of the game was an eighty-two-yard touchdown pass to Davis, who had been Mr. Inside at Army to Doc Blanchard's Mr. Outside.

Cleveland's respect for Tom Fears had made the play. Fears had set an NFL record that season with eighty-four catches and all Cleveland eyes were on him as he cut to the middle of the field. Davis hesitated two counts and curled into the area Fears had cleared. The linebacker who was supposed to cover Davis out of the backfield had gone with Fears, and Glen had an open path to the end zone.

The game symbolized the swing that pro football would take in the 1950s, when the passing game would be used to set up the run instead of the usual order. Both teams set their halfbacks out as receivers, leaving only the fullback to protect the passer.

They swapped touchdowns until a bad snap on an extra point attempt left the Rams ahead, 14–13. The lead changed hands twice, and with a minute and fifty seconds to play Graham got the ball at his own 32 yard line, trailing, 28–27, by the margin of that missed conversion.

"Nobody knew about sideline passes then, how to stop them," says Graham, "because this was our first year in the league and we had perfected it. Also, when a quarterback ran there was no one to cover him and you could pick up a few yards without anyone touching you." Graham began the series by running for fourteen yards. Then he threw to the left sideline to Rex Bumgardner, the right side to flanker Dub Jones, and then to Bumgardner again, who tumbled out of bounds at the Rams 11.

"Bumgardner made just one helluva catch right on his fingertips to set up the field goal," said Graham. When Lou Groza kicked it, only twenty-eight seconds showed on the clock. The Rams had one last shot. They called on Norm Van Brocklin, who had been kept out of the game with a rib injury.

From his 46, the Dutchman tried a bomb to Glen Davis at the goal line and Warren Lahr intercepted for the Browns. Few games ever saw a more dramatic game-ending play. "The thing that scared me about that pass," said Graham, "is what Davis did to Lahr. He tried to wrestle the ball from him in the air, and they were both heading for the end zone. They got into the end zone and Davis threw him down. What if the referee had signaled a safety? He didn't, because the momentum and Davis had carried Lahr in there, but I've seen crazier calls."

Brown left it to others to analyze his success. "When I think back," he says, "it never entered my mind that I wasn't right. The game was such an obsession with me. I could go into a game and actually visualize ahead of time the things that would happen—I suppose you get that way when you are involved in calling the plays. Obsessed is the word for it."

One of the things Brown was surest about was the wisdom of sending in plays to his quarterback. "It was never because Otto wasn't bright, because he certainly was. But nobody under the pressure of performing can give as much thought to play selection as he should. We were feeding in information from all our coaches in the press box, and we even had one sitting in the end zone. I was a quarterback myself—not a very good one—and in those days when you couldn't think of anything else, you'd run off tackle. What does a quarterback see when he makes a handoff? What part of the defense does he see? He doesn't see much. Field level is the worst vantage point in the stadium. Besides, I always felt that a coach calling the plays takes a lot of heat off the quarterback—and a lot of coaches don't want the responsibility. I didn't care. The players perform and get the credit. If people wanted to blast me for a dumb call, I could take it."

Brown had the one indispensable asset for his string of championships: the championship quarterback. When Graham defeated the Rams in 1955 and retired, the record he left behind— ten consecutive title games and seven wins—would be his legacy. It is quite possibly a record that will never be contested.

Brown says: "Otto Graham had the finest peripheral vision I've ever witnessed, and that is a very big factor in a quarterback. You know, he was an all-American in basketball and one year he played with Rochester in the NBA. He was a tremendous playmaker. I watched him in a game one night and I wasn't aware of him scoring, yet he ended up with twenty points. His hand-and-eye coordination was most unusual, and he was bigger and faster than you thought. Find another quarterback who took his team to as many championships.

"Otto was my greatest player because he played the most important position. He was the crux of how we got to things. I don't discount Marion Motley, Dante Lavelli, or Jim Brown. But the guy that was the engineer, the guy with the touch that pulled us out of many situations was Otto Graham."

After the war, Motley, the great fullback, and center Bill Willis at Cleveland reintegrated pro football, coming into the league in 1946 as Kenny Washington and Woody Strode were joining the Rams in Los Angeles. They were the first four blacks to be signed by the pros since 1933. Given the temper of the times, pro football had four Jackie Robinsons. Washington, who had been Jackie's college running mate at UCLA, played only three years. Strode lasted just one, then became an accomplished actor in Hollywood.

The steps taken to erase the traces of the color line were small ones, and slow. But they were also the hardest and the most meaningful because they were the first. On the Cleveland Browns, Coach Paul Brown had a rule. Whenever a rookie from the South reported, he had to first look up Marion Motley and Bill Willis, introduce himself and shake hands. There was no pretense that the gesture was voluntary. But it broke the ice and it worked.

Graham didn't always agree with the way Paul Brown ran his football team. He chafed at times under the play-calling system and he resented the discipline the coach rigidly enforced—until years later when Graham became a head coach himself with the Washington Redskins. "I was a clean-cut kid," says Otto. "I went to bed nights and got my rest, didn't drink, didn't smoke. When they came around to check my room I resented it. They knew I was in there. But what I didn't appreciate is that you have to check *every* guy—as an equal. You have to have discipline to the lowest denominator. If you've got an animal on the team you have to keep in a cage, then everybody has to go in a cage. I found out you have to crack down on guys—and that if you didn't have a curfew there would be a dozen guys who would go out the night before a game and get loaded.

"Paul Brown was just light-years ahead of everybody. I'm grateful I got to play under him. I learned an awful lot about football, about organization, about life. There were times when I hated his guts. I could have killed him. Other times I felt something close to love. All I know is, when I got into coaching I found myself doing and saying the same things that used to make me so mad at him.

"One night I ran out of the pocket a couple of times for what I considered a very valid reason. I didn't want to get my bones broken. He took me out, sent in George Ratterman, and walked over to one of his assistants five, six feet away from me. Loud enough for me to hear him, he said, 'At least, now we have someone in there with the guts to stay in the pocket.'

"Paul ran the game from the sideline like a computer, but at the oddest moments he would surprise you. During the championship game in 1950, I came out in the fourth quarter, two points behind, a minute and a half to go, after fumbling at the end of a good gain on a draw play. If I could have found a hole I'd have crawled in. As I crossed the sideline Paul came over to me, put his arm around my shoulder, and said, 'Don't worry, Ots. We're going to get them anyway.' He was right. We did get the ball back and we beat them on Groza's field goal with a few seconds left.

"When Paul began calling the plays from the bench I disagreed, but the whole thing was exaggerated over the years. I didn't like it, but I didn't resent it. Calling a play is nothing more than a guess. You see those movies where the quarterback raises up from the huddle, looks at the defense, then ducks down and calls the play. Well, that's baloney. Paul could see as much or more from the sideline than I could from the huddle. My complaint was that he didn't want me to audible. He did let me check off now and then, but I had to be *right*. The rest of the time, Paul called the plays and the record shows he called 'em pretty good.

"He thought of everything. He wanted us to have a familial

relationship, see, but he went to lengths to keep the wives from bickering with each other: 'Why won't your husband throw to my husband?' When they set aside the players' tickets for our home games, Paul used to personally separate the wives and had them sitting all over the stadium.

"Paul originated the notorious Tuesday Rule—no sex for all the married men after Tuesday. 'Save yourself for the game,' he'd tell us. We kidded about that. I guess it shows the morality of that time. Paul didn't recognize that sex existed outside of marriage. I kept asking him, 'What about the single guys?' and he'd never answer me.

"I don't think it is stretching the truth to say that he redesigned the game. He was the first to make football a year-round job for his coaches. The first to take his players to a hotel the night before a game in *their* hometown to get them away from the kids and the neighbors and distractions.

"We were the first team to carry notebooks. We'd start off each year talking about the most basic of fundamentals. He'd dictate to us and we'd write it down, things like how to do your calisthenics, the right way to touch your toes, how to form a huddle. Gawdamighty, after ten years I was still writing it all down. It was like being in the navy and hearing the same lecture on how to make hospital corners on your bed sheets. But you remembered.

"I got clobbered in one game and had to have a bunch of stitches taken on my lip inside my mouth. Paul had the equipment guy weld a bar across my helmet. It was so thick I could hardly see around it to pass. But I think that's how the face mask started."

Graham retains a sharp image of the game that used to be. "Every old-timer will always tell you how things were different in *his* time, but one thing I'm convinced of—we were more of a team. We cared about our teammates. Nobody was selfish. There was none of this, 'Well, I gained a hundred yards, so it was a great game and too bad we lost.' "

After he retired, Graham coached the college all-stars for thirteen years in their annual battle against the defending NFL

champions. "Every year," he says, "there were more prima donnas than there were the year before. All talking about the money
they had.

"I would have played just for the fun of it, and a lot of guys
felt that way then. I'd be out there hunched over the ball and
before calling the signals I'd wink at a guy across the way,
somebody I knew, letting him know we were coming right at
him. One time after Don Shula was traded to Baltimore, I looked
at him and winked and nodded—and then I completed a pass
right over him.

"But I was never that relaxed before a game. My stomach was
twisted in knots, and I went to the bathroom every five minutes.
Our pregame meal used to be steak and potato, no butter, dry
toast with no butter, and I'd choke on it. Never could get it
down. So I'd have a Hershey bar and an orange. Only one game
in my life I didn't get excited. That was the year I came back, in
1955, after I'd retired after the 1954 season. Paul called me up
the next summer and I came back. I woke up the morning of
my first game back and I told myself I was doing the Browns a
favor, so relax and enjoy it. I ate the pregame meal with no
trouble, and then went out and played the worst game of my
life. The papers were kind to me, saying I'd had a long layoff,
missed camp, but that wasn't it. Deep down I knew the reason
was my pregame attitude. After that, it was back to the Hershey bars."

There was no secret ingredient that made the Browns or himself a winner, says Graham. "I don't remember being obsessed
with football. I don't think we talked about it, or thought about
it, any more than the players today. We argued about the same
things as everybody else: the movies, women, politics, music.
The younger guys would bring their record players to camp.
Mostly it was rock and roll, except for Abe Gibron, who was
Lebanese. Abe was always playing those old Arab records, with
lots of wailing. You kept expecting to see a snake climb out
of a box.

"I don't know that we worked any harder than other teams.

We just had the greatest coach in the world, great players, and a lot of luck—particularly, luck that we all came together for those ten years."

The Browns did do at least one thing differently from other pro teams. Paul Brown had the quaint idea that his players should see a movie together the night before a game. "The players on the other teams used to laugh at us," Otto Graham remembered, "but we would whomp their ass on Sunday."

By the end of the decade Graham was comfortably retired and Milt Plum was the Cleveland quarterback. The code of Paul Brown was as stringent as ever.

In 1959 the Browns needed a win over the Steelers to keep pace with the Giants in the title race. These were the Bobby Layne Steelers, and adding pressure to the game was the talk that Buddy Parker had Paul Browns' number, the only coach in the league with an edge over him.

Cleveland's lanky Ray Renfro caught three touchdown passes, all bombs from Plum, but Layne put together a long drive against the clock. The Steelers scored to go ahead, 21–20, with only a few seconds left.

Everyone in the stadium knew what play Brown would call. Plum heaved the ball as far as he could—witnesses said the pass traveled seventy yards in the air—to a streaking Renfro down the left sideline. "It came down just about perfect," said Ray, "just on my fingertips. But when I hauled it into me, I was running so hard my knee came up and hit the ball and the ball went flying. The game was over.

"Renfro was standing there, sucking air and feeling cursed, when Paul grabbed his arm. He had run down the field to get to him. 'Renfro!' he said—he seldom yelled, but there was electricity in his voice. 'Renfro! You're through. You're all washed up. *You can't make the big play anymore!*' "

Decades later, the three touchdown passes Renfro caught that day were still the Cleveland record.

CATCH A
RISING STARR

Anyone who studies the reputation of Bart Starr—so efficient, so consistent, so patient—runs the risk of missing the best part of him. You miss the man.

It is clear from what he said in his prime as a player, and what he says now, that Starr in many ways agreed with the estimates of him. He never felt he had the heroic qualities of, say, John Unitas. He typed himself as colorless, if not humorless. He was not a naturally gifted performer, but one who worked slavishly to improve his skills. He learned to rely on his own deep and deceptive stock of raw nerve.

About the job of playing quarterback, Starr was purely and simply a fanatic. Sincerity is a fine quality, but it won't win many football games.

In many ways it is hard to get a handle on this unfailingly polite Alabaman with the perfect quarterback's name: *Bart Starr!* A musical name, a tall and evocative and yet a very sober name. It has flags in it and even a little circus. One would expect a Bart Starr to be flamboyant or at least dynamic. Instead, what the Green Bay Packers inherited in 1956 was a fellow of legendary niceness who never, ever went through the motions. It would take the Packers five years to discover that much.

Vince Lombardi answered the call in 1959, the most important arrival in Green Bay since Jacob Astor rode into town on a load of furs. You have to remember what the place was like when Lombardi blew in from an assistant coaching job in New York. In those years in Green Bay, when you saw someone on the street not wearing a mackinaw, you knew he was from out of town. Most police calls were to investigate complaints that a neighbor had shoveled snow onto the next yard. The population was sixty-three thousand, and there wasn't much to do except worry about the Packers. But by the mid-1960s, Green Bay called itself Title Town, U.S.A.

Lombardi was part missionary and part Machiavelli. He inherited a garbage dump, a team that had lost fifteen of its last sixteen games. Punishment was one of his favorite themes. As a coach he punished himself and he punished his players. A specialist in machinelike detail, he hammered and hammered, impressing his troops with the idea that winning is a habit that must be developed and sustained.

The Packers did not experience a losing season in the next ten years. When he left, Vince went out with a record unmatched by any other coach: 141 victories, 39 losses, 4 ties. The Packers had won five league titles and two Super Bowls.

Students of Lombardi declared Starr to be his masterwork, his personal monument in Green Bay, a manufactured superquarterback who pressed the buttons the coach had programmed. It was Starr who scored the touchdown that beat Dallas on the last day of 1967, in the snow and ice and fog, with one yard and thirteen seconds to go, with Green Bay trailing by three points in the conference final.

At game time the weather was thirteen below zero. The officials couldn't blow their whistles; the metal tore the skin from their lips. In this game the Packers did not become the Packers on finesse. Twice they went right at Dallas and twice the Cowboys stopped them. There was no way for Donny Anderson, their running back, to build up momentum on a field glazed with ice. Now there were at least three alternatives: (1) attempt a field goal to send the game into overtime, (2) throw a pass—an incompletion would stop the clock and still leave time to kick, or (3) put it all on the line in one more test, us or them, one more game-ending run, winner take all.

During a time-out, Starr went to the sideline and told his coach he could keep the ball and score. He didn't say "I think" or "I might." He said, "I can sneak the ball in," and Lombardi said, "You can? Then do it and let's get the hell out of here."

Of course, the rest is taught to Green Bay school kids before they learn the Pledge of Allegiance. Center Ken Bowman and guard Jerry Kramer double-teamed Jethro Pugh, and Starr swung to his right and plowed into the end zone. Does anyone remember if the Packers tried the extra point? They did not. The final score was 21–17.

Does anyone remember that the Packers blew a fourteen-point lead? Of course not. All they remember is that one play and one yard away, the Packers didn't get cute. For Lombardi there was really no choice. You don't build a dynasty on his kind of philosophy and then take the easy way, not when it is all there in front of you.

The Packers went on to overpower Oakland in the second Super Bowl as easily as they had handled Kansas City in the first. Before anyone else, Lombardi knew that age and success had taken a toll and the era was ending. Injuries had forced Vince to use six different backfields that season and during one stretch he lost Starr for five games.

Paul Hornung and Jim Taylor were gone. Lombardi was retiring to the front office and within a year would leave for Washington. In three he would be dead of cancer.

The "Ice Bowl" game against Dallas ever since has been referred to as a microcosm of all Lombardi stood for and believed. Starr used the phrase to describe his own career. For drama, for the arctic hardships of the day, for the heavyweight ending, the game clearly outstripped even Green Bay's two Super Bowl victories. Lombardi and Starr huddling in the icy twilight, the lead block by Kramer, these were the lasting images that emerged from the fog and snow.

This may smack of revisionist history, but some would come to feel that Starr was a great leader not because of Lombardi, but in spite of it. Nor is this judgment meant to be a negative one. In the mid-1960s, Starr asserted himself, took charge in the huddle, scolded and corrected and drove his teammates. Isn't this what a quarterback is paid to do? Yes, but imagine the power of will that was required when the most dominant coach in the game was a sideline away.

Bullied by Lombardi, geared to begging for his approval, the Packers would not give their respect to one without a steely character. And Starr had this quality. His problem was expressing it. Modest, intelligent, courteous, with a deep religious faith—these were the words his friends used to describe Bart.

"There is a softness in him," said Jerry Kramer. "A sort of gentle manliness. But there is also an iron-hard spirit. I recall when we were playing the Bears . . . Bill George came through and hit Bart in the mouth. A real good shot. Blood all over. 'That'll take care you, kid,' George said. You should have seen Bart. He snarled right back. Challenged him right there. 'You big SOB,' Bart said. And he was ready to fight. That's one thing about this game. You have to be ready to fight and Bart was."

Much of Green Bay's success was tied to Starr's understanding of his coach. Cool and unruffled, Bart realized that temper must not be met with temper. So he played away from the moods of Lombardi, for whom he had enormous respect as a teacher and tactician. The combination of Vince's brains and Bart's execution won an awful lot of games.

And what is this area of football intellect if not a marriage? As in real life, the oracles tell us two people of the same nature should seldom wed. A pair of hotheads fight and a pair of calm ones get bored.

You try to see Lombardi through the eyes of Starr, as the shy, acquiescent, self-conscious young man he once was. Performing in front of the new coach for the first time, in a scrimmage, Starr threw a poor pass into a crowd, the kind of pass Lombardi would not tolerate. "One more like that," Vince roared, "and you're through here."

It was the first pass the coach had seen him throw. "He scared me to death."

Of course, Lombardi spared no one. Jerry Kramer jumped offsides once and Vince screamed at him: "The concentration span of a college student is fifteen to twenty minutes. A high school student, ten to fifteen minutes. A kid in grammar school, maybe one minute. Now where the hell does that leave you?"

And in training camp one night, Marie Lombardi sat next to her husband during the evening meal. When she asked a waiter for a scoop of vanilla ice cream for her apple pie, he slapped the table and glared at her. "No! When you eat with the team, you eat what the team eats." He sent her dessert back to the kitchen.

Starr never quite shed the feeling that he was fortunate to be there at all. He was content to sit on the bench, behind Tobin Rote and Lamar McHan, picking up tips, making no waves, more or less resigned to the notion that he did not deserve to start. In his book, *Run to Daylight*, Lombardi said:

"When I joined this team, the opinion around here and in the league was that Starr would never make it. They said he couldn't throw well enough and wasn't tough enough, that he had no confidence in himself and no one had confidence in him . . .

"After looking at the movies that first preseason, I came to the conclusion that he did have the ability—the arm, the ball-handling techniques, and the intelligence—but what he needed was confidence."

Lombardi did not exactly give Bart's confidence an instant boost by trading for McHan and making him the starting quarterback. Starr, in fact, was running third string behind the anonymous Joe Francis. Bart was disappointed but took refuge in his glad-to-be-here attitude. In truth, he felt unprepared. He had been benched as a senior at Alabama by a new coach, Ears Whitworth, who had decided to play his sophomores. Starr was a long time recovering from that demotion. "I was not," he said, "emotionally mature."

He didn't expect to stick with the Packers, who drafted him in the seventeenth round. One good half in a preseason game against the Giants may have saved him. He was sort of surprised to still be around five years later. There had been one highlight: He passed for 320 yards in a 1958 loss to the Colts, who were on their way to the championship.

He was rooming in those years with Tobin Rote, "one of the toughest guys who ever played, an unbelievable competitor. He helped me as much as anyone ever did. We'd talk half the night on the road. I developed a great respect for what Tobin went through. The Packers were not strong or well staffed, there wasn't anywhere near the team balance I would enjoy under Lombardi. In one game Rote was knocked goofy and they had to help him to the sidelines. Frankly, I was a little thrilled. I got into the huddle and I thought, 'Well, it looks I'm going to get to play for a while.' And on the next play Tobin was right back in there. I took one snap."

In the middle of the 1959 season, the Packers lost Lamar McHan with a separated shoulder. Joe Francis finished the game as Starr never left the bench. That was as low as a low point can get. But later in the season he opened against the Redskins and guided the Packers to a 21–0 win. For the Packers, and for Starr, the game was a turning point. They won their last four and finished with a 7–5 record, their best since 1945.

Starr emerged as the ideal quarterback to test the Lombardi theory: The team that errs least wins the most. Power and precision became the Packer trademarks—they almost never gambled. Vince implored his backs to run to daylight, and in Paul Hornung and Jim Taylor he had the big backs to make the system work.

If the press and the public perceived Starr as a robot, but one with an accurate arm, he didn't seem to mind. "If people called me an extension of Lombardi," he says now, "well, I kind of feel that I was. Those statements didn't degrade me a bit. I took it as a compliment. I was extremely lucky because, by the time Coach Lombardi came to the Packers, I was receptive to his message. I was ready to play."

Starr grew. His outbursts were rare but they commanded attention. Once, reserve tackle Steve Wright missed his block on a Pittsburgh defensive end, Lloyd Voss, and Voss not only reached Starr but delivered an openhanded blow across his mouth. In the huddle, Bart's eyes flashed as he said: "Steve Wright, you ought to be ashamed of yourself, letting Lloyd Voss in here. I'll tell you one thing. If I see that guy in here again, I'm going to kick somebody in the can. Not him. You. I'm going to kick you in the can in front of fifty-two thousand people."

Voss did not get through again.

"The fact is, once the game started, I led them," says Starr. "I did it my own way, but I did it. You have to prove yourself. You could define leadership a lot of ways, but in the end it has to be measured by performance. You can't lead from the bench. You can't lead when you play poorly. I was a quiet leader because that was my style, that was my personality, and the results are there."

Starr and Otto Graham had this in common: They were not the rebellious type, and both were programmed by coaches who were in their time the sport's most demanding. Bart sees the similarity, but takes a tiny bite out of the myth when he suggests that preparation, not inspiration, made Paul Brown and Vince Lombardi tick. "Both went to extremes," he said, "to prepare their players and their coaching staffs. There was never a doubt in my mind what Coach Lombardi wanted done. I can't speak for Otto in his days, but we just killed teams using audibles. The defenses were not as well disguised. You could read them instantly when you walked to the line of scrimmage. I'd see something and check off . . . we made a living doing that."

Starr is considered by many the finest third-down quarterback who ever lived. That skill and others were more sharply appreciated as he moved out from under the shadow of Baltimore's virtuoso, Johnny Unitas.

"Unitas was a star when I was still sitting on the bench," he says. "I studied film of him for two years before I became a starter, just trying to improve myself. We played them twice a year, and it was always special. I knew I was going against the best quarterback in the game.

"I never felt that I was shortchanged in the recognition I received. I had a great team and a great coach around me. I think Tom Landry and Roger Staubach meshed brilliantly in Dallas. Roger executed the Cowboy system as well as a quarterback can. To me that said it all: Here was the system and here was the leader and, holy mackerel, when they were clicking it was impressive to watch.

"I always regretted that when Lombardi went to Washington he was a sick man. I've told Sonny Jurgensen, I wish he could have played for the Lombardi I saw in Green Bay. No telling how many titles they would have won. Jurgensen is one who comes to mind when you think of a quarterback with a great arm, whose timing was unlucky. He never had the system, or the supporting cast, or the right coach in his prime."

If we read Bart correctly, he seems to be suggesting that given time Vince would have ridden Sonny's arm to even higher altitudes. It is an oddly generous thing to say, even from one famed for his modesty.

Starr capped his career by being chosen the MVP of each of the first two Super Bowls. Against Kansas City in January of 1967, he burned the Chiefs seven times on third-down passes. One of them went for thirty-seven yards and a first-quarter touchdown to Max McGee, who reached back and speared the ball with one hand. Another set the stage for a fourteen-yard scoring run by fullback Jim Taylor as the Packers led by four at the half. They broke it open in the third quarter and went on to win, 35–10. "The only difference I can see between the two leagues," said a Kansas City lineman, "is Bart Starr."

The Packers had acquired an aura. Before the game a defensive tackle for the Chiefs, Jerry Mays, spoke of his admiration for Forrest Gregg, who had played some years ahead of him at SMU. When the Packers were lining up on the goal line, Jerry Kramer turned to Gregg, who played beside him, and whispered, "I'll get number seventy-eight, and you take the guy whose hero you are."

Starr did not have a great day against the Raiders the next year. He didn't need one. His good, solid, steady games were a form of art and that was what Green Bay required to put away a physical Oakland team, 33–14. The key play came on Green Bay's third possession, after the Packers had settled twice for field goals by Don Chandler. Oakland blitzed and Starr picked it up. He spotted Boyd Dowler open behind the cornerback and unloaded a pass that went sixty-two yards for a touchdown.

Still, there are other dimensions to Bart Starr and to his story. He was primed for a productive career in business when he agreed in 1974 to accept the Packers' coaching job. He had caved in at last to the public pleas, to the intermittent pressure that had existed through most of the Dan Devine regime. The Packer faithful dreamed of a restoration, a return to the glory years of

Lombardi, and who better to lead them than the player who was the symbol of those seasons. After all, he was Vincent's creation.

But there was one small oversight. The directors of the team, the fans, and to a lesser degree, Bart himself had managed to ignore the fact that he had almost no experience. He had coached the Packer quarterbacks for two fleeting seasons.

The town of Green Bay celebrated the return of one of their own, but Starr discovered to his dismay and his regret, sometimes you can't go home again. He could not turn the Packers into contenders, though in four of his last five seasons they finished .500 or better. He held the job nine years and he said later, privately, to close friends: "I didn't know anything when they begged me to take the job. By the time they fired me, I had finally learned how to coach."

It was a sad and painful twist in what had been a football fairy tale. Lombardi ruled the icy Wisconsin village like a Duke of a duchy, but Green Bay turned on Starr. It was his Siberia. He was fired Christmas week in 1983 and replaced by Forrest Gregg, who didn't sign on for the duration either. Gregg had been a successful head coach with the Browns and guided the Bengals to the Super Bowl.

He misread the situation in Green Bay, however. The game had changed. The money had changed. The players had changed. Only Green Bay itself was still unchanged from the 1960s. Gregg quit after the 1987 season to return to his alma mater, SMU, rebuilding from zero after being the first school in history to receive the death penalty for repeated recruiting violations.

There was a moment exquisitely awkward and sensitive in October 1984, when twenty-nine members of the first Super Bowl champions showed up in Green Bay for a reunion. They had not met as a group in eighteen years and a few of them had decided it was time.

The big suspense was whether or not Bart Starr would make an appearance. His home was then in Phoenix, where he headed a local group hoping to attract an NFL expansion franchise (an effort disbanded after the Cardinals moved from St. Louis). Although he kept an office in Milwaukee and a ranch house in nearby De Pere, he had not been back to Green Bay since his firing. No one doubted that the hurt and the resentment were still there.

He went, of course, not out of a sense of debt to the franchise but because his old teammates urged him, and he still cared about the fans, most of them. He flew into town the day before the game and went first to his empty house, where he thought about the first time he had invited Coach Lombardi to visit. Vince had sat down in the living room, in front of the fireplace, and told Bart and Cherry Starr what a lovely home they had. Bart had said simply, "Thank you. We owe it all to you." And Lombardi had taken out a handkerchief and wiped tears from his eyes.

The 1967 champions were to be introduced on the field before the Packers met the San Diego Chargers in their sixth game. The team was 1–5. It was not a perfect time for a festive occasion.

Just before the ceremonies started, the Packers finished their warm-ups and the players came through the tunnel leading to the locker room, passing in front of the old-timers. Forrest Gregg saw Bart Starr and stopped. They were two graying, fifty-year-old men who had been friends and teammates for fourteen years. One can only imagine the array of emotions that filled them both. Players were brushing by them on both sides, and Starr said quietly, "Good luck."

If ever a man looked as if he wished he knew the magic words, it was Forrest Gregg at that moment. He couldn't get the words out. He said, "Thanks," and when the two men brushed hands there was a light metallic click, the sound of Super Bowl rings connecting.

Starr doesn't talk about the reunion or his firing. "There just isn't anything I care to say," he explained. "I didn't know how to handle it at the time. I didn't go in there reluctantly. I was proud to get the job. But I felt like they knew what they were getting. My regret was that I hadn't had time to prepare myself. If I had sought the job, I would have first apprenticed under the best coaches in the business. When I went in there, I would have been qualified. I would have been ready to win."

The quietness of Starr should never be taken for an absence of thought or feeling. He has provided a hopeful example of how to cope when a bad or tragic thing happens to good people. In July 1988, his younger son, Bret, twenty-four, was found dead in his apartment in Tampa. The cause of death was cardiac arrest brought on by a toxic reaction to a minimal amount of cocaine.

Bart had described in his autobiography how his son had rebelled in his teens, rejected sports, dropped out of college, drifted, and finally fought hard to break his drug addiction. By Christmas 1985, the Starrs had thought he had turned a corner.

If he was reluctant to discuss his firing in Green Bay, Bart talked openly about Bret's death. If that position struck anyone as odd, he didn't know Bart Starr. On the one hand, his dismissal by the Packers affected no one else and he chose not to share his hurt. Drugs are a social problem and he felt an obligation to speak out.

Bret Starr died because he wasn't aware of the deadly reaction a small amount of cocaine might cause in a system cleansed of drugs. He was, in a sense, allergic to it. His doctors said that tests disclosed only "traces" of cocaine. It was just enough to kill him.

In the year after Bret's death, Bart and his wife, Cherry, traveled around the country speaking to groups on drug awareness. "We knew for a fact that Bret had been clean for over twenty months," said Starr. "He had been seeing a sports psychologist in Tampa, was subject to random testing.

"I asked him when I wrote the book how he felt about my mentioning his problem. He said, sure, that I ought to write about it. After his death I felt a heightened need to do more. The medical examiner in Tampa heard I was making speeches. He called and said, 'If you take no other message out there, please get this one across: It doesn't take an overdose to kill a person who has been chemically dependent and gotten off it. A taste will do it.' We believe that was what Bret did. It must have seemed harmless.

"Of course, we have second-guessed ourselves to tears at times. That isn't healthy but everybody does it. I have often wondered how much my coaching affected him, how much time it took away from him. My older son, Bart Jr., who is now thirty-two, came along when I was a player, and the Packers were enjoying their great successes. He hung around the locker room.

"When Bret came along, his big brother had been a fine golfer, a fine athlete, had a golf scholarship at Alabama. Bret could have been good at anything he tried. He had the instincts. I believe he didn't try because he was intimidated by the two of us who preceded him. For him the atmosphere [in Green Bay] was not very positive. It can't be fun to go to the stadium and hear your dad picked apart.

"Cherry has probably had the best perspective on what happened. 'We did the best we knew how and if we failed it was an honest failure. Bret knew how much we loved him and cared for him, he told us so in a letter he wrote us. He didn't have to guess, our family shared our love and I drew strength from that. A loss like that, well, you can make yourself sick trying to find some hope in it. But you do find that a lot people are thinking of you. There were thousands of letters. It took months just to read them."

It has been expressed many times, in many ways, the unique and terrible pain of a parent burying a child, a father burying a twenty-four-year-old son. Bart doesn't trivialize it by saying that the adversity he faced in football helped him cope. If you are Bart Starr, you reach out to others. You just go on. You don't quit.

He didn't learn that lesson from Vince Lombardi of course. It was in him all along, but these were principles Lombardi stressed and reinforced. And in a grieving time, they helped.

THE VINDICATION

No one, not even Unitas, came to the fullness of his glory in a manner more dramatic, or more troubling, than Len Dawson. In what should have been the triumphant week of his life, Dawson found his name smeared, his honesty questioned, his reputation and his future threatened.

His was a textbook case of how an athlete with an impeccable record can be drawn unaware into a spiderweb of intrigue, rumor, and the criminal justice system.

For the second time in four years, Dawson had quarterbacked the Kansas City Chiefs to the Super Bowl. They had lost the historic first one to the Green Bay Packers in the first face-off between champions of the once warring leagues. They had endured the taunts of pro football's older guard. And then in January 1970 they were back.

The year before, the New York Jets had shocked the Colts to give the patrons of the AFL their turn to howl and set the stage for the realignment of the leagues. So this one was a sentimental journey: Having come in peace for all mankind, the Chiefs would carry the flag of the sovereign American Football League for the last time. Minnesota, led by Indian Joe Kapp, a quarterback who liked to run over linebackers, was favored by twelve points.

Five days before the game, Len Dawson was patiently waiting for his wife and children to join him in New Orleans, the town that gave birth to the blues. The scene was as normal as the scene ever gets the week of a Super Bowl, but around the country events were converging that would leave the Kansas City quarterback twisting in the wind.

The story began with a man named Donald Dawson, no relation to Len, a kind of Damon Runyon character. He acquired the nickname Dice because he often won at craps, sometimes with loaded dice. He had a reputation as a "mechanic" at cards, a dealer of stacked decks. He was a golf hustler and bookmaker who cultivated the country club set around Detroit and Miami Beach.

He owned an elegant restaurant, The Fox and Hounds, in Bloomfield Hills, Michigan, and it became popular with the sports crowd. Dice Dawson was connected. When James Cavanaugh was mayor of Detroit, he was an occasional guest for dinner in the mayor's residence.

One of Dice Dawson's top clients was a wealthy trucker named Howard Sober, seventy-four, who had been introduced to him in 1967 by Dizzy Dean, the Hall of Fame pitcher. In two years Sober lost roughly a million dollars in bets he booked with Dawson. It was Sober, not Dawson, the Internal Revenue Service was tailing. When he tipped a skycap fifty dollars to phone in a two-thousand-dollar bet to Dawson, the IRS recovered the note.

An IRS investigation into Sober's affairs turned up enough information on Dice Dawson to attract the interest of a Department of Justice strike force on organized crime. Their agents traced nineteen hundred phone calls Dawson had placed to sports figures, most of them to horse owners, jockeys, and trainers, some to bookies and mobsters, and a few to active players and at least one college coach.

These calls included three each to the homes of Len Dawson and Bill Munson, quarterback of the Lions; and five to Karl Sweetan, a backup then with the Rams, two of them to bars in Texas and Louisiana. In addition, there were some sixty calls to Frank Kush, the head coach of the University of Arizona, to both his home and office numbers.

What was said in any of these conversations was unknown, and a request by the Justice Department to put a tap on Dice Dawson's telephone line was tabled by the department's top echelon.

On New Year's Day in 1970, federal agents arrested Dice Dawson and eight others in Michigan, seizing $450,000 in checks and $171,000 in cash. Subsequent arrests in Las Vegas, New York, and Biloxi, Mississippi, brought to fourteen the number of suspects charged with violating interstate gambling laws.

In a televised press conference, a U.S. attorney named James Ritchie promptly announced, "Statements made by some of those arrested and seized records indicate a national scheme involving famous figures in baseball and football and hundreds of trainers and jockeys." The claim was an obvious, inflated, bloated attempt at headline grabbing. And it worked.

Five days before the Super Bowl game, NBC's respected *Huntley-Brinkley Report* obtained and broadcast the names of Len Dawson, Munson, Sweetan, and Kush, and said they were expected to be called as witnesses when a federal grand jury in Detroit began hearing evidence against Donald "Dice" Dawson.

Commissioner Pete Rozelle rushed to the defense of the players, pointing out that nothing had yet surfaced that would provide grounds for disciplinary action. All the players agreed to submit to lie detector tests; Len Dawson, in fact, had secretly taken and passed a test a year earlier when the Chiefs had been the subject of point-spread rumors.

Len had acknowledged knowing the other Dawson "for about ten years." He knew him as the owner of a fine restaurant, he said. Their only conversations in recent years had been brief. In a couple of the calls, Dice asked Len how his knees were. One call was simply to offer his sympathies over the death of Len's father.

Len Dawson was waiting with some of his teammates for an elevator in his motel that Tuesday, when Jim Schaaf, the Kansas City publicity director, beckoned him over to a quiet spot against the wall. It was hard to miss the look of alarm on the broad face of Schaaf, himself a onetime Notre Dame lineman. In a voice just above a whisper, Schaaf told Dawson that his name had been dragged into a gambling scandal; the story moving now on the news wires. There would be more that night on the *Huntley-Brinkley Report*.

Schaaf might as well have been speaking in Swahili. Dawson had him repeat every word. He didn't know what he was supposed to say; what could a federal investigation possibly have to do with him? His mind raced quickly to the only issue that mattered: Was there any chance these charges could keep him from playing Sunday?

Schaaf didn't know. He touched Dawson's arm, a protective gesture, and told him to stay out of the lobby. "It might be a good idea," he said, "if you changed rooms. In a few minutes this place will be swarming with reporters."

It occurred to Schaaf that he needed to find Coach Hank Stram before the press did. Stram, portly, cocky, a fashion plate, had been Dawson's backfield coach at Purdue, had recruited him out of high school. After Lenny vegetated for five years in the NFL, Stram gave his career a new life with the team then known as the Dallas Texans. Schaaf led Dawson back into the dining room and found Stram lingering over his lunch. Lenny looked on, dazed, as Hank absorbed the snippets of information. "I agree with Jim," he said. "For the time being, you'll be better off in the room we set aside for looking at films. No one will find you there."

Dawson was all but at sea. He wondered if he should call his wife. What would he tell her? What would his teammates think? He didn't know who his accusers were or exactly what had been alleged. What if he had to leave the team, fly to Detroit to testify? Blindly he made his way to the film room. He was glad to be alone, to have a few minutes to collect himself.

The door kept opening and players piled in. He had forgotten that a team meeting had been called to review a Minnesota playoff film. He looked around the room, he searched the faces of the team's other quarterbacks—Jacky Lee, Mike Livingston, and Tom Flores. It was quickly apparent that no one had heard anything.

Dawson had no sense of how much time passed before the projector snapped off and the lights came up. He saw Jim Schaaf duck into the room and whisper to Stram. The coach slapped his hands and said, "Okay, that's it. Len, stick around for a minute, will you?"

The Chiefs were virtually keeping an open line to Pete Rozelle's office in New York, but so far the picture was no clearer than it had been when the story first exploded. Stram and Dawson dawdled in the film room another hour, replayed the game film that Lenny again watched with unseeing eyes. Finally Stram said, "Hell, we can't sit here all day. We all need some rest."

It was decided that Dawson would slip into the room reserved for Stram's kids, adjoining his own. The two of them ran up three flights of stairs, Stram puffing slightly. He let Dawson in with his key, told him to get his mind off things and try to rest. Lenny sat on the side of the bed, kicked off his shoes, and thought, "Boy, that's easy for him to say."

When the burly Schaaf returned to his own hotel suite, two writers were waiting for him. "Will there be a lot more coming?" he asked as he unlocked his door.

"I'm afraid so, Jimmy," said one of the reporters.

Schaaf nodded, walked to the phone, and picked up the receiver. "Hello, room service?" he said. "Send up five pounds of shrimp remoulade." It was going to be a long night and bumpy night.

Dawson couldn't sleep, couldn't rest, couldn't read. He kept hearing the phone ring in the other room. Then Stram opened the inside door and said, "The league security people want to talk to you. How do you feel about that?"

"It's all right with me," said Len. "I've got nothing to hide and I want to find out what I'm being accused of . . ."

Then a debate developed over where the interview should take place. Jack Danahy, the head of NFL security, was at the Roosevelt, the headquarters hotel for the game. Five hundred writers were registered there. Scratch the Roosevelt. Danahy ruled out the team's motel, fearing the writers would see him leaving and follow in hot pursuit. Then Stram delivered an ultimatum: "It's here or nowhere. Lenny stays with the team. He eats with the team. I'm not going to disrupt our whole schedule and get the squad upset over something we know nothing about . . . you want to see Lenny, you come to him."

The meeting was arranged for after dinner. Dawson again had to sneak down hallways and staircases and by then the word had spread among his teammates. Everyone tried to act normally. No one spoke. Dawson had the uncomfortable feeling of many eyes watching him move toward a table. He sat with the coaches, but when the food came he was unable to choke down more than a bite. He pushed his plate away and, over and over, stirred his coffee with a spoon. He checked his watch.

It was time to leave. He left the dining room through the kitchen and went around the back of the motel to the room the security people had occupied. Jack Danahy, a lawyer and former FBI agent, was waiting for him. His face, his eyes, were cold and serious. "I have to ask you some sensitive and personal questions," he said, "and I want you to answer me truthfully. We want to help you, do you understand?"

Dawson nodded. "Yes, I do," he said. "I've always told the truth and I have nothing to hide."

"Do you know a Donald Dawson?"

"Yes, I do."

"How well do you know him?"

"He's just a casual acquaintance, nothing more. He owns a restaurant in Detroit. I met him ten or eleven years ago when I was playing with Pittsburgh."

"How many times have you been around him?"

"About four or five times."

"When was the last time you spoke to him?"

"I talked to him on the telephone last November after my father had died. I was in Alliance, Ohio, for the funeral. He contacted my sister to find out where I could be reached and offered his condolences." Lenny mentioned the calls inquiring about a knee injury he had suffered early in the season. Dice Dawson's concern, he felt, was personal. "At no time did he seek other information that might be useful in gambling."

Of course, some would argue that the condition of a starting quarterback's knee can be useful, but Lenny's injury was no secret.

After a few more minutes of questioning, Jack Danahy said, "I believe what you've told us. I'm confident you had no connection with any of the gamblers, other than knowing Donald Dawson. We'll back you all the way on this."

Len Dawson's relief was in proportion to his puzzlement. No specific accusation had been made against him, and yet it was on the networks that he would be subpoenaed by a federal grand jury in Detroit.

"For now, don't worry about that," said Danahy. "We'll take it from here. Get some rest now."

Late Tuesday night, an official statement was released by the league office expressing confidence in Len Dawson's innocence. The statement added that he had cooperated with the league in similar circumstances in 1968, a fact that until then was unknown to the press. Dawson squirmed when he heard about this gratuitous disclosure. He consoled himself with the thought that the league's spokesmen must know what they were doing. He began to think about getting some sleep.

Minutes later there were knocks at his door. His hiding place had been discovered. A gaggle of reporters had appeared to take his own statement. He asked for time to confer with Stram and Jim Schaaf. The writers agreed. "Hey," said one, "we all know the pressure you're under."

The Chiefs worked out a strategy. Dawson would appear in the press room, deliver a brief, carefully worded statement, and leave. He would not submit to a press conference where the questions might run through the night. Lenny understood that there was a legitimate story here, one magnified by the Super Bowl backdrop. But he had to get it behind him. He needed to concentrate on the game.

Phone calls went back and forth to key people within the league, testing words, getting feedback. It was nearly 11:00 P.M. when Dawson walked into Jim Schaaf's suite, by now overflowing with writers. Slowly Lenny read the statement, describing his relationship with Dice Dawson, denying that he had been involved in, or was aware of, gambling activities by any parties known to him. He had not been contacted by the investigators in Detroit or by the Justice Department, and hoped that "any reference to me in this matter has been coincidental and unfounded. For my part this affair is now over with."

A path was cleared to the elevator and without another word, Len Dawson walked out of the room.

Twelve hours had passed since Jim Schaaf stopped him in the hall after lunch. He switched rooms again, and only after he locked the door behind him did he realize he had not yet talked to his wife, Jackie, in Kansas City. Her voice was hoarse when she answered the phone.

"Are you all right, honey?" she asked.

"Considering what I've been through," he said, "I'm okay. There's really nothing to worry about because I haven't done anything."

She had been told the news by one of the editors of the *Kansas City Star*. When Jackie insisted there had to be some mistake, the editor suggested, not unkindly, that she might want to talk to the family lawyer. Like everyone else, all the lawyer knew was what he had heard on television.

Jackie and the two children were due to arrive Friday. Len urged her to leave sooner to avoid any crank calls or harassment at home. She told him not to worry, that she could handle matters there and the children were taking it fine. She had told them to ignore the stories, stressing, "Your daddy wouldn't do anything wrong."

Dawson spent a sleepless night. Every time he felt himself dozing off, a thought turned over and he snapped awake. The next thing he knew, the sun was streaming through his window.

Wednesday is perhaps the biggest day of a usual football week, the day the offense puts in its heaviest hours and checks out the game plan. For the first time in his eight years with the club, Dawson felt timid about going on the field. That morning his name was plastered across every sports page in the land—and a few front pages.

Len bumped into Stram on their way to breakfast, and Hank raised the idea of his talking to the squad. Dawson concurred. He felt it essential that his teammates hear from him that there was nothing to the rumors swirling around the city, and that his mind was on winning the Super Bowl.

In the absolute stillness of the room, he read the statement, looked up, and said: "The reason I wanted to talk to you like this was to make sure the situation didn't prey on your minds the rest of the week. I wanted to bring everything out in the open and discuss it so we could lay it to rest once and for all and concentrate on the Minnesota Vikings and the Super Bowl. I am dedicated to that purpose. Despite all the ugly diversions we've encountered, we've all got to go forward together."

His words were greeted by the silence of a forest. He looked around uncertainly. Did they believe him, or would they use his predicament to conclude that it was all over now, the quarterback was so jittery and jumpy he couldn't play his game. He had the feeling that whatever he did now, he would be second-guessed. He mumbled, "That's all I have to say," and started toward the exit.

As Dawson was walking away, Bobby Bell, their big, raging defensive end, stood and said, "Don't worry about a thing, Lenny. We believe you. We'll all be fighting for you out there." Behind Bell, Dawson heard Jerry Mays say, "I'd bet my life on that guy, the type of individual he is." There were no fireworks, no emotional display, just a quiet, solid front of support.

Press conferences are a daily event, if not a twice-daily event, the week before a Super Bowl. Stram laid down the ground rules for Wednesday's session: no questions to Dawson about the gambling investigation; he had made his statement the previous night and he, and the team, would stand on that.

The first question posed to Dawson was "How do you think the gambling accusations will affect your performance Sunday?" At which point Stram threatened to clear the room. That subject was closed. The Chiefs had lost one day of preparation, they were not going to lose another. A defiant Stram added, "I don't think it's necessary for Len to be subjected to any more of this." The rest of the questions were related to the Vikings and the game.

Meanwhile, Jackie Dawson had to take Lennie Jr. out of grade school after a day of merciless teasing. His classmates wanted to know how much money his daddy made betting on games. Still she was determined to arrive as scheduled on Friday. They were not going to hide or sneak out of town.

Dawson was exhausted, nearly drained, after the day's workout. He had lost eight pounds, down to 178, and he felt listless. The scent of trouble was all around the Chiefs. Johnny Robinson, their best defensive back, had suffered a reaction to a shot he had taken to deaden the pain of his injured ribs. E. J. Holub, the big center, was playing on swollen knees that had to be drained.

Worried about his weight loss, Dawson ordered a steak that night in his room and finished half of it. He asked the team doctor for a sleeping pill and went to bed, waking up twice in half an hour when the phone rang in spite of his orders to the switchboard. One call was particularly cruel: The caller had told the operator he was Len Dawson's father.

Only one thing kept the week from unraveling completely: watching the Vikings on film, in particular the ends, Carl Eller and Jim Marshall; and the tackles, Alan Page and Gary Larsen. The Viking defense had acquired a suitable nickname: the Purple People Eaters. Dawson looked for flaws, for any weakness or habits he might exploit. He found none.

Minnesota was tall and quick on the front line; they batted down a lot of passes. Forty-eight hours before the kickoff, Len Dawson realized that the game would be settled in a textbook way: Minnesota's pass rush against Kansas City's offense of the 1970s.

So Stram had labeled it. Hank had designed his offense to take advantage of the nimbleness Dawson showed as a rollout quarterback at Purdue. In pro football terms, his concepts were radical. He found the traditional format too rigid, dropping the passer straight back into a protective pocket. Hank envisioned a passing game that was flexible, elastic. Dawson was the ideal man to run it.

The Stram theory was based on a movable pocket. Sometimes the passer would drop straight back. Sometimes he would roll to his right or left, tight or deep, with his blockers setting up pockets at various, predetermined spots, confusing blitzers and charging linemen.

Studying the film, rerunning frame after frame, Dawson saw that Eller and Marshall were quick enough to catch ball carriers from behind on plays directed away from them. This told him two things: (1) it would be futile to attempt to run sweeps, and (2) the Minnesota ends had no responsibility against reverses. He watched their front four swat passes away and knew they would have to be double-teamed, keeping their hands busy. He saw he could throw in front of the cornerbacks, who liked to play deep. He made a mental note: If he was patient, Otis Taylor or Frank Pitts might take the pass on a five-yard curl, break a tackle, and peel off long yardage.

The night before the game, Dawson was satisfied he had done all he could do under the circumstances. He was tired, edgy, impatient. He skipped the sleeping pill, unwilling to risk waking up drowsy. He didn't expect to sleep soundly. He didn't expect to have diarrhea either, and have to make four or five trips to the bathroom, but he did. He didn't know if he had a touch of flu or a case of nerves, but he gave up trying to sleep. He turned on an overhead light and studied the game plan one more time.

Would Hollywood have bought this script? Not a chance. Behind the almost flawless direction of Len Dawson, the Chiefs upset the Vikings, 23–7, in Super Bowl IV. Lenny said later he actually had no problem blocking out the rumors and suspicions. "You sit down with the playbook and the game plan," he said, "you sit there and think about Carl Eller, eighty-one . . . Alan Page, eighty-eight . . . you got a lot on your mind. You don't need more."

Dawson kept the Vikings off-balance all day, notably on two touchdown plays, a five-yard run by Mike Garrett and a forty-six-yard pass to Otis Taylor, and a series of reverses featuring flanker Frank Pitts. Quarterbacks are always in the spotlight. For Len Dawson this one was more like a searchlight. He did not gloat or appear bitter, because that is not his style. He seemed relieved rather than elated.

Hank Stram did not feel the same restraint. "I thought Len Dawson showed the great toughness he has," said the Kansas City coach. "To be able to express his ability the way he did after what happened earlier in the week was truly remarkable."

His teammates made it clear where they stood. "It made us angry," said Jerry Mays. "It didn't get us down. We were just angry. The press kept bringing it up and hounding him. It made us rally around him, admire him more, pull for him harder."

As an interesting sidelight, Stram had agreed to wear a microphone, the first time in history a coach had been wired for sound during a championship game. Certain of his spontaneous comments would be used on the sound track of the highlights movie by the NFL Films divison. Forgetting the mike, Stram was beside himself as the score mounted, calling out encouragement to Dawson, turning to the bench to toss off a gleeful aside: "We're beating their corners like a drum . . . this is better than stealing."

Thus did Kansas City pay off a four-year-old debt. Dawson would go on to give the Chiefs six more quality years, even in his last season in 1975 finishing third in the NFL in passing. But in the view of many, that performance, in those conditions, qualified him for the Hall of Fame.

He was voted the game's most valuable player. He went to the air only seventeen times, completing twelve, but controlled the tempo. He did not play like a man unable to eat or sleep, who had been linked however thinly or unfairly to a gambling scandal. And asked in the locker room what he did to combat the pressure, Dawson replied, "We just now got through combating it. We won the game."

☆ 12 ☆ THE SURVIVORS

When Archie Manning was quarterbacking the New Orleans Saints, he ran a football camp in Alabama, where one summer he brought in Terry Bradshaw of the Pittsburgh Steelers as a guest instructor.

Here's how the dialogue went as Manning, with Bradshaw at his side, told his campers of some bad habits to avoid:

Manning: "One bad habit is taking a false step forward when you take the snap from center."

Bradshaw: "I do that."

Manning (ignoring him): "Quarterbacks also tend to look at the ground when they drop back in the pocket."

Bradshaw: "I do that."

Manning: "Another bad habit is patting the football before throwing the pass."

Bradshaw: "I do that."

Manning: "So you see, if you have these bad habits, all you'll do is win four Super Bowls. If you don't have these bad habits, maybe you'll go eight-and-eight."

No quarterback had so many things go wrong and yet turn out so right as Terry Bradshaw—the first to wear four Super

Bowl rings, the MVP in two of them (a distinction he shared with Bart Starr). In 1989 he received the official stamp of approval: his induction into the Pro Football Hall of Fame.

As a rookie in 1970, Bradshaw joined a woeful Steelers team in the middle of a sixteen-game losing streak. The first player picked in the draft, the product of little Louisiana Tech was compared to Ozark Ike, Li'l Abner, and Sammy Baugh. He was depicted as a sort of Joe Palooka of quarterbacks, in contrast to Joe Namath's Easy Rider.

The notion that a rookie quarterback, supported by three rookie ends and two castoff backs, would lead the downtrodden Steelers back to instant glory was laughable. His most interesting statistic was the fact that he had gone steady with the last two Miss Teenage Americas, and married one of them, Melissa Babish.

His second most interesting stat was his ability to find the goal line. Unfortunately the goal line had been his own. He was tackled for a safety in each of his first three games, all of them losses. No pro football observer could ever remember that happening.

Bradshaw reported to the Steelers with obvious handicaps. He was an upright, clean-cut, clean-living, and, yes, Bible-toting Southerner who represented a sharp departure from a Pittsburgh tradition that dated back to Bobby Layne. The Steelers hadn't won a title in thirty-seven years, but they enjoyed a reputation as brawlers and patrons of the happy hour.

(Years earlier another wholesome rookie came under Layne's spell on the Detroit Lions. Layne had called a quarterback meeting at the most convenient place, the Stadium Bar. Bobby and the veteran Tobin Rote were joined at a rear table by this crew cut rookie from Occidental College. His name was, and is, Jack Kemp, and he was so in awe to be sitting in the presence of these two old pros that he never uttered a word. He just sipped silently on his Coca-Cola through a straw and listened. Finally Layne and Rote finished their strategy session and Layne ordered another round. He looked at Kemp, gurgling his last drops of soda through the straw, and shook his head. "Kid," he grumbled, "if you want to make it in this league, you're gonna have to learn to drink." Kemp never did develop a major-league thirst, but he made it later in the American Football League, although not as big as he would make it in politics.)

Bradshaw did not fit the mold of Layne or the Steelers, although for a time he tried mightily. No matter. He was shaky on the field, and recognition was slow in coming. He did not make an all-pro team until he was thirty. Pittsburgh did not exactly grasp him to its soul with hoops of steel.

Pro scouts had described him as the kind of prospect "who comes along every ten or twelve years." The only question was whether the Steelers would trade his draft rights for established players. The Cardinals, among others, offered four starters. The venerable Art Rooney, for the only time in his Pittsburgh ownership, intervened in the draft and insisted that the team keep Bradshaw.

"I was tired," Rooney said, "of giving away great players and suffering through fifteen years of them coming back to town with other teams." (The list of quarterbacks let go by the Steelers includes Unitas, Dawson, Kemp, Bill Nelsen, and Earl Morrall.) Added Rooney: "We even had the rights to Sid Luckman and lost those. I didn't want to see it happen again."

Rooney's intervention seemed less than divine that first season. Bradshaw's small-college background had ill prepared him for reading complicated NFL defenses and much of the time he seemed bewildered on the field. The other knock against him was that he had too much arm and too little touch. "He threw every pass as hard as he could throw," said Dick Hoak, a former teammate and later a Steeler coach, "whether it was for ten feet or a hundred yards." He was erratic and thin-skinned. In his first regular season start, Coach Chuck Noll benched him in the third quarter—he had gone 4-for-16—and Bradshaw spent the rest of the game with his face buried in his hands.

In New York, Noll humiliated him on the sidelines, grabbing him by the shoulders and spinning him around. "There was a lot of pain in those growing stages," he says now. "I wouldn't want to go through it again, but I wouldn't change it. It had to happen. There are a lot of scars, but the good times erased most of it. They're just flashbacks now. Being fined in my rookie year for being two minutes late to a meeting. The fans booing me when I was injured. Being pulled from a game early, put back in, and pulled again. Losing my job to Joe Gilliam. The Dumb Image in the papers, Ozark Ike, all those great descriptions of me . . ."

Bradshaw was born in Shreveport, not exactly the backwoods, and his grandparents were farmers but he wanted to be a rancher. He had thinning blond hair and pale blue eyes and a thick, country twang. He could throw the ball a mile, but he smiled a lot and struck just about everybody—his teammates, the media, the fans—as naïve. And this is not an ideal quality in a quarterback.

"I talked slow," says Terry, "so people perceived me as stupid. The week of the Super Bowl in 1975, the press kept asking me what kind of grades I made in high school. Did I really graduate from college? What kind of courses did I take? They made me out to be a moron."

His rookie season he completed only 38 percent of his passes, threw for six touchdowns, and led the league in interceptions with twenty-four. He suffered from the presence on the team of Terry Hanratty, an all-American quarterback from Notre Dame, who had been a high school star in western Pennsylvania. In short, from the start, he was not a Pittsburgh kind of guy, until they noticed that no matter how many times he got knocked down, or how hard, he kept bouncing back. Art Rooney, once a neighbor of Harry K. Thaw, the man who killed the architect Stanford White over the affections of Evelyn Nesbitt, said of Terry, "Thaw didn't get the abuse that Bradshaw went through."

Terry's second season held out promise. The Steelers won six and lost eight, their best record in eight years. He married his Miss Teenage America. In 1972 Franco Harris, the Penn State halfback, son of a black army sergeant and an Italian mother, joined the team and attracted his own fan club: Franco's Italian Army. The Steelers won eleven games and stunned Oakland in the first round of the playoffs on a last-second catch by Franco

of a deflected pass—known in pro football lore as the Immaculate Reception.

Pittsburgh had turned it around, but the life of Terry Bradshaw went haywire. It isn't likely that any other quarterback so
beset by doubts would wind up achieving more than Terry
Bradshaw. Here was a fellow who had been hurled into the lineup
as a rookie, who endured waves of criticism, and then in his
fourth season lost his starting job—and his wife. In 1973 his
shoulder troubled him and he was replaced by Gilliam. He fought
his way back into the lineup and then threw seven interceptions
in two games. In a wild playoff loss to Oakland, 33–14, he had
three more passes picked off.

"Losing my job to Gilliam," he admits, "that was really painful, when that old pride and ego get stepped on. No longer are
you important. All the self-doubt—the feeling you don't have
what it takes—comes back to haunt you.

"I was just as erratic off the field. I lived only for Terry Bradshaw. I tried to be 'one of the boys' and went to every honky-
tonk I could find. I chased women and behaved in a way that
was totally alien to anything I had known. My whole life was
out of control."

He scraped bottom that season, at one point listed as the third-
string quarterback. Terry wallowed in self-pity: "All I did was
mope around and feel sorry for myself. Someone would write
something unflattering about me in the newspapers and I'd be
mad at him. Someone would make an unkind remark on television and I'd flare up again. I just figured the whole world was
down on me and the Pittsburgh fans were leading the jeers. I
had no close friends. I had no spiritual counselor. I wasn't both-
ering to attend church and I rarely prayed. And I knew the guys
on the club figured I was the biggest hypocrite in the world."

He credits his revival on the field to the renewal of his religious faith. Some of his teammates take a more pragmatic view.
Said one, Paul Martha, who became an attorney: "Terry had
just been divorced, he was going bald, everybody was saying he
was dumb. He looked the situation over and said, 'The hell with
it. I'm just gonna play football. That's all I have left.' "

Still, like Roger Staubach, he made a point of expressing his gratitude to God with occasionally painful results. After one Super Bowl, a writer cut off his remarks with "We're not interested in that garbage." Bradshaw responded with sympathy, not anger. "That's sad," he said. "Football is just a fleeting thing. Football doesn't fill that void in your heart and inside you." And he had a similar experience during another Super Bowl week. "I started talking about Jesus," he said, "and they turned off the cameras."

Bradshaw started the back-to-back victories over Minnesota (16–6) and Dallas (21–17) in Super Bowls IX and X. He never felt fully deserving about the first one, given Gilliam's role in getting them there. In the 1976 game he answered his critics in a game-winning play, passing to Lynn Swann for sixty-four yards against a well-read safety blitz. He hit Swann in the space vacated by the Dallas safety, Cliff Harris, who at the same instant hit Bradshaw, knocking him cold. He left the game with a concussion, but got up—to resounding cheers.

By 1979 he had gone through another marriage and divorce, this time to ice-skating star JoJo Starbuck. Both were born-again Christians, but they couldn't overcome the career conflicts. Terry took to making slow, mournful drives from his penthouse home to Three Rivers Stadium, listening to Larry Gatlin songs on his tape deck and getting angry honks from the motorists backed up behind him.

He lost twenty-three pounds during training camp, the result of a lingering virus. His teammates watched him closely, worried about him. "In 1974," recalled Rocky Bleier, the gutsy running back who did a tour in Vietnam, "his intensity wasn't there. He didn't seem to be up for the game. You could tell by the way he got dressed, by his manner. You knew there was something missing. It wasn't easy to get to know Terry. He would tell you things, he was easygoing but not buddy-buddy. He seemed to be going through a whole guilt syndrome."

There was a key difference, however, from his tailspin of 1974. He had learned not to take his private setbacks onto the field with him. "At that point," said Bleier, "I think Brad had the ability to put up a wall and not let these things affect him. We all knew if his head wasn't there, we were in for a long, hard day."

In January 1979 he and the Steelers moved into a class of their own with a win in Super Bowl XIII, if you're keeping score in Latin. Dallas was again the opposition and Terry took the game into his big farm-boy hands, for the first time in his career passing for more than three hundred yards. Those who questioned his intelligence now had their answer. He owned the smartest arm in pro football. In a 35–31 victory, the super shoot-out the fans had been craving, he outpitched the classy Staubauch, four touchdowns to three. "The thing I didn't want to change was what got me here," he said. "That's play-action passes, throwing the ball. I was gonna play my game."

He stood alone now as a quarterback whose team had won three Super Bowls, but he clung to a modesty that was genuine. Don't put him in a class with his heroes, Graham, Starr, and Namath, he pleaded. He was a good workman on a great team, throwing to those superb receivers, Lynn Swann and John Stallworth, and blessed with a defense that could score points, the Iron Curtain. "Ground under for so many years," wrote veteran *Los Angeles Times* analyst Bob Oates, "Bradshaw has trouble to this day thinking of himself as a champion."

His insecurity was a combination of several things: his slow acceptance in Pittsburgh, his hot-and-cold dealings with Chuck Noll, his failed marriages, his faltering attempts as a country singer and reluctant actor.

Each Super Bowl became a kind of turning point. "Staubach was from the Naval Academy," he says, "so the matchup in Super Bowl Ten was supposed to be brains against the country boy. We won, and people began to realize that what had been said of me was just a crock.

"Thirteen turned me into a legitimate star. All of a sudden, the accolades and the opportunities poured in. Fourteen cemented all this. My name was in bronze. The change came about because I had won the big one. You can throw for a lot of yardage—that's easy in the NFL. But very few can consistently win championships, beat the odds, beat the best. I did that, so now I was labeled a winner. Sports isn't about IQ. It's about winning and losing."

Sports Illustrated chose him as its Sportsman of the Year for 1979. He was even named one of the fashion industry's ten best-dressed men. "Wasn't that a hoot?" he said. "That just cracked me up. All I ever wear are cowboy boots and shirts and jeans and hats."

The third week of January 1980 was when Bradshaw revealed his superstitious side. The Steelers were heavily favored over an ordinary Rams team which squeezed into the playoffs with a 9–7 record. Pat Haden had broken a finger, leaving the quarterback job to the untested Vince Ferragamo the final four games. Los Angeles won three of them, relying on defense and ball control.

Before the game, Terry made the mistake of catching a movie with one of his backups, Mike Kruczek. The movie was called *Heaven Can Wait,* a remake of a classic about a man whose death and heavenly ascent turn out to be a mistake. In the original, the main character is sent back to earth in the body of a boxer. In the remake, Warren Beatty returns as a quarterback . . . who leads the Los Angeles Rams to a victory over the Steelers. "All week," said Kruczek, "this fear ate at him that we were going to get upset by the Rams."

"Everything," said Bradshaw, "was pointing toward a disaster. I'm surprised they didn't have that movie on our sets in the hotel room." And there were other, discouraging signs. Three L.A. assistant coaches had been with the Steelers and knew the system. Rain in the area around Pasadena had turned the practice field to muck. Bradshaw felt his practices were poor and his worries deepened.

He was intercepted three times in the first half and the Rams led, 13–10, at halftime. When the Rams were primed to pull it off, Bradshaw twice brought the Steelers from behind. Heaven could wait.

Early in the third quarter, he picked up the blitz, called an audible, and hit Lynn Swann on a post pattern for forty-seven yards and a score. Terry was buried on the play. "I heard the crowd yell," he said later, "and someone told me Swannie made a helluva catch."

The Steelers were down, 19–17, in the fourth quarter, facing third and nine on their own 27, when Chuck Noll sent in a play. Bradshaw grimaced. In the Steelers' playbook it was identified as 60 Prevent Slot Hook and Go, with Stallworth playing both roles—the hooker and the goer. "I ran that play eight times in practice," said Bradshaw, "and never could make it go." This time it went. "I just unloaded. They had him double-covered, but he went deep and made a great catch." Stallworth pulled in the pass over his shoulder for seventy-three yards and a touchdown. Jack Lambert picked off a Ferragamo pass and Bradshaw drove the Steelers to the score that put the game away, 31–19.

Finally he and Pittsburgh understood each other. "This is a blue-collar, shot-and-a-beer town," he says. "The fans get up for big games. They're like us. They're good, honest-working people who come out to be entertained. They lead a tough life and they like a team with a tough defense because that's where character shows. We had it. We played tough and we played hard. We had guys with names like Dirt Winston and Mean Joe Green and Mad Dog White. They called Jack Lambert 'Fangs.' Pittsburgh names. And I tell you, it gets cold up there for our fans those last few games of the season. That gets them all wound up and they would get us all wound up. I don't know how much they identified with me, but I do think they at last accepted me. Anyway, they stuck with me."

In his time Bradshaw was one of the most popular players in the league. He was good-humored, friendly, always smiling, seldom complaining. No one had a bad word for him. He was Houston's favorite opposing quarterback, although twice he kept the Oilers out of the Super Bowl. In the 1980 season opener, Bradshaw broke out of the clutches of a 280-pound tackle, Mike Stensrud, and passed for fifty yards and a touchdown to the leaping Stallworth.

The Oilers felt the play should have been whistled dead. "But I'll give Bradshaw credit," said Bum Phillips, "for breaking out of the tackler's grasp. Dan Pastorini couldn't have done it. Ken Stabler couldn't have done it. Terry's a big, strong boy."

Says Bradshaw: "I learned three things about football a long time ago. Number one, if defensive backs were great receivers, then they'd be playing on offense; number two, when your receiver sticks his hand up, he wants you to throw the ball to him; number three, if it was eighty-two, don't worry, just throw it. Nobody was going to outjump John Stallworth."

That Pittsburgh was slow to discover his positive qualities remained a mystery to many.

"He took a beating from the fans early," says Myron Cope, whose radio talk show reflects the pulse of the city. "He got worked over so badly he became a kind of a recluse for a while. He wasn't a mill worker's guy, a Pittsburgh guy. He was a rancher, for God's sake. But in time they loved him because he was a winner and—this is very important—because he's a tough guy. You hurt him and he's back."

"I guess you develop a hard crust," says Bradshaw. "You almost have to to survive. The football cronies, the Christian people, you get everyone judging you differently—to be the perfect person, to fill their needs. I stopped trying. I had to; it was driving me crazy."

He needed the approval, but of more importance Terry had matured. He had dabbled in the arts, appearing in a Burt Reynolds movie called *Hooper,* and kept a few club dates with his pal Larry Gatlin. But he had no urge to retire from football. "There's the emotional-physical side," he said, "and the economic side. Emotionally, you work all your life to realize a dream. Economically, everything an athlete makes on the side is a byproduct of his football ability."

In time he would discover that show business was, if anything, more cutthroat than football. He had a role in another Reynolds film, *The Cannonball Run,* and costarred with Mel Tillis in a tacky, short-lived TV series, *The Stockers.* He cut a gospel album and decided to leave the country-and-western field to Merle Haggard and Willie Nelson. The final blow came when his producer, a man he considered a close friend, sent a Mail-o-Gram to tell him his recording contract had been canceled. "I kind of got a taste of how cold people could be in the entertainment business," he said.

Between the end of his playing days in 1983 and his election to the Hall of Fame six years later, Bradshaw made a successful transition to the television booth as a network analyst. He was not a natural in the role, but he worked at it and improved.

You wondered if many in the audience were suprised at the substance of what Terry Bradshaw had to say: "There are a lot of quarterbacks who can throw the ball between the twenties and can't get it in the end zone. There are a lot of them who can play well for sixteen games and then they get in the playoffs and stink up the joint. Some play well when they're ahead and some can't. Some play better when they are in a pressure situation. The NFL is full of all these types of people.

"Boomer Esiason struggled through the playoffs in 1988, because of injury or whatever, and when the Bengals lost to San Francisco in the Super Bowl everyone said, 'Well, what if?' But there are no 'ifs' in this. You won't win with an average game from your quarterback.

"Great quarterbacks have an ingredient I consider the most important of all—poise. It's like when a guy gets a lot of criticism in the media or starts hearing the boos from the crowd. Watch what they say when that happens, how they respond. Is it, 'Hey, why are you guys doing this to me?' And does he stop talking to the media, all that kind of reaction? Does he start pointing fingers?

"Or watch the guy who just sits back and says, 'Yeah, I've really been stinking up the place.' If he's fairly levelheaded, a guy who can't be rattled by what people think of him, who can handle criticism, those are the ones who are going to excel in the big games.

"I was playing tennis one afternoon with a friend who was beating me pretty handily. I just started talking to him, talking a lot of trash. All of a sudden he was saying, 'Stop talking. Stop talking so much and just play the game.' I won the next three sets and he just kept begging me to stop talking. I told him, 'I can't beat you, so I'm going to talk you to death.'

"You've got to be able to take the talk around you, all the distractions, and concentrate on the game and nothing else. That's poise. I don't recall ever losing my poise, really. But I've been embarrassed.

"The worst time was when my false teeth fell out when we were playing Philadelphia. I came up to the line and was yelling out the signals and my bridge popped out. I just remember thinking, Bill Bergey, the linebacker, was right in the middle and I had to scramble around on the ground and get them before he saw them. I knew he'd stomp on them if he saw them. I was lucky. I slipped them back in my mouth before anybody realized what had happened.

"I've had my share of embarrassing moments. Once I got hit so hard my jockstrap—my plastic cup—just exploded. There was this noise like a small explosion and several guys turned and looked at me. I didn't know what to say."

Clearly Terry can't be hurt anymore. He doesn't try to hide the pure delight he takes in the game that was: "Football is basically a serious game. But I remember being in a big fight, in the middle of a pile, and I was just whaling away, beating up what I thought was a human being. It ended up that it was just the leg of Buck Buchanan [of Kansas City]."

He still isn't sure how to define his relationship with his former coach, Chuck Noll. When the Steelers released him, he said he felt he could still play, and he didn't think—correctly, as it turned out—that the Steelers were able to replace him. Noll let him leave without any words of sentiment or appreciation. What he did say seemed to suggest that Bradshaw was trying to undermine his old team.

"Chuck was in some ways a negative influence on me. Oh, everyone knows the stories. He was just a negative motivator. I learned a lot of football from him, about defense, about the running game, so it wasn't all negative. People have asked me If I would rather have had another coach. But you can't argue with four Super Bowls. I don't think anyone would want to change anything after what we accomplished.

"Chuck was tough, a tough man. If you were a weak person, if you were easily intimidated, he'd dominate you. He would steamroller you. In some ways, that's just what we needed. We fought. Who doesn't? I just disagreed with the way Chuck handled people. He was not a good person with people. He would just cut away at someone, hit a nerve, it didn't seem to matter. Me and Franco kind of lashed out at him a few times because he was so cold to his players. I heard from a source later that was the way Chuck wanted us to think of him. I don't know. I haven't figured out how that was supposed to motivate us. Maybe it did."

He played fourteen seasons, and he isn't quite prepared to think of them yet as "the good old days." But Bradshaw is aware that he has crossed an invisible line, the one that marks the end of one generation and the start of another. In short, playing quarterback today is a jelly roll compared to when he was breaking in. For this, in large part, rather indiscreetly, he blames his present employers.

"They ought to knock off all the rule changes," he says. "They have just become a bunch of pussies out there. Television has screwed them up. The TV money made them all millionaires and then they decided that since they were making so much money they had to start protecting them. Some of these guys are so worried about their investments they can't concentrate on the game. I'm sick of all the rules protecting the quarterbacks; the in-the-grasp rule, the elimination of the bump-and-run. Snake [Stabler] and I talk about what it was like all the time, back in the days of the bump-and-run and you had to get the ball off in three seconds. You were lucky to gain a hundred and fifty yards in a game then. Now these guys all throw for three hundred yards and never get their suits dirty. It's all based on TV, what the TV moguls want."

Not a day goes by that Bradshaw doesn't think about the game. He can't help it, he has all these reminders. "I just had an MRI [Memory Resonance Imaging] exam on my lower back. It bothers me all the time. My wrist aches constantly where I broke it. I broke my neck once and that gives me a lot of pain. I crawl out of bed every morning and have to roll on the floor and twist and turn and pop my body to get myself going. But that's just part of the game."

Yes, of course, but does he ever regret the price he paid, the pain, the misery, the memories that don't quite mend? And Bradshaw answered, as most quarterbacks do, in the tone they would use if you asked if they would rather have been born in Mongolia: "Oh no, no regrets. It's the greatest thing that ever happened to me, playing in the pros. The most intense emotional experience I've ever had, other than my wife and kids. It was the great passion of my life." He paused and reflected for a moment before adding: "I guess that proves how crazy we are."

UPS AND
DOWNS

Around the time Jim Plunkett retired, not entirely of his own will, John Madden corrected a fellow who tried to tell him that Plunkett was a "rags to riches" story. "No," said Madden, whose Raider team salvaged his career, "it's a 'riches to rags to riches' story." Actually Madden just missed. Jim Plunkett came out of the barrios of San Jose to win the Heisman Trophy at Stanford and go to the pros as that rare art object, the first pick in the draft.

Traded by the Patriots, cut by the 49ers, waived through the National Football League, he caught on with the Raiders and led them to two Super Bowl victories. So when you think about it, you see that his was a story twice-told: "rags to riches," and back to "rags to riches." And when the Los Angeles Raiders released him in August 1988, Plunkett really could not complain. With his arm and his heart he had purchased another ten seasons after nearly everyone had written him off.

As a rookie in 1971 with the struggling Patriots, he took a fearful punishment each week. A friend would keep him company each Monday as he tried to walk off the soreness. They would stroll through town, beside the Charles River, in silence except when they came to a curb, then Plunkett would take his friend's elbow and say, softly, "Up," or "Down." The gesture puzzled and amused the friend, until he learned that Plunkett's mother and father were both legally blind, and this was the way he had guided them on the streets at home. His father had died in 1969.

The family was on welfare when Jim was growing up, and his early goal was simply "to get them the hell out of it." He sold papers, pumped gas, delivered groceries, and developed into a fine athlete.

And a fine, sensitive adult. He was proud to dramatize his Mexican-American heritage, as golf's Lee Trevino did, for a very distinct reason: to encourage others to broaden their vistas in a changing society.

No one ever said it would be easy for Jim Plunkett. After the 49ers released him, he signed with the Raiders, who kept him on the bench for all of the 1978 season. He finally got his chance six games into the 1980 schedule after Dan Pastorini broke his leg.

And suddenly there he was, in January 1981 in the Superdome, feeling the pressure around him. The Raiders led the Philadelphia Eagles by a touchdown and the play was breaking down. Plunkett was looking for Bob Chandler. "But he was covered," Jim said later. "Then I saw Kenny King wave his arm. He was behind the cornerback. All I did was get the ball over the man covering Kenny. What a catch he made! Then he outran everybody in the secondary."

The first quarter play traveled eighty yards and Oakland—the team had not yet gone Hollywood—went on to win it in a breeze, 27–10. That was the key play, the kind Plunkett had made all year, turning bad plays into good ones, making chicken salad out of chicken feathers.

He passed that day for 261 yards and three touchdowns. He showered, dressed, snapped a gold chain around his neck, and walked into the interview room to meet the press. He approached the platform, missed the first step, and tripped, crashing to the floor on his face. It was a colorful entrance, one of the few times that he had been down all day.

But he knew what it meant to get off the floor. He had thought about quitting when the 49ers pink-slipped him. "When you get cut," he said, "you begin to think. I did my thinking over a lot of beer. I got pretty low." Which made the rebound all the higher of course. Three years later, with the Raiders then comfortably resettled in Los Angeles, Plunkett was the winning quarterback in another Super Bowl. They buried the Redskins, 38–9.

It was a terrific roller coaster ride while it lasted. In time the Raiders found themselves in an alien position, having to reshape a roster grown old. Few teams feel they can do it around a forty-year-old quarterback. Plunkett was persuaded to retire.

Part of our fascination with sport is getting to see a kind of life cycle: the birth of a career, the flowering, and the exit. In the case of Jim Plunkett, everyone got double his money's worth.

ANYTHING
FOR BILLY

Billy Kilmer could qualify for most of the chapters in this book. He was a leader, a backup, a party animal, a fierce competitor, a stubby castoff who didn't fit the mold of the classic quarterback, but he took his team to the Super Bowl. Most of all, he was a survivor.

There are two kinds of survivors in pro football. One endures as a professional, moving from one team to another, losing ground and regaining it, in or out of favor, hanging on to a job. The other has to overcome a devastating injury, severe enough to end a career or shorten it.

Kilmer was both kinds. He was as close to a one-legged quarterback as the league ever saw. On a December night in 1962, Billy's car missed an off ramp on a California freeway, plunged to the ground, burst through a wire fence, and landed half-submerged in a ditch full of stagnant water. He was pinned in the wreckage for almost an hour, his right leg nearly torn from the socket until the Highway Patrol dragged him out and carted him off to the nearest emergency ward.

"He'll probably lose that leg," a patrolman told reporters after the crash. His doctors considered amputating it below the knee—the polluted water had infected a compound fracture of the ankle. He kept the leg, but the doctors advised him to forget about football.

Red Hickey, then coach of the San Francisco 49ers, visited Kilmer often during his months in a hospital. "He was lying in the hospital bed," recalled Hickey, "making plans to be a sports car driver if he could never play football again. He swore he'd play again but I didn't see how. He was going to walk with a limp the rest of his life."

The Billy Kilmers of this world are made of fairly stern stuff. Six months after the accident he was on crutches. He spent a year in rehabilitation, during which he grew fat but hardly lazy. He missed the 1963 season and the next year, incredibly, he rejoined the team. He didn't play much, not for three seasons, but Billy was back.

The injury had robbed him of his great gifts as a runner. In 1960 as a tailback in the Single-wing formation at UCLA, he had led the nation in total offense. Drafted by San Francisco, he became the central figure in Red Hickey's grand experiment with the Shotgun formation, pro football's only departure from the T since the early 1940s.

Hickey built the Shotgun offense around Kilmer to take advantage of his running ability on the option play. The results were fabulous at first. In the end, though, the Shotgun cost Hickey his job. Rival teams learned to defend against it, and he had traded Y. A. Tittle, made expendable by the new offense.

The 49ers used three quarterbacks. John Brodie would pass and Kilmer was the running threat. Bobby Waters did both, but since he didn't pass as well as Brodie or run as well as Kilmer, he served mainly as a diversion.

In 1961 the 49ers won four of their first five games and led the division in every category. Then they met the Chicago Bears, whose resident genius, Clark Shaughnessy, designed a defense tailor-made to stop it. The simplest feature of this otherwise complex strategy was the stationing of a linebacker, Bill George, over the center, who had to keep his head down to snap the ball to the tailback. George streaked up the middle on every play and the Bears won easily, 31–0.

Hickey, the Shotgun, and, finally, the gimpy Kilmer disappeared. Only Billy really materialized again, although the Shotgun made a cameo appearance with the Cowboys in 1964, is today the formation of choice on third and long, and was used with some frequency by Denver in 1988 and 1989.

Kilmer asked the 49ers to include him in the expansion pool in 1967, and he was picked by the New Orleans Saints. There Kilmer won the starting job from Gary Cuozzo, who had cost the Saints a first-round draft choice in a deal with the Colts.

So Billy was reincarnated as a T formation quarterback on an expansion football team in the best party town in America. Predictably, the Saints were awful and the fans, bred on centuries-old traditions of exuberance and a complete lack of inhibitions, booed Kilmer without mercy.

Before one game a banner in the stands caught Billy's eye. Kilmer for Mayor it proclaimed, a lonely signpost amid a multitude of jeers. "When I saw it," he admitted, "I thought it was a compliment. Then I realized the mayor was the only man in New Orleans who was booed more than me."

How bad was it? "Kilmer," said the Saints' publicist, Ed Sinton, "has been booed worse than a stadium cop taking a game ball away from a kid on crutches."

Quarterbacks are in general agreement in their position on public booing. They don't like it. Kilmer, however, admired the spirit behind the assault. "I liked the New Orleans breed of fan," he said. "They root harder than in most places . . . they are almost part of the game. I'm an emotional person . . . I stomp and rave when a play fails and many of the fans didn't understand. I was taking the failure out on myself, not another player.

All the fans wanted was a winner. So did I."

There was one brief, shining moment for Kilmer in New Orleans. In 1969 he threw six touchdown passes, one shy of the record, in a crazy 51–42 victory over the St. Louis Cardinals. The win ended a six-game losing streak.

At the end of that season the Saints sent him to Washington, where he hooked up with George Allen and his Over-the-Hill Gang. After eight years, the florid face still somehow reflected the innocence of youth and the hard uses of maturity. He was frequently, and accurately, likened to Bobby Layne. Both threw an occasional knuckleball to their receivers and both were celebrities in the local saloon society.

George Allen once received a call to get his quarterback out of jail. He had been arrested for causing a disturbance in a diner, around four in the morning, when he had tried to pay for a cup of coffee with the only currency he had, a hundred-dollar bill. Allen encouraged his players to think big. The incident blew over, Kilmer started the next game, and the Redskins won.

He lacked the arm and the form that made coaches gasp, but he had one lovely quality, he was indestructible. He took his minimal talent for throwing the ball and through sheer will and effort he kept improving. He reduced his drop-back time, quickened his release, fine-tuned his touch until he became a rated passer with a 60 percent completion rate.

He competed with Sonny Jurgensen and eventually gave way to Joe Theismann, but in between, in January 1973, he started at quarterback for the Redskins against the Miami Dolphins. Kilmer was intercepted three times, and Miami, behind a flawless Bob Griese, won, 14–7, to finish the most remarkable season in memory: seventeen wins in a row.

Billy retired in 1977, at thirty-eight, an impressive feat for a fellow who was not a natural thrower and had almost lost a leg. His will, his soul, his zest for the game and for living, were the tools in his survival kit. "One good thing came out of the car accident," said Billy Kilmer. "They quit trying to make a running back out of me."

☆13☆ TOP GUNS, YOUNG GUNS

No quarterback in memory ever raised the art of illusion to the levels Joe Montana has. You begin with the name, which sounds western, macho, Marlboro Mannish. Yes, you can picture a Joe Montana reaching for greatness in pro football. How many quarterbacks, after all, have an entire state named after them?

Then there is the matter of his physique. He is listed on the San Francisco roster as six feet two and 190 pounds and yet he looks so skinny, almost fragile. His teammates feel even more protective of him than teams normally do about their quarterbacks. As Bubba Paris, the 300-pound offensive tackle, who in his spare time writes poetry, put it:

"You look at Joe and he's about the size of my youngest son. When the pass rushers beat on him and he gets up like nothing happened, you feel bad. There is a nonverbal communication. His eyes are telling you, 'I depend on you.' You do everything in your heart not to let it happen again."

The prudent observer does not ask Bubba to produce his youngest son for the sake of comparison. One accepts as part of his mystique that Montana will never be mistaken for Arnold Schwarzenegger. All around the league you hear the same refrain, have heard it for years: that Joe doesn't have the strongest arm, or the quickest release, or the fastest feet. What he has is the ability to pump himself up and take his game to another level when all the worldly goods are on the line.

"If the Forty-niners are the team of the eighties," says their former coach, Bill Walsh, "and they are, then Joe Montana was the quarterback of the eighties." No argument. No contest. Montana is the comeback king of his era, just as Layne and Unitas and Staubach were in theirs. A kind of a mythic quality surrounds his career. It helps, of course, to have blond hair and icy-blue eyes and pockets always filled with four-leaf clovers. Montana does not just win football games. He delivers them from evil.

It also helps to be a product of Notre Dame, attached to the legends of Rockne and Gipp, the Four Horsemen, Angelo Bertelli, and Johnny Lujack and all the other saints who walk forever along the misty banks of the Wabash. Right here it needs to be noted that such talk, such references, make Montana uncomfortable. "I go to the store, buy milk, and forget the bread," he says. "I try to hammer a nail and I hit my thumb. Do legends do that?"

No one rushes Joe Montana. Standing in the pocket or heading for Canton, Ohio, home of the Pro Football Hall of Fame, he will take his own sweet time. And sweet times they have been. In the Montana decade, the 49ers won three Super Bowl triumphs—he was the MVP in two of them—and enjoyed nine winning seasons out of ten. The one exception came in a fraction of a season, a 3–6 record in strike-torn 1982.

With his uncanny sense of timing, Montana established himself as the 49ers' starter by the end of the 1980 season, his second. He was still there nine years later to ring out the decade. No other quarterback came close to matching his tenure.

Yet Joe Cool didn't sail through the 1980s unchallenged. He had to contend with the entire Class of 1983, the richest group of quarterbacks ever to join the pros out of one draft. In the order of their selection, they were John Elway of the Broncos (drafted by the Colts and then traded), Todd Blackledge of the Chiefs, Jim Kelly of the Buffalo Bills, Tony Eason of the Patriots,

Ken O'Brien of the Jets, and Dan Marino of the Dolphins. By the end of the decade, all six were still in the league.

Elway, Marino, and Eason had played in losing Super Bowls. Kelly had become a star in Buffalo. O'Brien, an unknown when the Jets plucked him out of California-Davis, led the NFL in passing in 1985, his first full season as a starter. A year later he guided the Jets to ten wins in their first eleven games before the team went into a nosedive. Only Blackledge failed to complete a full season as a starting quarterback. Five more were taken later in the same draft, and three of those are still around in backup roles: Babe Laufenberg, Gary Kubiak, and Tom Ramsey.

Most NFL teams would make a pact with the devil to obtain a franchise quarterback (and depending on which agent they were dealing with, no doubt some teams felt they had). Cincinnati found its man in the left-handed Boomer Esiason. Cleveland tapped Bernie Kosar off the University of Miami assembly line in 1985. Vinny Testaverde won the Heisman in 1986 and went to Tampa Bay as the first pick in the draft.

In the Montana decade, three quarterbacks had a career year. Jim McMahon, Phil Simms, and Doug Williams each won the Super Bowl—for the Bears, Giants, and Redskins—and became temporarily godlike. Houston brought down Warren Moon from Canada and defrosted him. Later the Oilers drafted Jim Everett out of Purdue and traded him to the Rams when the two sides couldn't come to terms. The Eagles got lucky in Las Vegas, signing Nevada's Randall Cunningham, touted by Coach Buddy Ryan as the quarterback of the nineties. Green Bay, looking for the kind of meaningful relationship it has not had since Bart Starr, took the wraps off an unheralded Don Majkowski (pronounced Ma-KOW-ski), nicknamed Magic. Dallas had high hopes for Troy Aikman, the first pick in the 1989 draft, if he lives.

When Montana came into the league in 1979, this was the scene: Terry Bradshaw had reached the end of his remarkable run of four Super Bowl victories with Pittsburgh. Dallas would say good-bye to Roger Staubach. Bob Griese had one more season left in Miami. It was the prime of Ken Anderson in Cincinnati and Brian Sipe in Cleveland. Joe Theismann made

Washington a winner. Dan Fouts was racking up numbers that looked like zip codes in San Diego. Archie Manning was taking his lumps in New Orleans.

If there were any experts forecasting immortality for Joe Montana, no record of it exists. It was John Brodie, the former 49ers quarterback, who urged Bill Walsh to draft Montana. Walsh was high on Phil Simms, who figured to be gone by the time the 49ers picked, and Steve Dils, who had played for him at Stanford. Then Walsh watched Joe work out and liked his quick feet and the way he set up to throw. The 49ers grabbed Montana on the third round, the eighty-second player picked. The rap against Joe at Notre Dame was his casual attitude toward practice and his inconsistency. Walsh was intrigued. "If he could be great for one game," he wondered, "why not two, why not more? He was willing to learn. That was easy to tell."

No one around the team knew what to expect. Randy Cross, the veteran guard, remembers his first thought when he saw the spindly Montana: "Who's this, the new punter?"

Also new to the team that summer of 1979 was the quarterback coach, a fellow named Sam Wyche. A few years earlier Sam had been a backup quarterback for the Bengals when Walsh was the offensive coordinator there. At his first 49ers minicamp, Wyche found himself working with the starter, Steve DeBerg, who the season before had been a 60 percent passer. "My first day," recalled Sam, "we were on the field and I was stepping out there to show DeBerg how to hold the ball and how to follow through and keep his feet balanced. Bill walked up and separated us, whispering something like, 'Why don't you let Steve warm up for a minute first?' Like, we don't need to overcoach him just yet. I guess I must have been pretty nervous, and Bill sensed it right off."

The rookie Montana wasn't nervous at all. His role was to stand around and watch. Nor was that a new role for him. At Notre Dame he had been ranked last among the three quarterbacks on the freshman roster. (Funny about football myths. By the time Joe was a certified NFL hero, the popular version of his college debut had six quarterbacks ahead of him.)

Still, it was lonely on the bench. In his second semester he married a beauty from his hometown in Pennsylvania, Monongahela, or Mon City as the locals called it. His teammates, his academic counselor, and others tried to discourage him, but kids married young in Mon City and not many went off to college. The former Kim Moses landed a job in the sports information office at Notre Dame, where she could keep track of her husband's clippings. They were a little slow in coming. Joe, the uninspired practice field performer, didn't start for the Irish and Coach Dan Devine until the fourth game of his junior year. As a spot player, at coming off the bench, he all but rewrote the storybook.

In six games in which he played a total of fewer than forty minutes, he rallied the Irish from eighty-eight points behind and won them all. As a sophomore, his team trailed North Carolina by eight, and Joe led them to a 21–14 win in the space of sixty-two seconds. Against Purdue, as a junior, he entered the game as Notre Dame's fourth sub quarterback and passed them to seventeen points and a 31–24 victory. And so it went.

His reputation as a fourth-quarter miracle maker, however, actually dates back to his final college game, the 1979 Cotton Bowl against the University of Houston. The scene was Siberian, seventeen degrees with thirty-mile-an-hour winds sending snow flurries swirling across the field. Montana was cut and bleeding from raw rock salt on the field, and he left the game in the third quarter, suffering from hypothermia. His body temperature was down to ninety-six degrees; he was wrapped in blankets and still shaking while a doctor forced hot chicken soup into him.

By the time he returned to the field, Notre Dame trailed, 34–12, and the snow made it nearly impossible to see the line of scrimmage, or for the fans to tell the players apart. Montana went to work, and with time running out Notre Dame had drawn to within 34–27, inside the Houston 10. Joe whipped what would have been a touchdown pass to Kris Haines in the end zone, but the receiver slipped and the ball fell incomplete. The clock stopped with four seconds left. In the huddle Montana told Haines not to worry, he was coming right back with the same pass. This time Haines held on for the score. With no time on the clock, Joe hit Haines again for a two-point conversion and Notre Dame won, 35–34.

It was a glorious way to wind up a college career, except for one flaw. His marriage had fallen apart. It probably was doomed well before Joe landed in Dallas, and his picture appeared in the papers with all those Cotton Bowl princesses. Playing quarterback can be hard. Playing the quarterback's wife can be harder.

Walsh and the 49ers were unclear about what to expect from him. Pro football teams do not build their game plans around sorcery, and the impossible was what Montana did best. "An average arm," noted Sam Wyche. "Street ball," said running back Wendell Tyler, picking up on Joe's improvisational skills. As a rookie, he threw only twenty-three passes and studied Steve DeBerg as the 49ers suffered through a 2–14 season. Walsh had decided there was something special about the lean and enigmatic kid from Namath country—the Pennsylvania coal fields. And he set out to protect him. At the start of his second year, Montana would rarely enter a game unless the 49ers were across midfield. Once Walsh subbed him for DeBerg on the goal line, and Joe scored on a rollout. His ego unharmed, he returned to the bench.

The grooming of Joe Montana continued into the 1980 season, an up-and-down one for the 49ers. At halftime of their fourteenth week, they trailed the New Orleans Saints, 35–7. In the second half Montana put together four touchdown drives that totaled 331 yards. He ran for one score and passed for two, and the 49ers won in overtime, 38–35. In his fifth start Joe had pulled off the greatest comeback of the NFL's modern times. No other team had come from that far behind to win.

In the garment industry, they save their raves for the man who can close a sale. In a league that had seen some great closers, Montana would be there again—and again.

In the off-season Bill Walsh traded Steve DeBerg to Denver. He turned the offense over to Montana and began to refine the play-action, ball-control passing game that would become known as the San Francisco System. It was a scheme that thrived on touch passes, short- and medium-range. Over the years, Joe's success would attract a curious criticism: that he was a creation of the system. Those who bought this argument missed the point, if they believed it devalued his accomplishments. "Sometimes," said Sam Wyche, "Joe just makes things happen that really don't have much to do with the system. But the system is suited for Joe's best abilities, with a series of options on each play. He is a master at selecting the correct option."

It became quickly apparent that such questions do not offend Montana. They do not even interest him. He is an intensely private fellow who isn't keen on abstract ideas. He needs the immediacy of the game and the finality of the scoreboard.

At the same time Walsh disposed of DeBerg, he drafted half of a defensive backfield in rookies Ronnie Lott and Eric Wright. The pieces were falling into place for a fairy-tale year. Before anyone seemed to know it, the 49ers finished 13–3 in 1981, Montana's first full season as a starter, and were facing the Dallas Cowboys for the conference championship.

In the final minutes San Francisco had to go eighty-nine yards against a defense that featured Randy White and Too Tall Jones— and, of course, they did. With the ball at the 6 yard line, Montana had to give ground and scramble. He was being chased toward the sideline when he pump-faked, then threw off the wrong foot. In the end zone Dwight Clark leapt high above a Dallas defensive back and made what San Franciscans still call "the Catch." The extra point gave the 49ers a 28–27 win and their first trip to the Super Bowl. "I thought the pass was high and out of reach," said Montana, "but I heard the crowd roar. I didn't know what kind of catch it was until I saw a replay in the locker room. I couldn't believe it."

That reaction was often shared or exceeded by the opposition. The 49ers held off the Cincinnati Bengals, 26–21, in Super Bowl XVI, in a duel of teams not expected to be there. Montana won the most valuable player award.

It was about this time that his teammates began to refer to him as Joe Cool, and a newspaper contest to select a suitable nickname drew ten thousand replies. One reader suggested that what he actually needed was a name that sounded real, and he proposed that Montana be called David W. Gibson. For better or worse, nothing caught on.

Three years later the 49ers were being described as a power-house. The team had matured, rolling through the regular season with a 15–1 record. Not even the breakup of his second marriage could throw Montana off his game.

In January 1985 the 49ers returned to the Super Bowl to meet the Miami Dolphins. But the star attraction in Game XIX, played in Palo Alto, was Dan Marino, who had been burning out scoreboards all over the league. In his second season, Danny Boy had gone where no quarterback had gone before him, throwing for over five thousand yards and forty-eight touchdowns.

San Francisco dominated the Dolphins, 38–16, controlling the ball for more than thirty-seven minutes and harassing Marino as no team had all year. The game was over by the second period, during which the 49ers scored three touchdowns. By the fourth quarter the *San Francisco Chronicle* had airlifted editions to Stanford Stadium with a headline proclaiming: "THE 49ERS WIN IT ALL." Fans were treated to the rare experience of reading about the game before it had ended. And for the second time, Montana was voted the MVP, a distinction he now shared with Bart Starr and Terry Bradshaw.

Not long after Super Bowl XIX, Montana married for the third time. He had met his bride, Jennifer Wallace, an actress-model, when the two of them taped a commercial for Schick razor blades. According to one account, the company was considering a number of other athletes, including Danny White of the Cowboys. Joe's agent suggested that the director put up a video of Montana next to one of Jennifer, who had already appeared in the role of the Schick sheriff. When they did, the agent beamed. "Now look at that," he said. "Is that a match?"

Yes, it was. Jennifer says she had to pinch Joe's bottom to get him to loosen up enough to complete the commercial. The script ended with Joe asking, "What am I wanted for now, Sheriff?" And her reply: "To take me to the dance, Joe Montana."

Quarterbacks and singing cowboys usually get the girl, but not many marry the Schick sheriff. What came across the TV screen was a pleasant fellow who faintly resembles Barry Manilow. He is close to his parents, but he accepts the fact that not everyone in his hometown approves of his marriages or his California living. There were awkward moments the first time he visited Mon City with Jennifer. "It's very hard to go back, anywhere," he says. "It really is. But Mon City is not the kind of place people who leave go back to . . . not in spirit, not all the way. I know what the people probably think."

Even as he gained more recognition as a great player, we hardly knew him. He is still modest and shy and uncomfortable with being interviewed, not exactly the qualities you associate with his line of work.

Once he steps on a football field, though, Montana is a man transformed. Icy calm, he is the picture of confidence. He leads. He implores. He takes over. Once after the Cowboys had been quoted as saying they didn't respect the 49ers, he rifled a touchdown pass to Dwight Clark, ran over to Too Tall Jones, and said, "Respect that!"

Setbacks, personal or professional, were temporary things to Montana. He majored in happy endings. The first real crisis of his football career came in 1986 when he injured his back in the opening game and missed half the season. He underwent surgery to remove a ruptured disc and to widen his spinal canal. His doctors doubted he would play again that year, or any year. Clark and Ronnie Lott visited him in the hospital a few days after his operation. "Joe had to use a walker to see us to the elevator," said Lott, "and it exhausted him. As soon as the door closed, Dwight and I looked at each other and both of us were thinking, 'No way. Ever.' It was scary and really sad."

Eight weeks later Joe Montana started against the St. Louis Cardinals. It seemed sheer madness to take such a chance with anything as serious as a back injury. All Montana did was pass for three touchdowns, and the 49ers scored on seven out of nine possessions to win, 43–17. He met every test. He had been decked while throwing a forty-yard touchdown strike to Jerry Rice, and Bubba Baker, the Cardinals' defensive end, stood over him. "You're a helluva man," said Baker, then turned and walked away.

As he always did, Montana had carefully weighed the odds. "The doctor told me," he said, "that of the people who had the surgery I had, seventy percent need surgery again down the line. It could be twenty years, it could be tomorrow. Hopefully, I'll be one of the thirty percent who don't need it at all. That's the way I approached it."

He was back, but not everyone seemed sure, including his coach, Joe feared. He reached a low point in the 1987 divisional playoff game against the Vikings, when he was sacked four times, intercepted for a forty-five-yard touchdown return, held to 109 yards in the air, and then replaced with Steve Young in the third quarter, down 27–10. "When Joe was pulled from that Minnesota game," said Dwight Clark, "my comment was 'This is bull.' Here is the greatest comeback quarterback of all time. If anyone is going to pull it out, it's Joe."

The 1988 season started under a cloud of uncertainty. "Before training camp opened," said Montana, "there were already rumors I might be traded. And that was after I had maybe my best year ever. I threw thirty-one touchdown passes and we were thirteen–two. Then in camp I didn't get as much playing time as in the past. They said I didn't need it, that they wanted to give Steve Young more time to see what he could do. That was fine with me. But you always wonder, 'Are they phasing me out?' "

Young, a splendid athlete who would be number one on many teams, received some starts when Walsh decided that Montana was too banged-up to play effectively. Montana claimed otherwise. "I felt the benching wasn't because of my health," he said, "and I sensed there was a push for Steve at that time."

As he struggled to keep his case in perspective, Montana remembered a message from Y. A. Tittle, who told him: "When you're young, they love you. When you're in the middle, they hate you. But when you're old, they love you again."

Admit it or not, Joe had to cope with a bruised elbow and an aching back, and he was weakened by a stomach flu. The pivotal game for Montana and the team would come against the Redskins on a Monday night in late November. The 49ers were third in the NFC west with a 6–5 record, but that night the offense clicked. Joe passed for two touchdowns, one an eighty-yard bomb to Jerry Rice, and ran for another as San Francisco wasted the defending world champs, 37–21.

They were on their way back to the Super Bowl in Miami, against a Cincinnati team coached by Joe's former quarterback guru, Sam Wyche. As he had against Marino, Montana would be taking on another young gun, that season's top-rated passer, Boomer Esiason.

If any doubt existed, the last drive of Super Bowl XXIII would confirm Montana's arrival as a classic quarterback. This was the setting: Cincinnati had taken the lead, 16–13, on a forty-yard field goal by Jim Breech. Night had fallen on a game that had started at teatime under a dazzling Florida sun.

When a penalty pushed the 49ers back to the 8 yard line on the kickoff, they were ninety-two yards from the other end zone and had three minutes and ten seconds left on the clock. Shrieks of optimism rose from the Cincinnati bench. "I heard somebody screaming, 'We got 'em!' " Cris Collinsworth, the veteran Bengals receiver, said. "I yelled, 'Will you see if number Sixteen is in the huddle?' He said, 'Yeah.' I said, 'Then we haven't got 'em . . .' "

The record and storybooks are, of course, loaded with long and legendary winning drives: Johnny Unitas against the Giants in sudden death in 1958; John Elway and the Broncos going coast to coast, ninety-eight yards, to tie and later beat Cleveland in the AFC playoffs in 1986; and Montana himself marching the 49ers to their first Super Bowl in 1982, with Clark's catch in the corner of the end zone beating Dallas and signaling the decline of the Cowboys.

But, as late, great, game-winning drives go, this one was the Mona Lisa—because this one happened in the Super Bowl, the largest aquarium in sports. On San Francisco's side of the stadium, déjà vu was breaking out all over. Cornerback Don Griffin hugged Ronnie Lott. "You gotta believe," he shouted over the noise of the crowd. "We're gonna win this one."

"It was eerie," said Lott. "The same thing happened in 1981 against Dallas. Archie Reese came up to me and said the same thing, same words."

In the huddle Joe Montana also remembered the comeback against Dallas. "Here we go again," he thought to himself. He started the drive with three safe, short passes to three different receivers for eight, seven, and seven yards. "I was a little cautious there," he confided later. It was an explanation, not an apology. He had thrown ninety-three passes in three Super Bowls without an interception, and he didn't build that record by being impatient or stupid.

Until that drive the Bengals had stopped the 49ers on nine of twelve third-down conversions. Now every play, in effect, was third and long.

On the entire drive the 49ers ran the ball only twice, Roger Craig getting a yard the first time, then four yards and a first down at the San Francisco 35. There the 49ers lined up in a slot formation and Montana saw what he wanted: The Bengals were in man-for-man coverage. Jerry Rice beat his defender and stepped out of bounds at the Cincinnati 48.

"When the drive started," Randy Cross said, "we were thinking field goal [and a tie]. But once we crossed the fifty we were going for the throat."

The veteran center had announced his retirement before the game, but he had more than a sentimental interest in how it might end. His low snap on a missed field goal in the first half was the difference on the scoreboard.

A curl pass to Craig was good for a thirteen-yard gain to the 35, and the 49ers had another first down. Here Montana would have an instant of breathtaking clarity. Other athletes have described such a moment, a feeling, an experience, an almost trancelike state . . . time suspended . . . the players moving as if in slow motion.

Joe Montana went beyond that point in Super Bowl XXIII. He almost fainted. "We got the tie," he remembers thinking.

But the win was still there in front of him. As he ducked under center, he could feel the adrenaline pumping wildly. He had been changing the plays at the line of scrimmage, repeating his signals, bellowing them, so his teammates could hear over the Niagara of noise in Miami's new Joe Robbie Stadium.

"I was short of breath," he said, "and when I screamed the next play I got dizzy . . . like I was blacking out. Then my vision blurred. I figured maybe I was hyperventilating. So I stood there with my hands under center for what seemed like an hour, trying to decide: Should I go ahead, or shouldn't I? My head cleared a little, so I figured by the time I got the ball back and read the defense I'd be okay. But the second I stepped back into the pocket, the fuzziness returned. Jerry Rice got open breaking outside, but all I saw was the red blur of his shirt. So I threw it away, out of bounds. I couldn't risk an interception because I knew I wasn't all there.

"I looked to the sidelines and started pointing circles to my head to let Bill know I was dizzy on that play. But he wasn't watching me. Then I realized if he thought something was wrong he might take me out. So I went back to the huddle and I was all right. It was the strangest feeling I've ever had on the field. You can see it on the videotape. I was in another world."

If Montana felt temporarily faint, he was not the sole licensee. The crowd was right there with him.

Facing second and ten from the 35, the 49ers were penalized ten yards for having an ineligible receiver downfield. The guilty party was Randy Cross, who earlier had been flagged for holding. His was going to be a farewell to remember.

Then came the most critical play of the drive, on second and twenty from the 45. Once more Montana went over the middle to Rice, who made the catch as three defensive backs converged on him. The play gained twenty-seven yards and only a last-man tackle by Rickey Dixon prevented a touchdown.

Reggie Williams, the Cincinnati linebacker, said, "That was the play that broke our backs." Cornerback Ray Horton added: "It was the play of the game. We were in perfect coverage for it. I should have made the interception."

A pass to Craig was good for eight yards, and the 49ers called their last time-out with thirty-nine seconds left, facing second and two at the 10 yard line.

In the San Francisco playbook the pass is called "20 halfback curl, X up," and the primary receiver is Craig, who breaks to the outside to split the safeties, then cuts back to the inside. John Taylor, the split end, runs underneath. If the safety goes with Craig, Taylor usually is open.

The Bengals were running out of guesses. "Our last chance," said Sam Wyche, "was to defend against Jerry Rice. I thought when it came down to one play, they would go to Rice."

Taylor lined up at tight end, with Rice in motion to that side. "When he went," said Ray Horton, "I had to widen out a little bit. It gave Taylor more room to operate. He shot right inside. Before I could react, the ball was in the air."

A shrill cry escaped from the throat of Cincinnati safety David Fulcher, "Nooooo!" He saw what was happening and came hard, but he had too much ground to make up. "Two steps," he said. "That's all. Two steps too late. I've watched the replay dozens of times. If they could rewind the tape, I'd know what to do now."

Taylor caught the pass that won the game, 20–16, with thirty-four ticks left on the clock. Nobody touched him. One would hesitate to suggest that Taylor's moment of fame was a fragile one, but when a panel of analysts wrapped up the game on television, Miami head coach Don Shula kept referring to him as "Turner."

Taylor's catch was his first reception of the game, although he had set a Super Bowl record with a forty-five-yard punt return earlier. His other claim to fame was that he sold cars in the off-season for a dealership owned by former baseball great Reggie Jackson.

Montana had made it all the way back. On that final drive he had moved them ninety-two yards, completing eight of nine passes. In the crucible, he was nearly perfect. He had buried like an old bone the indignity of being relieved in the playoff loss to Minnesota in 1987. "Getting pulled was tough," he said, "but the hardest part was after the game people talked as if I couldn't do it anymore. It wasn't like I was being judged on a bad year. I was being judged on half a game."

He had rebounded to give as poised a performance as a quarterback had given on pro football's holy day. It wasn't just his numbers—a record 357 yards passing, on twenty-three completions in thirty-six attempts—that impressed us. It was the way he seemed to revel in the pressure as the clock ticked away. Now we knew why Bill Walsh called him the "most instinctive quarterback ever to play the game."

Montana's best instinct that day, of course, was to throw to Jerry Rice, the receiver with the extra gear, who tied the record for catches with eleven and broke the record of most yards, 215. Rice was voted the game's most valuable player.

In the end Montana's drive was guaranteed to grow in memory because the Super Bowl magnifies such things. All day he hung tough in the pocket, and he threw almost every pass in the book. He threw them deep and he dumped them off, he threw outs and slants. And, most important, he threw them straight.

"If every game was a Super Bowl," said Randy Cross, "Joe Montana would be undefeated."

Boomer Esiason, it turned out, was held back by a tender shoulder. Still the Bengals held the ball for nine minutes on a drive that ended in one of their three field goals. They led the 49ers three times, once on a ninety-three-yard kickoff return by Stanford Jennings, whose wife had given birth to a baby girl the day before. Cincinnati lost what many thought had been the best Super Bowl ever played. They lost it hard and late and they lost it honest.

For Bill Walsh, it was a big enough win to retire on, and he announced his decision a few days later. He was succeeded as head coach of the 49ers by the lower-keyed George Seifert, the team's defensive coordinator. The change was significant because the 49ers would be taking dead aim at the last true dynasty the league had known, the Pittsburgh Steelers, the team of the Seventies, the only team to win four Super Bowls.

The Steelers had packed their success in a remarkable six-year run, keeping intact a basic cast of nineteen players. The 49ers had undergone an almost complete turnover. Only five players were still there who wore the rings from 1981, and now their overhaul included a new coach.

Of course, they still had Montana, who approached every camp, played every game, as though he had to fight for his job. No one remembered Joe ever being really booed in San Francisco. And if the criteria were hard luck, he wouldn't qualify among the NFL's top fifty quarterbacks. But as most of the great ones do, he feels accountable for every defeat.

"There were times after losses," he says, "when I didn't want to leave my house. Once, we were trying to get my daughter Alexandra to the hospital because she was very sick. As we were backing out of our driveway a bus loaded with people stopped in front of our house, and the driver pinched her nose and pointed at me, like, "You stink, Montana!" I was embarrassed for my family and for myself. I thought, 'God, did I play *that* bad?' "

For years sportswriters and other intellectuals have wondered how this blond-haired introvert turns himself into the swashbuckling Joe Montana we see in the arena. He doesn't know either. "Dwight Clark," he says, "once told my wife, Jennifer, 'If you were on the field with Joe you wouldn't recognize him.' In real life, I'm a more relaxed, everything's-going-to-be-O.K. kind of guy. I don't like conflict. Yet on the field I enter another dimension of my personality. I attack conflict there head-on.

"I've always believed I could walk onto a football field and make things happen. I will find a way to get the job done. I will find a way to get the ball to the secondary receiver or the third receiver, or to scramble long enough for someone else to react and get free. I see myself as maybe not the greatest thrower or the fastest runner, but a good, solid, all-around quarterback for this system. Maybe I wouldn't fit into another system. I've wondered about that. But I've always felt, within myself, I can find a way to win."

He had done so often enough, well enough, to establish the 49ers as the winningest team of the 1980s. Along the way he would compile the stats that made him the passer with the highest average for accuracy, the lowest percentage of interceptions, and the highest overall rating in NFL history.

The season began with some observers wondering whether Montana could maintain the pace. Randall Cunningham of the Eagles, Jim Everett of the Rams, Miami's Dan Marino, or Buffalo's Jim Kelly were seen as potential challengers.

As the 49ers put together one crisp performance after another, on their way to a 17–2 season, Montana at thirty-three was quite simply at the top of his form. This is how the season unfolded:

- Montana brought them from behind in the fourth quarter in four of their first five games.
- With Joe hobbled by knee and rib injuries, Steve Young quarterbacked the 49ers to three straight wins over the Cowboys, Patriots, and Jets. Montana returned to pass for three touchdowns in an easy victory over the Saints.
- Having lost twice by five points, to the Rams (13–12) and the surprising Packers (21–17), San Francisco would not lose again, winning its last five games.
- Among Montana's highlights were that he threw four touchdown passes in the fourth quarter to beat the Eagles, and three touchdown passes with no interceptions against the Saints (twice), the Falcons, and Giants. As teammate Matt Millen put it, "He is having a career year in a career that has been unbelievable."

Montana finished the regular season with a quarterback rating of 112.4, breaking the record (110.4) set by Cleveland's Milt Plum in 1960. The ratings are based on a formula understood only by engineers at NASA, but which is applied to pass attempts, completions, interceptions, and touchdowns.

As the 49ers turned their attention to the playoffs, Montana had list makers scurrying to revise their ledgers. Said George Allen, the former coach of the Rams and Redskins, "A few years ago I rated the top one hundred quarterbacks in the history of pro football. I rated Unitas number one. But if Montana wins his fourth Super Bowl, I'll have to put him up there.''

About the same time, Steve Sabol and his staff at NFL Films were discussing what to do about their popular video, *Greatest Quarterbacks of All Time*. Said Sabol: ''We're redoing it. Montana has to be reevaluated, his position in history. Bradshaw did win four Super Bowls in six years to Montana's three in eight. But the Steelers' first two were testimony to their great defense more than Bradshaw's brilliance. Montana is the pivotal person in all three of the Forty-niners' championships.

''We did a poll with all the coaches, asking them what criteria they would use to judge the great quarterbacks. They said over-whelmingly, 'Whether he wins.' In redoing the video, Montana is going to move up. Perhaps to the top.''

We are, of course, a nation of list makers. We do this in the same spirit in which Leporello, the servant of Don Giovanni, kept score of his master's conquests while the Don concentrated on enjoying them.

Not to put too fine a point on it, but the goal for Montana and the 49ers was now nothing less than immortality. They blew past the Vikings, 41–13, and the Rams, 30–3, and found them-selves favored by up to twelve and a half points over the Denver Broncos, champions of the AFC. Denver carried a burden of its own: lopsided defeats in three previous Super Bowls, by mar-gins of thirty-two, nineteen, and seventeen points. Only Min-nesota had lost four. What you had here were two teams heading in polar opposite directions, toward fame or infamy.

Denver pinned its hopes on a do-everything quarterback, John Elway, and a hard-hitting secondary. The oddsmakers and foot-ball people gave the Broncos almost no chance to win, and the only real uncertainty dealt with whether they could keep the game from becoming a blowout. For once, the experts were dead right.

New Orleans was to be the backdrop for Super Bowl XXIV. At the end of a long and merciless day, Montana had played the game of his life, and the 49ers made Denver pay for every mis-step, every hesitation, every impure thought. The final score was 55–10, the worst mismatch in twenty-four years of Super Sundays.

Montana passed for five touchdowns, three to Jerry Rice, as the 49ers joined Pittsburgh as the only teams to win four Super Bowls, and the first to repeat since the Steelers did it ten years ago. Forty-eight records were broken, tied, or extended. Montana went into the books for most touchdown passes, most consecutive passes completed (thirteen), and career marks for yardage, attempts, and completions. In four Super Bowls, he has thrown 122 passes for eleven touchdowns and no interceptions. By a unanimous vote, he became the first three-time winner of the most valuable player award.

Poor Elway, looking tight and confused, spent most of the day overthrowing or underthrowing his receivers, who compensated by dropping some that were on target. He was intercepted twice and fumbled once, setting up three touchdowns, was sacked for a twelve-yard loss, and had trouble getting the snap from center. He tried three shovel passes to his running backs in the first half, an odd piece of strategy, and completed one. It may have been a blessing that the Broncos had the ball for only twenty minutes.

To imagine a disaster on a scale grander than this one, General Custer would have had to make his last stand on the *Titanic*.

Denver trailed by 7–3 when Bobby Humphrey, playing with a flak jacket protecting two broken ribs, fumbled at his own 45. Montana turned that miscue into a quick score, drilling his tight end, Brent Jones, for the last seven yards. At halftime the 49ers led, 27–3. The score mounted to 41–3 in the third quarter on Montana's thirty-five-yard pass to John Taylor, last year's unsung hero.

With nine minutes left in the game, both starting quarterbacks had turned the game over to their backups. Montana operated behind an offensive line that never allowed him to get hit, much less sacked. "I think I was touched once," he said.

He was on this day without argument the best quarterback of his time. The next question is whether he is the best of everyone's time. "I'm one who answers yes," said John Madden, the former Raiders' coach turned CBS analyst. "You usually wait until the end of a guy's career to say he's the best, but I think we can say it about Montana." And from George Young, the New York Giants' general manager: "You can talk all you want about numbers. Greatness is about winning. And winning is what Montana has been all about."

Montana has as many Super Bowl rings now as Bradshaw and is compared to Baugh and Unitas and Namath, who was the original Super Joe. Namath was Montana's boyhood hero. Only the two of them won a national championship in college and a Super Bowl in the pros.

Montana has the same quick drop and setup as Namath, but his feet are nimble and his ability to scramble separate them. "He's Fred Astaire," says Joe Willie.

All of the praise, the measuring, the scrutiny, Montana can easily do without. "I don't think about history or records or how I want to be remembered," he says. "I happen to be in a sport that has a Hall of Fame. But right now I'm more concerned with how I'm judged by my peers."

Montana did not pick up the cry in the San Francisco locker room of "three-peat!" or the reference to a fifth Super Bowl ring, "one for the thumb," a slogan the Steelers couldn't fulfill. That sort of demonstration isn't his style. But you study Joe Montana and you may get a glimpse of what propels him. He simply wants to go on. He sees retirement as a form of failure— a time when you begin the rest of your workaday life, when you forget about the one thing you always wanted to be.

"I'm not retiring," he said in January 1990. "I'm not even thinking about it. In sports, when it's over, it's cold turkey. You're finished. You don't come back. You play from the time you're eight years old, and then you're done forever."

EPILOGUE— HOW THEY RATE

Some thirty quarterbacks were assembled in the nation's capital one night a year or so ago to honor themselves. The occasion was the Washington Quarterback Club's National Awards dinner. They ranged from Otto Graham, who began his career in the 1940s, to Jim Kelly and Jim McMahon, who represented the arms and mouths of the 1980s.

At one table the guests began to argue over which city in America was the toughest on quarterbacks. There were votes for New York, where the fans booed Phil Simms on his way to a Super Bowl season, and strong support for Chicago and San Francisco. One gentleman took up for Dallas. "When Don Meredith was playing for the Cowboys," he recalled, "he got booed one night in a restaurant." Another party was able to top that one. "In Detroit," he claimed, "Bobby Layne once got booed in the men's room." Others chimed in. When Dan Pastorini broke his leg in his first year in Oakland, the crowd cheered. Now that is world-class cruelty.

There is no longer any purpose in pointing out the unfairness of this treatment. Quarterbacks know when they accept the job that they will not be coddled, not by the fans and surely not by

★**317**

the defense. "It's like a gunfighter," Joe Theismann was saying. "You know sooner or later something might happen."

You get an insight into the pressures on a quarterback, and the way they judge each other, when you examine the dialogue between John Elway and Terry Bradshaw that enlivened the days leading up to Super Bowl XXIV. Some thought they heard, in Terry's words, a proud and sensitive man telling the world he had paid bigger dues than Elway had in Denver.

Bradshaw had taken note of Elway's complaint that he felt suffocated at times by the Denver fans and media. He had been criticized by one paper as a poor tipper and another sent out a reporter to see what kind of candy he gave away at Halloween. They learned that he did not pass out a candy bar he endorsed.

Trivia? Silliness? Of course. But it does seem to go with the territory. Bradshaw, who had overcome years of second-guessing in Pittsburgh, said that "John's problem is that he has been babied. He has been babied by the city until this year when they jumped his ass. Babied by the coaches a little bit. It's just too easy. Too many things bother John that shouldn't. The candy bars and stuff like that. You're making two million dollars a year. Hell, things shouldn't bother you when you're making two million a year. Wait till you go out and get a real job."

Bradshaw said later that he meant his criticism more in the form of a challenge. "I think John has got to get tougher emotionally. In Pittsburgh I had a talk with the wall. I challenged myself: 'By God, I'm going to make it. I'm going to make them eat their words. I'm going to show them. I'm going to go out there and win Super Bowls and pack my bags and get my ass out of this place, and I ain't coming back.'

"The people only care about winning championships. They don't care about your candy bar endorsements. They don't care about your Mercedes Benz and your television show. None of that. How many rings do you got? I [Elway] ain't got none. That's the bottom line."

"Elway is a very good quarterback," said one NFL coach, "who has a chance to be great. But he has to be more consistent. And he has to win a Super Bowl ring. He knows it. That's the only way to silence the critics."

The obvious defense of Elway, if he needs one, is that he has never been surrounded by a great cast of players. The reality is that only a few whose names are in the Hall of Fame were not.

Great teams need great quarterbacks. In the 1950s there were the Cleveland Browns and Otto Graham, reaching ten straight championship games and winning seven. The 1960s brought you the Green Bay Packers and Bart Starr, winning the first two Super Bowls for the man with the jack-o'-lantern smile, Vince Lombardi. The 1970s? Clearly the property of the Pittsburgh Steelers and their blond bomber, Terry Bradshaw.

The rest of the vote is in and it is nearly unanimous. The San Francisco 49ers are in a class with all the teams of legend, and Joe Montana is the quarterback for all the ages. "I don't know if he is the best in any one category," says his old coach, Bill Walsh, "but if you put it all together he's the best all-around quarterback that ever was." George Allen rated Montana first in technique, setting up, balance, and heart.

"Is Montana a better quarterback than me?" repeated Terry Bradshaw. "Yes, he is. He is way ahead of me on timing, on touch, on being able to throw every kind of pass. He rarely takes a sack. He can get rid of the ball on a two-step drop or a five-step drop and he senses the rush. But could this Forty-niner team beat our Steelers' team? The answer is no way. They have never faced a defense like our Steel Curtain."

This is, of course, by no means the end of the debate. It may be merely the beginning. But for now Montana has won.

★ TOP 20 CAREER PASSERS, YARDAGE ★
(Through 1989 Season)

Quarterback	Years	Attempts	Completions	TD	Interceptions	Percentage	Yards
1. Fran Tarkenton	18	6,467	3,686	342	266	57.0	47,003
2. Dan Fouts	16	5,604	3,297	254	242	58.8	43,040
3. Johnny Unitas	18	5,186	2,830	290	253	54.6	40,239
4. Jim Hart	18	5,076	2,593	209	247	51.1	34,665
5. John Hadl	15	4,637	2,363	244	268	50.4	33,503
6. Y. A. Tittle	16	4,395	2,427	242	248	55.2	33,070
7. Ken Anderson	16	4,475	2,654	197	160	59.3	32,838
8. Sonny Jurgensen	18	4,262	2,433	255	189	57.1	32,224
9. John Brodie	16	4,491	2,469	214	224	55.0	31,548
10. Joe Montana	11	4,059	2,593	216	107	63.2	31,254
11. Norm Snead	15	4,353	2,276	196	257	52.2	30,797
12. Roman Gabriel	15	4,498	2,366	201	149	52.6	29,444
13. Joe Ferguson	15	4,421	2,323	193	201	52.5	29,263
14. Len Dawson	19	3,741	2,136	239	183	57.1	28,711
15. Terry Bradshaw	13	3,901	2,105	212	210	54.0	27,989
16. Ken Stabler	14	3,793	2,270	194	222	59.8	27,938
17. Craig Morton	17	3,786	2,053	183	187	54.2	27,908
18. Dan Marino	7	3,650	2,174	220	125	60.2	27,853
19. Ron Jaworski	14	4,056	2,151	177	159	53.0	27,805
20. Joe Namath	12	3,762	1,886	173	220	50.1	27,663

(Minimum, 1,500 Attempts)

Quarterback	Years	Attempts	Completions	Yards	TD	Interceptions	Rating
1. Joe Montana	11	4,059	2,593	31,254	216	107	94.0
2. Dan Marino	7	3,650	2,174	27,853	220	125	89.3
3. Boomer Esiason	6	2,285	1,296	18,350	126	76	87.3
4. Otto Graham	10	2,626	1,464	23,584	174	135	86.6
5. Dave Krieg	10	2,843	1,644	20,858	169	116	83.7
6. Bernie Kosar	5	1,940	1,134	13,888	75	47	83.4
7. Roger Staubach	11	2,958	1,685	22,700	153	109	83.4
8. Ken O'Brien	8	2,467	1,471	17,589	96	68	83.0
9. Neil Lomax	8	3,153	1,817	22,700	136	90	82.7
10. Sonny Jurgensen	18	4,262	2,433	32,224	255	189	82.6
11. Len Dawson	19	3,741	2,136	28,711	239	183	82.5
12. Ken Anderson	16	4,475	2,654	32,838	197	160	81.9
13. Danny White	13	2,950	1,761	21,959	155	132	81.7
14. Tony Eason	7	1,536	898	10,987	61	50	80.3
15. Bart Starr	16	3,149	1,808	24,718	152	138	80.5
16. Fran Tarkenton	18	6,467	3,686	47,003	342	266	80.3
17. Dan Fouts	15	5,604	3,297	43,040	254	242	80.2
18. Jim McMahon	8	1,831	1,050	13,335	77	66	79.2
19. Bert Jones	10	2,551	1,430	18,190	124	101	78.2
20. Johnny Unitas	18	5,186	2,830	40,239	290	253	78.2

★ TOP 20 CAREER LEADERS, TOUCHDOWN PASSES ★
(Through 1989 Season)

Quarterback	Touchdowns	Quarterback	Touchdowns
Frank Tarkenton	342	John Brodie	214
Johnny Unitas	290	Terry Bradshaw	212
Sonny Jurgensen	255	Jim Hart	209
Dan Fouts	254	Roman Gabriel	201
John Hadl	244	Ken Anderson	197
Y. A. Tittle	242	Norm Snead	196
George Blanda	236	Ken Stabler	194
Len Dawson	239	Joe Ferguson	193
Dan Marino	220	Craig Morton	183
Joe Montana	216		

★ HALL OF FAME QUARTERBACKS ★
(Modern Era)

Quarterback	Height	Weight	College	Team
Sammy Baugh	6–2	180	TCU	Redskins
George Blanda	6–2	215	Kentucky	Bears, Colts, Oilers, Raiders
Terry Bradshaw	6–3	210	Louisiana Tech	Steelers
Len Dawson	6–0	190	Purdue	Steelers, Browns, Texans, Chiefs
Otto Graham	6–1	195	Northwestern	Browns
Bob Griese	6–1	190	Purdue	Dolphins
Sonny Jurgensen	6–0	203	Duke	Eagles, Redskins
Bobby Layne	6–2	190	Texas	Bears, Bulldogs, Lions, Steelers
Sid Luckman	6–0	195	Columbia	Bears
Joe Namath	6–2	200	Alabama	Jets, Rams
Bart Starr	6–1	200	Alabama	Packers
Roger Staubach	6–3	202	Navy	Cowboys
Fran Tarkenton	6–0	185	Georgia	Vikings, Giants
Y. A. Tittle	6–0	200	LSU	Colts, 49ers, Giants
Johnny Unitas	6–1	195	Louisville	Colts, Chargers
Norm Van Brocklin	6–1	190	Oregon	Rams, Eagles
Bob Waterfield	6–2	200	UCLA	Rams

NOTES ON SOURCES

Portions of the chapters on Johnny Unitas and Bobby Layne appeared in articles by the author first published in the National Football League magazine, *PRO!*, and reprinted in his book *The Golden Age of Pro Football*.

Members of the Pro Football Hall of Fame were sounding boards for opinions and ratings of the great quarterbacks over the years, and were a source of important background and details. Myron Cope was an authority on Sammy Baugh and Layne; John Steadman on Unitas; Bob Oates, Sr., on Bob Waterfield and Norm Van Brocklin in their Los Angeles heyday. The work of such other Hall of Fame panelists as Edwin Pope, Ray Didinger, Will McDonough, Jerry Greene, and Larry Felser was extremely helpful.

At the outset of our research, the files of a longtime co-worker and friend, the late Steve Perkins, were available and provided insights into the Dallas Cowboys. A story by William Gildea in *The Washington Post* gave a clear picture of the unusual history of Babe Laufenberg. Background on Gary Kubiak came from Jack Disney, then with the *Los Angeles Herald-Examiner*.

In the verification of facts, scores, and highlights, the Elias Sports Bureau and the research department at *Sports Illustrated* were open and accommodating.

INDEX